Chanteuse in the City

Chanteuse in the City

The Realist Singer in French Film

KELLEY CONWAY

University of California Press

BERKELEY   LOS ANGELES   LONDON

University of California Press
Berkeley and Los Angeles, California

University of California Press, Ltd.
London, England

Chapter 4 was previously published, in slightly different form, as "Diva
in the Spotlight: Music Hall to Cinema," in *Gender and French Cinema*,
edited by Alex Hughes and James S. Williams (New York: Berg, 2001),
35–61. Portions of chapters 3 and 5 were previously published as "Les
«goualeuses» de l'écran," in *Le Cinema au rendez-vous des arts: France,
années 20 et 30*, edited by Emmanuelle Toulet (Paris: Bibliothèque
nationale de France, 1995), 162–71, and as "Flower of the Asphalt: The
chanteuse réaliste in 1930s French Cinema," in *Soundtrack Available:
Essays on Film and Popular Music*, edited by Pamela Robertson Wojcik
and Arthur Knight (Durham, N.C.: Duke University Press, 2001), 134–60.

Library of Congress Cataloging-in-Publication Data

Conway, Kelley, 1963–.
  Chanteuse in the city : the realist singer in French film / Kelley
Conway.
    p.   cm.
  Includes bibliographical references (p.), filmography (p.) and index.
  ISBN 0–520–24019–7 (alk. paper)
  ISBN 0–520–24407–9 (pbk. : alk. paper)
    1. Popular music—France—History and criticism.   2. Motion picture
music—France—History and criticism.   3. Woman singers—France.
4. Motion pictures—France—History.   I. Title.
ML3489.C66   2004
782.42164'082'0944—dc22   2004000621

Manufactured in the United States of America
13   12   11   10   09   08   07   06   05   04
10   9   8   7   6   5   4   3   2   1

For Patrick, Sullivan, and Charlotte

Contents

Acknowledgments

This book began as a dissertation in the Department of Film and Television at UCLA, where I had the great fortune to have as my advisor a fellow francophile. Janet Bergstrom offered precious advice, encouragement, and friendship over this project's trajectory. I am grateful also for the enthusiasm and support of the other members of my dissertation committee at UCLA, Kathryn Norberg, Peter Wollen, and Steve Mamber.

David Gardner, more than anyone else, understands my passion for Montmartre, *music-hall*, and Mistinguett. I thank him for his expert and extensive help with editing and translation, for putting me up in his Marais apartment, and for cooking delicious French food for me. He is the best friend anyone could have.

For her extraordinary generosity and excellent advice, I thank Emmanuelle Toulet and her staff at the Bibliotheque de l'Arsenal. I am deeply grateful as well to all of the other archives in France that granted me access to rare films and precious documents: the Centre national du cinéma at Bois d'Arcy (Michelle Aubert, Eric Le Roy, and Daniel Courbet), the Cinémathèque française, the Bibliothèque du film, the Forum des images, and the Département de la phonothèque et de l'audiovisuel and the Département des estampes et de la photographie of the Bibliothèque nationale de France. Thanks also to Patrick Bensard of the Cinématheque de la danse for his counsel and to Pierre Philippe of Gaumont for sharing with me his documentary on French music hall, *Le Roman du music-hall*.

At the Université de Paris III, I benefited enormously from courses taught by Noël Burch, Michèle Lagny, and Geneviève Sellier. A special thanks to Ginette Vincendeau of the University of Warwick, who graciously provided me a copy of her groundbreaking dissertation on 1930s French cinema, and whose work continues to inspire me. For their precious help in finding illustrations, I thank Bernard Bastide, Giusy Basile, and Laurent Mannoni. Thanks also to Richard Abel for sharing his knowledge of Mistinguett's silent films with me. Jerilyn Goodman, Vicki Callahan, and Edward O'Neill each read the manuscript at crucial points in its development, offering sound advice and encouragement. Geneviève Drouot helped me decipher the slang in Aristide Bruant's songs.

I am very grateful to the many people and organizations who gave me the opportunity to present material from this book at conferences: Donald Crafton of the University of Notre Dame, Corey Creekmur and Lauren Rabinowitz of the University of Iowa, Janet Bergstrom of UCLA, the Society for Cinema Studies, and the Western Society for French History. A Fulbright Senior Specialist Grant allowed me to share my ideas with the faculty and students of the Université de Liège, where I was shown great hospitality by Geneviève Van Cauwenberge and Juliette d'Or.

Special thanks are due to the extraordinary teachers I have had over the years. My love of cinema was born at Carleton College, where Vern Bailey introduced me to the work of Jean Renoir and where John Schott's London Program convinced me of the rightness of a life in film. At the University of Iowa, Dudley Andrew shared with me his wealth of knowledge on French film and culture, Rick Altman sparked my interest in music and film, and Lauren Rabinowitz whetted my appetite for archival research.

At the University of Wisconsin–Madison, my intellectual life has been profoundly enriched by my colleagues and friends David Bordwell, Kristin Thompson, Lea Jacobs, Vance Kepley, Ben Singer, J. J. Murphy, Tino Balio, Susan Zaeske, Susan Bernstein, and Mary Louise Roberts.

Generous grants supporting my work came from the University of Wisconsin–Madison Graduate School and the Wisconsin Alumni Research Foundation, as well as the UCLA Center for the Study of Women. I am particularly grateful for the Charles Boyer Award, which made my initial research in Paris possible.

Thanks to the wonderful team at the University of California Press, Mary Francis, Richard Terdiman, Rachel Berchten, and the indefatigable Peter Dreyer. I appreciate the wonderfully helpful comments of the anonymous readers of my manuscript. A special thanks to Eric Smoodin who, upon hearing me describe my manuscript, spontaneously belted out a tune by Mistinguett.

Family members Jane, Jeff, David, and Dan Conway, Kristi Caldwell, and Karen Carr Lorence provided endless encouragement and good humor. My father, Robert Conway, was near the end of his life when he offered words of inspiration that spurred me to finish this book. His courage, optimism, and tenacity set an example that will nourish me for the rest of my life. A heartfelt thanks also to Catherine Romens and Catharine Gartelos, who cared for Sullivan and Charlotte with such love while I wrote. Finally, my deepest gratitude and love to Patrick Sweet for his unwavering support and for sharing my passion for Paris.

Introduction

When we think of 1930s French cinema, images of the dilemmas of masculinity are likely to dominate our memories. In *Le Jour se lève* (Marcel Carné, 1939), Jean Gabin barricades himself in his apartment after murdering a rival; in both *La Belle Équipe* (Julien Duvivier, 1936) and *Gueule d'amour* (Jean Grémillon, 1937), a virile male community is threatened or destroyed by a beautiful woman; in *La Grande Illusion* (Jean Renoir, 1937), an aristocratic officer creates a diversion so that two men can escape from a prison camp. Our general sense that this cinema tells stories primarily about men seems confirmed by a statistical analysis of the credits of feature films made in the 1930s.[1] The study reveals that, by far, male actors held the majority of the lead film roles in 1930s French film. Appearing in the top tier of the compilation are those actors who performed in more than thirty films each in the 1930s and who played the starring role in at least 80 percent of those films: Armand Bernard, Jules Berry, Albert Préjean, Charles Vanel, Henri Garat, Raimu, and Harry Baur.[2] There are no corresponding actresses with this same degree of visibility in 1930s French film.[3]

Striking though it is, this disparity in the number and size of roles played by men and women tells us very little about the decade's decidedly ambivalent and often dichotomous cinematic construction of femininity. French films of the 1930s tend to ask spectators to either desire or despise their female characters. This trait is reflected in the most familiar female "types" in 1930s French film: the ingenue and the *garce* (tart or bitch). The ingenue appears in both a passive guise (Annabella in Carné's *Hôtel du Nord* or Jacqueline Laurent in his *Le Jour se lève*) and a vivacious, "modern" version (Danielle Darrieux in *Un Mauvais Garçon* and *Club de femmes*). At the other end of the spectrum of female representation we find the malevolent seductresses incarnated by Viviane Romance in *La Belle Équipe*, Mireille Balin in *Gueule d'amour*, and Ginette Leclerc in *La Femme du boulanger*.

The ingenue typically serves as the object of desire of the film's much older, male lead. The *garce* possesses the power to disrupt the narrative, driving men to murder or suicide, but she has a rather flat, undeveloped quality, which we see in the ingenue as well, and which is defined exclusively by her relation to the male lead.

There are a few exceptions to this dichotomous representation of women. Arletty, a venerable symbol of working-class Paris in 1930s and 1940s cinema, is famous for her nasal argot and her bons mots in Carné's *Hôtel du Nord* and *Le Jour se lève*. As Madame Raymonde or Clara, she projects an appealing independence and complexity. In her 1940s films, Arletty exudes a kind of cool, enigmatic sexuality in Carné's *Les Visiteurs du soir* and *Les Enfants du paradis*. This ethereal quality makes of Arletty a kind of cipher, a particularly effective screen onto which spectators could project their fantasies about gender and national identity during the Occupation.[4]

The other major exception to the ingenue/*garce* dichotomy is Edwige Feuillère, the *aventurière* of 1930s cinema. She plays high-class thieves in *J'étais une aventurière* (Raymond Bernard, 1938) and *L'Honorable Catherine* (Marcel L'Herbier, 1943) in a comic register akin to that of American screwball comedy heroines. In the 1940s, Feuillère was dubbed the "grande dame" of French cinema as a result of her portrayals of strong, aristocratic women in *De Mayerling à Sarajevo* (Max Ophüls, 1940), *La Duchesse de Langeais* (Jacques de Baroncelli, 1941), and *L'Aigle à deux têtes* (Jean Cocteau, 1948).

Yet there is also a tradition of representation in 1930s French film that presents a version of femininity quite different from the gamine and the *garce*, one that is more developed than the exceptional roles of Arletty and Feuillère. This is the tradition of the *chanteuse réaliste* (realist singer). Ancestor of Edith Piaf, the realist singer performed songs about prostitution, urban poverty, and female desire in the *café-concert*, the cabaret, and the music hall beginning at the turn of the century, and, later, in the sound cinema. Unlike the ingenue, the realist singer is knowing and world-weary. Like the *garces* played by Balin and Romance, the realist singer is overtly sexual, but is much more likely to unite a working-class community than to destroy it. Like Arletty, the realist singer symbolizes the working class, but is earthier than the androgynous Dominique of *Les Visiteurs du soir* or the ethereal Garance of *Les Enfants du paradis*. By way of introduction, let us explore three "clips" featuring the realist singer.

A fugitive killer hides out in a shabby Montparnasse apartment, mesmerized by the sound of a woman singing in the room next door. The film is

Duvivier's *La Tête d'un homme* (1932), and the woman, described simply as "the weary woman" in the film's credits, is the realist singer Damia (1892–1978). Depressed for reasons we never learn, she sings plaintively "night invades me/all is fog/all is gray."[5] The killer imagines that this voice belongs to the woman he loves and that she is singing directly to him. In the end, the killer dies under the wheels of a car on a busy boulevard in nocturnal Montparnasse to the strains of Damia's song.

What does it mean, in a cinema dominated by male directors and actors, and by narratives that privilege male communities, when a woman begins to sing? Is Damia's performance best understood as the condensation of an exclusively male desire and anxiety? Or is Damia, dubbed the *tragédienne lyrique*, part of a historically specific tradition devoted to representing female loss and suffering? What can we say of the eerie separation of the singing voice and the female body in this film? What of the film's resolutely urban texture?

A gathering of prostitutes provides the setting for a song about the lives of streetwalkers in *Faubourg Montmartre* (Bernard, 1931), a film about two sisters trying to eke out a living in Paris. Here, a woman addresses other women; in a series of close-ups, the camera lingers on each listener's face as she stares at an aging, melancholy singer played by Odette Barencey. Barencey was a second-tier singer from the world of the café-concert, a modest entertainment space that emerged in eighteenth-century Paris and offered food, drink, and song to listeners of all social categories. Here, Barencey sings about the lives of prostitutes to an audience of prostitutes. "They stroll alongside shop windows/And seem to think of nothing/but showing their humble faces./But they are not bodies without souls/The little women."[6]

What does this striking sequence, which evokes the intimacy of the largely bygone café-concert, communicate about the film's other singing performance, a glitzy revue number in an upscale music hall featuring the music hall revue and film star Florelle? What does this film have to tell us about female desire and female community amid the pressures of urbanization?

A man's singing performance is upstaged in a surprising turnabout in Anatole Litvak's *Coeur de Lilas* (1932). Jean Gabin plays a petty gangster who moves about a working-class dance hall boasting of his erotic exploits with a woman who, because of her prodigious sexual dexterity, is dubbed the

"Rubber Kid." Without warning, a woman steps in to claim the sobriquet for herself, appropriating the song and identifying herself as the legendary "Môme Caoutchouc." She proceeds to relate her own story with great relish. "I can tell you, just between us/The rubber kid is yours truly/Oh yes, that's what they call me."[7] It makes no difference that the singer is an aging, unshapely prostitute; she nevertheless wants it known that the exploits were hers. The singer is Fréhel (1891–1951), *l'inoubliable inoubliée* (the unforgettable unforgotten), the comeback queen who reinvented herself in the 1920s after years of self-exile and drug addiction.

How important is Fréhel's biography to our understanding of this film? Is it significant that a woman usurps the place of a man in this singing performance? Why does *Coeur de Lilas* spend so much time evoking the working-class people and neighborhoods of Paris? In an attempt to respond to these and other questions, this book explores the realist singer in 1930s French cinema, as well as the cultural context that produced her. The figure of the realist singer, which evokes Paris *populaire* and a very particular version of femininity, resonates in an especially intense way during the period between the wars and functions as a flexible icon for a number of desires and tensions around gender and class. Her cultural construction, on- and offstage, within and beyond the diegesis, is rife with contradictions: she is powerful, yet frail, even wrecked; she is wealthy, but speaks to the poor; she grew up in poverty, but appeals to both the rich and the poor; she can be sexually aggressive, yet is often under the thumb of a man. She serves as an emblem of an emotional, nostalgic topography of Paris and lost sense of community already articulated after World War I, yet she also stands for a newer, more threatening conception of modern femininity associated with the twentieth century, the city, and mass culture.

The realist singer often appears only for the duration of her song performance in 1930s films. But the relatively meager screen time accorded Damia, Odette Barencey, and Fréhel in *La Tête d'un homme, Faubourg Montmartre*, and *Coeur de Lilas*, respectively, and in their other films, belies the evocative power possessed by the realist singer in French popular culture. The realist song became a staple of both live singing performance, starting in the 1890s, where it could be heard in the streets and courtyards of Paris—it was a mainstay of the street singer's repertoire—and in neighborhood café-concerts and opulent music halls like the Casino and the Folies-Bergère. By the 1930s, the realist song was available to listeners, not only in live performance, but on the phonograph, on the radio, and at the cinema. Fréhel, Damia, and Edith Piaf were the most famous realist singers, but there were many others: Yvonne George, Andrée Turcy, Germaine Lix,

Berthe Sylva, Lucienne Boyer, and Irène de Turcy. Many singers devoted only a portion of their repertoire to the realist song. Florelle, who sings a song in the realist tradition in *Le Crime de Monsieur Lange* (Jean Renoir, 1935), was better known as a revue star at the Casino music hall in the late 1920s. Marie Dubas, a celebrated comic singer on the music hall circuit, was known also for her performances of realist songs. Lys Gauty and Marianne Oswald, admired for their performances of the songs of Bertolt Brecht and Kurt Weill, also performed the realist song.

The realist singers usually possessed deep voices, typically mezzo-soprano or even contralto. Their voices were described by contemporary critics as *véritable, naturale,* and *brutale.* These were not the pretty, trained voices capable of glorious coloratura one heard at a performance of an Offenbach operetta, but, instead, rather nasal voices, which frequently ventured into the deeper chest tones and often broke, to great tragic effect, in the middle of a song. These were voices belonging to women perceived to have "lived." The bodies, as well as the voices, of the realist singers often departed from the normative codes of beauty in 1930s Paris. Fréhel, a slender, strikingly beautiful young woman in the teens, was overweight and alcoholic in the 1920s and 1930s. Damia's sleeveless black gowns revealed her muscular arms and her powerful, sculptural figure. Yvonne George (1896–1930), revered by Jean Cocteau, Robert Desnos, and Henri Jeanson for her performances of realist songs and authentic sailor songs, had a "Pierrot" figure with huge eyes, a pale complexion and a body wasted by consumption. Edith Piaf's disproportionately large head and sickly, stunted body, ravaged by drugs and illness, provided a striking contrast to her immensely powerful voice. Whether too fat, too strong, or too sickly, the realist singer is quite far from the standard 1930s female ideal of blond hair, a petite, yet curvy, figure, and the catlike face shared by Florelle, Annabella, Colette Darfeuil, and Nadia Sibirskaia.

The realist song is almost always about loss and tends to be intensely cynical about the possibility of romantic love and domestic stability. Sometimes called the *chanson vécue* ("lived" or "true to life" song), it typically chronicles the plight of a woman facing heartbreak and poverty. The song "Je t'aime d'amour"[8] in the film *Paris la nuit* (Henri Diamant-Berger, 1930) chronicles an innocent young girl's initiation into prostitution by the man she loves. Her lover is now tired of her; she threatens suicide. "L'Amour des hommes"[9] performed in the film *La Rue sans joie* (André Hugon, 1938) is about prostitutes who walk the streets in rain, snow, and wind. "We have souls, we seek love," the chanteuse tells us, but "men are all the same, blasé and vicious." Frequently, the realist singer's persona is submissive and fatalistic. The songs often tell the stories of passive, dependent women incapable of escaping their brutal men. Yet the realist singer is more than the mere victim her songs and film appearances might imply. She frankly expresses her sexual desires and the hope that true love is still possible. "Tu m'fais chaud, j'ai la fièvre" ("You make me hot, I have a fever"), the singer moans in *Paris la nuit.*

The intertexts of the singers' biographies also mitigate the passivity often expressed in the realist song. The characters of the songs who endure violence, betrayal, and prostitution for the love of their men are brought to life by performers renowned for their resilience, physical strength, powerful voices, and aesthetic innovation. Fréhel, celebrated endlessly in the 1920s and 1930s popular press for her comeback after a painful rupture with Maurice Chevalier and years of self-imposed exile in Eastern Europe, enjoyed great success with "Le Grand Frisé" (Big Curly).[10]

Il m'cogne, il m'démolit, il m'crève	He hits me, he demolishes me, he wears me out
Mais que voulez-vous, moi j'aim' ça.	But what do you want? Me, I like that.

Mistinguett, undoubtedly the single most powerful performer in French popular entertainment in the teens and the 1920s, and, from all accounts, a woman who dominated her lovers in real life, enjoyed a huge hit in 1920 with "Mon homme," an only slightly parodic realist song expressing devotion to her "man."[11]

Sur cette terr', ma seul' joie, mon seul bonheur	On this earth, my sole joy, my sole happiness
C'est mon homme.	Is my man.
J'ai donné tout c'que j'ai, mon amour et tout mon coeur	I've given everything I have, my love and all my heart
À mon homme . . .	To my man . . .

Likewise, the realist singer's robust voice and her (sometimes) large and powerful body modify the surface meaning of the realist song lyrics. Indeed, for all her apparent pessimism and passivity, the realist singer represents one of the few forums for the expression of female subjectivity in French popular culture in the 1920s and 1930s in France.

This study aims to shed light not only on the specific phenomenon of the realist singer but also on the incorporation of songs and singers more generally into 1930s French cinema, in which a remarkable number of songs made their way into both feature and short films. In the early years of sound cinema, feature films were preceded by three, four, or five short films, some of which were *chansons filmées* (filmed songs). The *chanson filmée*, which persisted until the 1950s, featured the performance of a song, either in a recording studio or on the stage of a music hall, sometimes with an audience and an orchestra in view.[12] The *chanson filmée* has, unfortunately, all but disappeared from the archives, but a description of *Tour de chant* (Alberto Cavalcanti, 1933) indicates that the realist song was among the musical genres filmed.[13]

Popular songs are everywhere in French feature-length films of the 1930s, as a discography published by the Bibliothèque nationale confirms.[14] Compiled through the analysis of the commercial catalogues published by record companies, the discography reveals that the 686 films inventoried (of the approximate 1,300 feature films made in 1930s France) contain an average of two to three songs per film.[15] A partial explanation for the prevalence of popular songs in 1930s French film is that the phonograph and radio were not in widespread use until the late 1930s.[16] Thus, it has been argued, the cinema provided the largest distribution network for songs in the early 1930s and was, in fact, the first medium to popularize recorded music.[17]

A more convincing explanation for the prevalence of songs in 1930s French cinema is that it allowed films to capitalize on the established appeal of music hall stars. The film industry did not hesitate to incorporate the realist singer into its narratives when sound cinema emerged. Fréhel appeared in fourteen films in the 1930s and three more in the 1940s, typically in secondary roles that were, nevertheless, quite important on a symbolic level. Damia appeared in five films in the 1930s. She is generally considered a lesser actress than Fréhel but played the lead in most of her films. Edith Piaf appeared in one film in 1936, at the beginning of her career, and in nine more in the 1940s and 1950s.[18]

Much more than a distribution mechanism for recorded music and a way to capitalize on the popularity of music hall stars, however, the realist singer in 1930s French films satisfies a hunger experienced by French audiences at this time. In order to understand the desires and anxieties inscribed in this figure, we must construct her history in French commercial entertainment that predates sound cinema. Long before she appeared in 1930s French films, the realist singer performed in the turn-of-the-century café-concert, music hall, and cabaret. As a tradition, the realist song hearkens back to that moment when, dressed like a down-and-out prostitute from the marginal quarters of Paris, Eugénie Buffet (1866–1934) first sang of the street, the poor, and prostitution at her debut performance at La Cigale in 1892. From there, the realist song evolved into a highly specific popular genre, which thrived at the turn of the century and then spiked in popularity again in the 1930s.

The realist song was part of a much larger body of texts in French culture that strove for a realistic depiction of underworld and working-class Paris. The penetrating gaze turned to the "lower depths" of Paris by this song genre constitutes an extension of the naturalist novels of Zola and the Goncourt brothers, nineteenth-century theatrical melodrama, and the anti-authoritarian and populist poetry in the songs of Richepin, Béranger, and Clément.[19] Additionally, as Vanessa Schwartz has shown, turn-of-the-century Paris offered crowds "spectacles of everyday life" of a burgeoning mass consumer culture at the morgue, the wax museum, and the panorama.[20] The photographs of Eugène Atget, Brassaï, André Warnaud, and André Kertész, regrettably beyond the scope of this study, likewise depict the marginalized landscapes of Paris and its socially dispossessed.[21] In the period between the wars, the populist novels and essays of Eugène Dabit, Pierre Mac Orlan, and Francis Carco modified and reinvigorated the representation of the marginal neighborhoods and inhabitants of Paris. Many of the novels written by Dabit, Mac Orlan, and Carco were, in fact, adapted to film and thus provide a direct link to poetic realist cinema, those German Expressionist–influenced films made in 1930s France that tell pessimistic stories set in an urban, industrial working-class, or criminal milieu.[22] Although part of a much larger discourse that romanticizes working-class and criminal Paris, the realist song and the realist singer are well worth examining for what they can tell us about the relationship, both contentious and mutually beneficial, between live modes of entertainment and the cinema, and about how this culture imagined working-class femininity.

Historians of French song usually trace the origins of the realist song to the late 1880s, when the songwriter, performer, and cabaret owner Aristide Bruant brought to popular song a new preoccupation with the material conditions of working-class Parisians. At his Montmartre cabarets, Bruant sang of *le peuple* with a mixture of irony and sincerity. He amused, offended, and moved the largely bourgeois audiences with his slang-filled "Dans la rue" (In the Street), "Rose blanche" (White Rose) and "À Saint-Lazare" (At the Saint-Lazare [a prison]).[23] The realist song in its initial incarnation, then, combined the melancholy and sentimentality of the traditional *chanson* with Bruant's attention to material conditions. Crucially, however, the realist song was quickly taken up by female performers exclusively—women who were understood by their fans to have lived tragic lives themselves. Edith Piaf, whose career stretched from the late 1930s to her death in 1963, was the last of the great realist singers, but the vogue for this figure reached its height in the 1920s and 1930s in the careers of Fréhel and Damia. Men generally wrote the realist songs, but women performed them, interpreted them, and, in a sense, "authored" them. The right to "author" the realist song was conferred upon the realist singer for two reasons, according to contemporary critics: she was "authentic," that is, she had "lived" these songs, had known poverty and prostitution herself; and she was an "artist" who created these characters using her performance skills, as well as her skills as an observer of human misery.

This study investigates not only the realist singer in her classic incarnation, described above (which would include Eugénie Buffet, Damia, Fréhel, Piaf), but also those singers who generate similar meanings about femininity, class, and the urban milieu. Although not generally labeled realist singers, Thérésa (1837–1913), Yvette Guilbert (1867–1944), Mistinguett (1873–1956), and even the African American performer Josephine Baker (1906–75), initiate or extend in some important way the model of the popular and populist chanteuse, and thus are addressed here.

METHOD

To ask the question of how the realist singer was meaningful to 1930s French cinema is to approach a beloved "golden age" of film in a new light. Until very recently, historians of 1930s French cinema have been intensely invested in a limited number of canonized works, notably poetic realist films, and certain (justifiably) lionized directors, such as Jean Renoir, Jean Vigo, Marcel Carné, Jacques Feyder, René Clair, and Julien Duvivier. In their treatment of 1930s French cinema, then, film historians tend to privilege aesthetic achievement in the films of a handful of directors. Accounts of this period tend to be organized chronologically, beginning with the transition from silent film to sound in 1929 and ending with the German Occupation. Typically, the extratextual contexts of 1930s French cinema discussed include political upheaval (the rise of fascism, the Popular Front, the coming of war) and the ongoing financial crises in the film industry, crystallized most flagrantly in the bankruptcy of the two giant film consortia Gaumont-Franco-Film-Aubert and Pathé-Nathan in the mid 1930s. But the main "story" is usually the movement from the "awkward" early sound films made in the late 1920s and the early 1930s to the innovations of Vigo, Clair, and Jean Renoir; or, in the latter half of the decade, from the optimism of the Popular Front films to the powerfully pessimistic vision offered by poetic realism.

My goal is not simply to write a more complete history of 1930s French cinema that would take into account a broader range of films or address the contributions of lesser-known directors more fully. Instead, my aim is a feminist cultural history of one aspect of 1930s French cinema: the representation of femininity, class, and the urban milieu as inscribed in the figure of the realist singer. Approaching this era of film history in this manner is, I believe, absolutely crucial, not only for generating new ideas about 1930s French cinema, but for extending recent feminist film criticism that attempts to build on early feminist film theory with historical research.

Such an approach invites us, first, to consider femininity in a body of films usually considered to be concerned primarily with masculinity and masculine communities. Looking at the realist singer requires also that we look at noncanonical films, for many films containing this figure are half-forgotten or utterly unknown, for a variety of reasons. This too moves us away from a strictly *auteur* or aesthetic approach. In writing a kind of "micro-history" of 1930s French film, I aim to avoid the positivist and teleological tendencies in many histories of the era in which the awkward beginnings of sound cinema give way to technical proficiency and dramatic power, climaxing in poetic realism. Instead of focusing only on films valued for their aesthetic qualities, this study moves in and out of the canon and cuts across genres, looking at classics like *Le Crime de Monsieur Lange* and *Pépé le Moko* from a new angle, and also lingering on precisely those "awkward" early sound films, such as *Faubourg Montmartre* and *Paris-Béguin*.

My project confirms several of the basic insights of feminist film theorists who began working in the 1970s, but it also takes part in some new directions in feminist film studies. Scholars working today on any aspect of gender and film are indebted to Laura Mulvey for her pioneering theory of sexual difference in the cinema. Mulvey's fundamental, still-powerful insights into cinema's representation of woman as visual spectacle provided a productive starting point for my thinking about the narrative and visual functions of the chanteuse. In particular, Mulvey's observation that the device of the show girl within the film narrative unites the gaze of the male characters and the gaze of the male spectators without breaking narrative verisimilitude reminded me that female singing performance within film narrative offers a particularly rich site for the examination of gender representation.[24] Her basic conception of the contradictory nature of female representation in the cinema, threatening and yet pleasurable to the male unconscious, is confirmed in many ways by my textual analyses of films featuring the realist singer. Performance numbers often seem to invite a presumed male spectator (and, often, a diegetic male spectator) to gaze upon the female protagonist in a gesture of voyeurism or fetishistic scopophilia.

And yet, the films often contain intriguing departures from this traditional structuring of looks, sometimes involving the eroticisation of a male character, as in *Le Bonheur* and *Coeur de Lilas,* and, at other times, featuring a charged exchange of gazes between the female performer and her diegetic female spectators (as in *Zouzou* and *Faubourg Montmartre*). These alternative structures of the look suggest that the cinematic gaze can and does respond to psychoanalytic scenarios other than those experienced by the typical male infant undergoing crises of individuation. Textual analysis informed by psychoanalysis, in my view, can still be profitably mobilized, and it has certainly moved well beyond the initial Lacanian frameworks that focus exclusively on the mechanism of the gaze and presuppose a male subject and spectator.[25]

However, my project departs in a significant way from the psychoanalytic model of feminist film criticism inaugurated in the 1970s in that it is a historical investigation of the realist singer's shifting representations in 1930s film and in live entertainment contexts. In this regard, my study is a response to the relative rigidity and ahistoricity of early psychoanalytic feminist theory and apparatus theory, both of which assume a passive spectator and a sexually and culturally undifferentiated audience.[26] My readings of films and star performance are informed by historical research that serves to challenge a conception of the cinema that posits woman as inevitably evoking lack, or that assumes that the effects of the cinematic apparatus are universal and unchanging.

In her evaluation of the various responses to the perceived limitations of 1970s theoretical approaches to the cinema, Judith Mayne usefully summarizes the types of questions typically asked by proponents of the historical models now dominant in film studies, questions with which my study of the realist singer is also concerned:

> What did film going represent for historically different audiences? Do different film genres address spectators in radically different ways? How are the cinema and individual films contextualized in a given culture? What are the different texts and institutions that define how individual films, groups of films, audiences, and film-going patterns are defined? In short, the central question raised is two-fold: what are the histories of spectatorship, and what is historical about spectatorship?[27]

In the effort to determine what is historical about spectatorship, feminist film historians have profitably combined textual analysis and the study of various contexts shaping the production of meaning of individual films, genres, and the work of directors at specific moments in history. Among the contexts deemed meaningful to such historians have been the mechanisms of censorship,[28] lesbian authorship in Hollywood cinema,[29] consumer culture,[30] and shifts in national identity.[31] Such work has implicitly informed my own.

Mayne usefully outlines the four major areas of research taken up by recent feminist film historians seeking to address the limitations of early feminist film theory: intertextuality, film exhibition, film as a particular public sphere, and film reception.[32] My work corresponds most closely to Mayne's category of intertextuality, which she defines broadly as "the ways in which film addresses its viewers across a wide range of texts."[33] This line of research can take the form of an extension of textual analysis to a group of films defined generically or historically, as in Mary Ann Doane's study of female subjectivity, consumer culture, and 1940s woman's films,[34] or in Rhona Berenstein's study of the horror genre, gender, and spectatorship.[35] Another productive branch of intertextual analysis has involved the extension of textual analysis "from the individual films to the various texts that accompany them," as in the many recent studies that draw upon fan magazines or as in star studies.[36] My study draws on both of these tendencies of intertextual work. First, it extends textual analysis to a group of films defined historically (1930s French films containing the figure of the realist singer), attending to salient patterns in visual style and narrative structure. Second, my analysis extends to nonfilm texts, such as popular songs, star biographies, fan magazines, newspaper reviews, and, above all, live performance modes, with the goal of reconstructing the realist singer's trajectory through French culture. French cinema of the 1930s, more than most, interacts significantly with other forms of popular entertainment and thus invites an intertextual approach. Cinema may have become the dominant form of popular entertainment by the early 1930s, but the café-concert, the music hall, street singing, and the dance hall were still important sources of pleasure, and each finds its way into 1930s films. Not only are the modes of performance found in the café-concert and the music hall, in particular, evident in 1930s cinema, but the very stars themselves, many of whom had been in the public eye since the early teens, extend their careers through cinema performances. I aim to show that the interaction between films and their spectators was determined in part by experience of these other forms of popular entertainment, as well as by foreknowledge and anticipation of the star. My analysis profits, in particular, then, from previous work on film stardom in that it reconstructs the star images of realist singers and music hall revue stars by analyzing the various texts and institutions through which the stars' images were created and circulated.[37]

Intertextual analysis as a method is not limited to feminist film studies, of course. Since the 1970s and early 1980s, an era that can be seen as the high point in the use of psychoanalytic and semiotic models, film studies has increasingly expanded its inquiry into the different fronts on which the production of meaning takes place. My study participates in this broad shift in film studies from the interpretation of the film text alone, using the tools of structuralism, semiotics, and psychoanalysis, to the search for meanings inflected by various contexts, such as film authorship, production, distribution, exhibition, and reception, as well as broader historical contexts. Influenced by cultural studies and cultural history, film scholars have begun to conceive of the meanings of a film, a genre, or a national cinema as contested, fluctuating, and historically specific. Tracing the realist singer's movements through the café-concert, the music hall, and the cinema helps us understand her contradictory and often unstable mixture of progressive and reactionary characteristics. On the one hand, the realist singer defies norms in the representation of class and gender, in the sense that she highlights social injustice, the plight of the prostitute, female sexual desire, and the strength to be found in female community. On the other hand, she reaffirms certain conservative notions circulating at this time regarding women's place and the nature of "the people" in general. Historical and intertextual analysis are thus required in order for us to see that the realist singer represents neither a clear-cut, nascent feminism nor a purely reactionary model of nineteenth-century gender norms in which men dominated women, but a combination of both.

Another way in which this book departs from early feminist film studies is that it examines a national cinema that differs considerably in structure and scale from the classical Hollywood cinema, the object of most 1970s feminist theoretical inquires. Here, I have benefited from Colin Crisp's excellent study of the French film industry.[38] My work is also informed by several recent studies of gender that engage the specific context of classic French cinema. As such work makes clear, there are many potential forms and goals of a feminist approach to French film. Such a project can involve writing about female filmmakers in the context of an industry and a culture that all but shut women out until the 1980s and 1990s, as Sandy Flitterman-Lewis does in her important study of Germaine Dulac, Marie Epstein, and Agnès Varda.[39] Feminist work on French film can also mean identifying a nascent feminist aesthetic in films made by men, as Geneviève Sellier does in her superb monograph on Jean Grémillon.[40] The writing of feminist film history can also involve interpreting narrative patterns that reflect and helped construct a patriarchal culture. Ginette Vincendeau does just this in her identification and analysis of a widespread pattern in 1930s French films that reflects an intensely patriarchal cultural context—the widespread, cross-generic formation of quasi-incestuous couples consisting of mature men and very young women.[41] A feminist film history might also explore those few "woman's films" films made in 1930s French cinema that aim to tell stories about women and to address female spectators.[42] Writing about masculinity is another manifestation of feminist film history, as we see in three important recent works addressing gender in French cinema: *Jean Gabin: Anatomie d'un mythe*, Claude Gauteur and Ginette Vincendeau's analysis of Jean Gabin's evolving star image; *Child of Paradise*, Edward Baron Turk's exploration of homosexuality in the films of Marcel Carné; and *La Drôle de guerre des sexes du cinéma français, 1930–1956*, Noël Burch and Geneviève Sellier's ambitious and provocative charting of the vicissitudes of patriarchy in French cinema.[43]

Vincendeau's impressive body of work on 1930s French film has proved a particularly important resource for my own investigation. My study of the realist singer, however, departs from her conception of 1930s cinema as, fundamentally, the "exploration and dramatization of masculinity."[44] Vincendeau marshals evidence of the fundamentally patriarchal nature of 1930s French cinema, noting that 99 percent of the films were produced, written, and directed by men and that relationships between male characters are consistently privileged in films such as *La Belle Équipe* and *Gueule d'amour*, as well as throughout entire genres, such as the *comique troupier* (military vaudeville comedy). Moreover, she argues, the male-female couplings of old men and young woman we see in films such as *Arlette et ses papas*, *La Femme du boulanger*, and *Vous n'avez rien à déclarer?* dominate the decade's film narratives, yielding regressive incest fantasies and reactionary politics. If I find Vincendeau's account of the many complex levels at which 1930s French cinema privileges masculinity to be entirely convincing, I choose, nonetheless, to focus on a particular construction of femininity, even if it might initially seem marginal in light of the decade's overall preoccupations.

Several groundbreaking works exploring the functions of music in film have appeared in recent years, including Claudia Gorbman's *Unheard Melodies*, Kathryn's Kalinak's *Settling the Score*, and Anahid Kassabian's *Hearing Film*. Additionally, two important anthologies addressing music and the cinema have expanded our conception of the possible functions of music in film: *Music and Cinema*, edited by James Buhler, Caryl Flinn, and David Neumeyer and *Soundtrack Available*, edited by Pamela Robertson Wojcik and Arthur Knight. All of these works have reinforced my sense of the importance of music in film, but two studies exploring the connections between music, moving images, and gender have been particularly suggestive for my study of the realist singer.

Caryl Flinn's *Strains of Utopia: Gender, Nostalgia, and Hollywood Film Music* establishes connections between romanticism in Hollywood film scores and a sense of utopia, nostalgia, and femininity. Flinn finds that in both music theory and in individual Hollywood films (particularly film noir and melodrama), music tends to be tied to a sense of utopia, and yet it also can evoke a sense of "lost pleasure and stability."[45] Flinn's work has been most suggestive for my own project in two ways: (1) in its consideration of not only nondiegetic music but also diegetic music (an element neglected by many scholars of film music); and (2) in its exploration of the association of music, femininity, and loss in film narratives that in some way confront the struggle over women's ability to "speak." In a particularly suggestive analysis, Flinn examines the repeated use of a diegetic song in the low-budget film noir *Detour* (Edgar Ulmer, 1945). After initially serving the utopian function of reminding the male protagonist of happier times spent with his fiancée, the song eventually evokes a loss of male subjectivity. In the course of his downward spiral, the protagonist accidentally strangles an aggressive and manipulative woman hitchhiker, thus divesting her of her ability to speak and "debas[ing] her for the control she wields over his unhappiness."[46] Flinn's work thus suggests, for me, that the nexus of music, femininity, loss, and imperiled male subjectivity I have identified in 1930s French films featuring the realist singer is potentially transcultural.

Another important influence on my study of the realist singer is Susan McClary's *Feminine Endings: Music, Gender, and Sexuality*, an exploration of the contributions of women in music, a field that traditionally has barred them from full participation. McClary analyzes the myriad ways in which music is "gendered," from its very codes to the discursive strategies of female composers and performers. At the same time, she avoids ascribing excessive agency to female musicians. For example, she argues that Madonna's deployment of musical codes defies tradition in their use of pitch and cadence and that, furthermore, Madonna creates "fluid identities" and "counternarratives" of female heterosexual desire in her interviews, music videos, and concert performances.[47] Yet, she also argues, Madonna is not a "solitary creator who ultimately determines fixed meanings for her pieces"; she is, rather, "best understood as a head of a corporation that produces images of her self-representation." This line of argumentation has inspired me to try to maintain a balanced understanding of the possibilities for the realist singers' agency and the constraints on that agency. The realist singers operated within a commercial system in which they functioned as commodities, and they performed songs usually written by men, in venues owned and operated by men. And yet, we must not lose sight of the realist singers' ambiguous textual functions, of their important role in creating and sustaining their own public images, or, more broadly, of the disturbance realist singers created in a cultural context in which women had very little political and economic power.

Dudley Andrew's *Mists of Regret: Culture and Sensibility in Classic French Film* has also shaped my study of the realist singer. Andrew's work combines careful analysis of individual films with a vivid portrait of the relevant contexts of poetic realist films: the films' production and reception, as well as their literary, artistic, and theatrical contexts. Although my study does not address the phenomenon of poetic realism directly, Andrew's work informs my own in many ways, for the realist singer frequently crosses the path of the poetic realist film. The realist song's emphasis on décor and atmosphere is shared by films such as Carné's *Hôtel du Nord* and *Le Jour se lève*. Its nostalgic sensibility—its longing for another time, another place, and a lost community—permeates films such as Duvivier's *Pépé le Moko* and *La Belle Équipe*. The outsiders given pride of place in the realist song—pimps, prostitutes, the poor, soldiers—populate *Jenny* (Carné, 1936), *La Bandera* (Duvivier, 1935), *Quai des brumes* (Carné, 1938), and *Hôtel du Nord*. The tragic destiny encountered by the realist song's narrator or her pimp likewise awaits the proletarian male protagonist of *Gueule d'amour*, *La Bête humaine* (Renoir, 1938), and *Le Dernier Tournant* (Pierre Chenal, 1939). Certainly, the realist song draws upon many of the same literary and visual sources informing poetic realism, and so we shall encounter the tropes of poetic realism with some frequency here. Indeed, given the appearance of the realist singer in several important poetic realist films and their precursors early in the decade, one might be inclined to conceive of her as the subjugated, female voice of poetic realism, the döppelganger of the doomed criminal-hero played so often by Jean Gabin. This study, however, veers away from poetic realism and its concerns, most obviously because the realist singer appears in many non-poetic-realist films in the 1930s. Moreover, the realist singer's genealogy, which I trace from the mid-nineteenth-century café-concert singer Thérésa to the 1920s revue star Mistinguett and beyond, stands quite apart from that of the male protagonist in poetic realism.

My analysis of the specific figure of the realist singer constitutes a tighter focus than the wide-ranging studies of Burch, Sellier, Flitterman-Lewis, Vincendeau, and Andrew. These scholars have made the specificity of my project possible by virtue of their willingness to take on the oeuvre of a director, entire genres or movements, or even decades of film history. Because others have taken the preliminary steps in gender analysis of 1930s French cinema, I am able to carve out a more specific area of investigation: the functions of the realist singer in French film and culture.

In another sense, however, my project is more broadly conceived than those of many other investigations in that it explores not only the cinematic incarnations of the realist singer, but also her movements through other forms of popular entertainment. Understanding the realist singer in film requires an exploration of her historical development in the café-concert and the music hall.[48] The café-concert of the 1860s, the context I explore first, offered food, drink, and song to a mixture of working-class and bourgeois spectators in performance spaces ranging from Latin Quarter dives to sumptuous song palaces clustered along the Champs Élysées and the *grands boulevards* of the Right Bank. The environment of the café-concert gave rise to the emergence of the first popular female singer, Thérésa. In her populism and her expertise at self-promotion, Thérésa was, I argue, the prototype of later realist singers like Damia and Fréhel.

In the 1880s, another type of popular entertainment began to emerge, the music hall. Offering variety acts and more monumental performance spaces, the music hall slowly began to displace the café-concert. By World War I, the centerpiece of the café-concert, the *tour de chant* ("singing turn," or the performance of several songs in a row by one singer) began to cede its centrality in an evening's entertainment to the revue, which offered kick lines, elaborate costumes, and complex sets, resulting in a new scale of spectacle. The revue also engendered a kind of female star, the *meneuse de revue* (revue star). Mistinguett, Josephine Baker, Florelle, and Jane Marnac led the sumptuous productions at music halls like the Folies-Bergère and the Casino de Paris in the teens, the 1920s, and the 1930s. The *meneuse de revue* did not simply displace the more modest performance mode of the realist singer; rather, she absorbed, distorted, and transformed the persona of café-concert realist singer, infusing spectacular performance with the populism and intimacy of the realist singer.

After exploring the realist singer's roots in the café-concert and music hall, I shall look closely at her film performances in order to answer a number of questions. How did the realist singer negotiate the contextual shifts from her public persona as a recognizable performer to her character within the film narrative and back again? Are the gender codes of a predominantly male cinema resistant to the more fluid and transgressive ambiguity of these charismatic, popular women, or are the narratives, and the gendered structure that underlies them, subverted in some residual (and partly unconscious) way? More broadly, what was the realist singer, an apparently anachronistic figure from the turn-of-the-century café-concert, doing in 1930s films? Why did this cinema, and 1930s French culture more generally, still need her?

In addition to exploring the intertextual influences on the representation of the realist singer and her textual functions in a number of 1930s films, I shall also explore some of her broader historical contexts. Given that one of the most salient meanings of the realist singer is her association with the city of Paris from the late nineteenth century to World War II, I should like to indicate my position in relation to the extensive debate on the Paris flâneur that has unfolded over the past twenty years in literary studies, sociology, and political philosophy.[49]

Flânerie is, in its most general sense, the act of strolling or sauntering idly. But in the recent critical literature, the flâneur is defined with more precision, usually (1) as a historical figure of nineteenth-century Paris whose wanderings through the city were facilitated by the rise of consumer capitalism and the construction of new urban spaces (notably the Paris arcades, Hausmann's wide boulevards, and the department store); and (2), in a much broader sense, as "an emblematic representative of modernity and personification of contemporary urbanity,"[50] not only in nineteenth-century Paris, but in other major cities and periods as well. This second, expanded definition emerges from the notion that the flâneur is a "man of the crowd" engaged in a new ways of observing the world around him and capable of "reap[ing] aesthetic meaning . . . from the spectacle of the teeming crowds."[51] This second definition has received the most attention, resulting in a voluminous literature on the metaphorical possibilities held by the flâneur in conceptualizing modernity and, in more recent literature, the gendered hierarchy of the modern city.

The classic flâneur is a bourgeois masculine figure, free of pressing financial concerns and family obligations. His female counterpart, the *flâneuse*, was considered nonexistent in the early critical literature due to women's restricted relationship to the urban environment in nineteenth-century Paris.[52] Janet Wolff contends, "There is no question of inventing the *flâneuse*; the essential point is that such a character was rendered impossible by the sexual divisions of the nineteenth century."[53] Susan Buck-Morss, likewise, disputes the existence of the flâneuse and points out that the closest female equivalent to the flâneur was the prostitute. "[T]he flâneur was simply the name of a man who loitered; but all women who loitered risked being seen as whores, as the term 'street-walker,' or 'tramp' applied to women makes clear."[54] However, scholars such as Deborah Parsons have begun to raise new questions about the flâneur: "Is the flâneur bourgeois or vagrant, authoritative or marginal, within or detached from the city crowd, masculine, feminine, or androgynous? And what does such a redefinition imply for theories of women's place in the urban landscape?"[55]

Scholars have suggested several candidates for the flâneuse. Anne Friedberg, for example, argues that the female window shopper was a flâneuse, emphasizing that new ways of looking were connected intimately to modern, urban modes of consumption brought about by the development of the department store, in particular.[56] Parsons argues convincingly that Virginia Woolf, Janet Flanner, Djuna Barnes, and Anaïs Nin and other novelists working in London and Paris from the 1880s to World War II can be considered flâneuses in that they observed, wrote about, and negotiated new, specifically urban identities for themselves.[57]

Is it useful to think of the realist singer as a kind of flâneuse? Yes, I would argue, but only in a limited sense. As a historical phenomenon, there is a connection between the realist singer and the flâneur, in that the realist singer engaged in urban wandering with the purpose of observing the variety of social types found on the streets of Paris. If we can believe the autobiographical accounts of singers like Eugénie Buffet and Mistinguett, realist singers strolled through poor or geographically marginal neighborhoods in search of evocative images, possible personae, and even the costumes of the streetwalker or the lowly seamstress. This wandering was quite purposeful, however, and thus seems to differ substantially from the aimless wandering of the male dandy or even from the middle-class female shopper's window-shopping. The realist singer's search for an atmosphere, a sensation, the texture of a voice, the choker ribbon of a prostitute, or even a violent encounter between a prostitute and her pimp (observed from a safe distance, of course) was carried out in the service of her art: the creation of a convincing persona she could present on the stage of the café-concert or the music hall.

The realist singer is less easily associated with the second meaning of the flâneur ("symbol of modernity"). True, like the flâneur (in his incarnation as "artist" celebrated by Baudelaire), the realist singer was seen by her contemporaries as emblematic of a certain urban "type" symbolizing Paris itself and capable of recounting something important about the contemporary urban landscape. But the "stories" she told about that landscape and its inhabitants (which included themes such as "poverty and violence pervade the city" and "Paris is changing, and not necessarily for the better") distance her from the figures of modernity, both male and female, who experienced the modern cityscape from an apolitical vantage point. The realist singer narrated the lives of prostitutes, pimps, sailors, and the poor: figures barred from the luxury of aimless wandering, distanced observation, and the excitement of shopping. Rather than serving as a symbol of the "new," modern city, she evokes nostalgia for preindustrial Paris and for a sense of community felt to be disappearing following urban "renewal."

Another reason for resisting the full absorption of the realist singer into the debates around flânerie and modernity is that the meanings generated by the realist singer are shaped by quite specific institutional contexts, namely, the spaces of popular entertainment (the café-concert, the music hall, the cinema). Likewise, a full understanding of the realist singer requires analysis of the specific textual forms that "produce" her: the fiction film or the popular song, for example. We should resist the reduction of the realist singer to one of a whole gallery of modern urban types (the flâneur, the ragpicker, the prostitute, etc.) or to a vague symbol of modernity. This stance does not, however, prevent us from seeing her as one, quite specific response to the changes brought about by modernity in the late nineteenth and early twentieth centuries in France. Indeed, the texts and contexts I analyze: the performances of the realist singer in 1930s films, music hall, and the café-concert; song lyrics; and the "star texts" around the singers, consisting of autobiography, music hall criticism, and film criticism, can be understood to signal an attempt to cope with loss (and the perception of loss) in the face of industrialization, urbanization, and new cultural roles for women. One way the texts accomplish this is by creating a nostalgic image of Paris (and, by extension, France), in which there exists a strong sense of community and working-class identity. In the context of large-scale cultural and economic shifts, popular entertainment undergoes a transformation beginning in the mid nineteenth century from human-scale, local attractions toward an increasingly spectacular mode reliant on new technologies. Spectators become increasingly "passive," it is generally thought, and audiences become increasingly mixed in terms of gender, class, and national identity. Performers and genres from earlier entertainment forms are called upon to assuage the anxiety generated by new technologies, changes in media, and shifts in audience composition.

The realist singer is an important part of these historical changes and symbolic operations. As this book will show, femininity is reconstructed in relation to changes in technology and society. The realist singer symbolizes, in part, the negative effects of urbanization. She expresses *and* masks social division by "performing" urban poverty and "overcoming" it at the same time through a rags-to-riches discourse. For audiences of the 1930s, she stands for a successful adaptation to the urban space of Paris in the face of economic depression and political upheaval, but is still, reassuringly, a "woman of the people" who can evoke the "good old days."

One of the main vectors through which I interpret the realist singer is the notion of "place," a concept broad enough to include the evocation of urban space, decor, and setting in the films themselves, the various institutional spaces of popular commercial entertainment, and a more metaphorical conception of space relating to French national identity. I argue that the realist singers embody a particular experience of the city of Paris, an experience that includes nostalgia for an idea of community believed to be found in working-class parts of Paris such as Belleville and La Villette; a voyeuristic look at prostitution on the darkened streets and among the shadows of the military fortifications of Paris; and the vicarious pleasure found in the experience of emotional, deeply felt texts (autobiographies, records, film performances, the music hall tour de chant), all of which—uncharacteristically, in the French context—assign a central place to women.

The genre of the realist song itself is noteworthy for its preoccupation with the topography of Paris.[58] The song titles themselves reflect this focus on "place": "Elle fréquentait la rue Pigalle" (She Hung Out on Pigalle Street),[59] "Entre Saint-Ouën et Clignancourt" (Between Saint-Ouën and Clignancourt),[60] and "À Paris dans chaque faubourg" (In Paris in Each *Faubourg*).[61] (*Faubourgs* were the villages on the periphery of Paris that were annexed by the city in 1860, bringing to twenty the number of *arrondissements* [districts]). The realist song is typically set in the poor neighborhoods on the periphery of Paris: Belleville, Ménilmontant, Montmartre, La Villette, La Chapelle, Les Lilas, and St. Denis. Other preferred settings are, simply, "the street" and "the fortifications." The specificity of place in songs about the poor begins in the songs of Aristide Bruant (1851–1925), whose 1889 collection of songs entitled *Dans les rues* (In the Streets) contains songs such as "À la Villette," "À Montrouge," "À la Chapelle," and "À Saint-Ouën,"—all working-class areas in or just outside of the city of Paris.

This emphasis on place persists in the 1930s films in which the realist singer appears, particularly in the poetic realist films. The rain-soaked streets of Paris and port towns, the cheap furnished hotel rooms, the working-class cafés and bistros, and the "Zone," a depressed, arguably dangerous, quarter on the periphery of Paris where the poor lived, are all evoked through both the diegetic performances of the realist song and films' settings. Whether set in La Villette (*Coeur de Lilas*), Montparnasse (*La Tête d'un homme*), or the Faubourg Montmartre (*Faubourg Montmartre*), the films addressed here use a sense of place to comment on the intractable nature of class boundaries, on the allure of the city, and on the shifting nature of national identity. More specifically, this preoccupation with the geography of Paris in songs and films reflects this culture's pleasure in "knowing" (and remembering) the city's marginal spaces that are in the midst of transformation by the forces of modernity. Such cultural artifacts promise a trip through the landscape of the city that leaves the path of the touristic or bourgeois Paris and allow one to celebrate, mourn, and romanticize the underworld and the working class. The incessant naming of places, the insistence on specificity here also, perhaps, reflects a need to "pin down" meanings about this ever-changing city and its various populations, which had experienced such tumult and change throughout the Third Republic.

For an understanding of the broader possibilities in what seems to be an essential connection between urban space and the realist singer, I was greatly helped by Adrian Rifkin's *Street Noises: Parisian Pleasure, 1900– 1940*. Rifkin explores the highly charged, historically varying relationship between Paris and *le peuple* in sources ranging from the writings of literary journalists about the Paris Zone and flea markets to the photographic montages and special reports of *Détective* magazine, Gustave Charpentier's operetta *Louise*, popular songs, and autobiographies of music hall performers. Rifkin holds that the discourses around Paris and *le peuple* are generally spoken in a male voice. With the exception of the American singer Josephine Baker, he argues, the chanteuse never manages to address the city of Paris as a lover.[62] Rifkin sees the female singer not so much as a "writer" of the city of Paris, but as herself "written" by other, male figures. Thérésa, the café-concert star of the mid nineteenth century was thus "written" by the journalist-ghostwriters who penned her memoir; Fréhel and Damia were "authored" by music hall critics like Gustave Fréjaville and Maurice Verne and the poet-flâneur Pierre Mac Orlan. These male authors, Rifkin argues, needed the female singer as a site on which to project their own desires for fame, scandal, and alterity.[63]

While Rifkin rightly notes the apparent pervasiveness of male authorship in the production of the female singer, there is another way in which we can view the realist singer. My own premise is that a sustained analysis of her performances—both on- and offstage—and the cultural contexts that shaped her reception can lead us to a different view, one that figures her in some sense as both "producer" and "produced." The chanteuse is both a product of discursive forces we might label "male" (forces that include male lyricists, male impresarios, male critics, and even male fantasy), and she is also at least partly responsible for the production of meanings associated with her public persona. Moreover, the realist singer's female fans were likely to have constructed interpretations of her performances and her personae that differed somewhat from those of her male spectators. While my primary interest is the cultural nexus that produced the representations of the realist singer, as opposed to reception or female spectatorship, I engage in speculation from time to time about how the realist singer's performance might have "spoken" to women.

This study argues that the realist singer is an "author," not only of her "self," but also, in a sense, of the city of Paris. One of the powerful elements of the realist singer's persona is her ability to evoke Paris. When Mistinguett sings "Ça c'est Paris," affirming that Paris is a blonde with an upturned nose and laughing eyes (her own appearance precisely), or when, in *Pépé le Moko*, Fréhel condenses her own past with that of the history of Paris and then grafts these two histories onto the film's narrative, both singers project themselves (or at least the ensemble of traits known as "Mistinguett" and "Fréhel") quite forcefully into the texts in question. Female performance, I argue, constitutes one way of "writing the city."

In Mulvey's "Visual Pleasure and Narrative Cinema," woman is spectacle, a textual manifestation of male anxiety. For Vincendeau, the generic patterns, male authorship, and implied spectators of 1930s French film are, primarily, manifestations of patriarchy. For Rifkin, the male bohemian usurps the place of the female singer-as-"author." In contrast, I conceive of the realist singer and her spectators as in possession of some agency in the production of her various meanings.

Chapter 1 establishes the template of the realist singer figure and shows how it evolved from the mid 1800s to the turn of the century. My search for the precursors of the realist singer in 1930s cinema begins in the 1860s, when women first occupied positions of centrality in commercial entertainment. Although women had obtained stardom in opera, theater, and ballet, it is the stars of the café-concert who, because of their mass appeal, their power within institutions of popular entertainment, and their perceived incarnation of the working class, provide the most direct antecedents to the popular singers and cinema actresses of the period between the wars.

The realist singer was perceived to have come (and usually did come, in fact) from the working class. This aspect of the singer's past was celebrated and used to establish her authenticity.[64] Popular with working-class and bourgeois audiences alike, she sang songs, and sometimes performed dances, that evoked the lives and geography of the Paris working class and the underworld. This lineage begins with Thérésa in the mid-1860s café-concert, continues with Eugénie Buffet, who created the genre of the *pier-reuse* (streetwalker), and intersects with the Montmartre cabaret tradition through Yvette Guilbert, the "turn-of-the-century *diseuse* [monologist]."

Chapter 2 continues the genealogy of the realist singer, this time within the context of the rise of the modern music hall. Against the backdrop of the music hall's shift in scale and technology, its incorporation of jazz and its emphasis on dance, and its appeal to an audience both more international and affluent, we shall look at the career of Mistinguett, "queen" of the music hall, who both absorbs and extends the realist singer legacy. Mistinguett incorporated the realist singer's persona and performance style into her singing and dancing, but also elaborated a quite different version of the Paris chanteuse, the glamorous and imperious *meneuse de revue*. Her one sound film, *Rigolboche,* bears all of the contradictions that such a combination could generate.

Chapter 3 argues that, contemporaneous with the now-dominant music hall, the legacy of the café-concert mode of sociability and female performance persists in the film performances of Fréhel, who expresses nostalgia for her own past, for the past of Paris, and for a diminishing sense of community, female and otherwise, in contemporary urban life. *Pépé le Moko* contains the template of this set of meanings around the realist singer, while *L'Entraîneuse, Coeur de Lilas,* and *Le Crime de Monsieur Lange* supplement the template with alternative models of femininity as well as different visions of class constraints. The realist singer, I attempt to show here, is not only the projection of male fantasy we see in Mac Orlan's writing and in Carco's *Prisons de femmes,* but can be seen to "author" her own version of the city of Paris.

Chapter 4 examines the legacy of the music hall in 1930s French film, when the music hall itself had been displaced by the sound cinema as the primary form of popular entertainment. I begin with *Faubourg Mont-martre,* which contains both the realist singer and the revue star as secondary characters, and continue with analyses of *Zouzou, Paris-Béguin,* and *Le Bonheur,* films that feature the music hall queen as protagonist. The "star" characters in *Zouzou* and *Paris-Béguin* are, in fact, played by real stars of the Paris music hall revue, Josephine Baker and Jane Marnac. To varying degrees, by incorporating the remnants of the realist singer persona into their female characters, these films mourn the decline of earlier, more human-scale forms of entertainment, yet they also celebrate (and, in effect, mourn) the music hall. Moreover, the films comment quite self-consciously on the music hall as a social space and on the regimes of "looking" engendered by both the music hall and the cinema.

Chapter 5 analyzes 1930s films that directly address the modern technologies of sound and image recording—photography and cinema—as opposed to the live forms of entertainment represented in the films of chapters 3 and 4. In *Sola, La Tête d'un homme,* and *Prix de beauté,* both the entertainment context represented and the representation of the realist singer had changed dramatically. Far from representing the lost sense of working-class community or the romanticized underworld of Paris during the era before World War I, as we see her doing in chapter 3, and far from expressing the desire for the aura of the realist singer in the modern music hall, as in chapter 4, the female singer examined in chapter 5 generates male anxiety and even madness. The singers played by Damia and Louise Brooks evoke a revised model of femininity, one that is linked specifically in the films' narratives, visual style, and aural style to the new technologies of sound cinema and the phonograph. The Conclusion explores what had become of the realist singer by the late 1930s. Her legacy, I argue, persists into the 1960s through Edith Piaf, yet is absorbed into the persona and film roles of a man: Jean Gabin.

In sum, this book strives to trace the historical development of the realist singer through the café-concert and music hall and untangle her symbolic complexities in 1930s French cinema. This figure offers the possibility of understanding not only her construction as an ambiguous force operating from the margins of French society and its narratives, but also the probability that those narratives, and the society beyond it, are inherently unstable and far more ambivalent in their construction of class and gender than previous writing suggests. I envision this work as part of an ongoing project of a long overdue rewriting of the history of the "golden era" of French cinema, one that takes into account both the construction of femininity within the narratives and the broader impact of female performers in French culture.

1 · Caf'-Conc'

The Rise of the Unruly Woman

Around 1865, the journalist Louis Veuillot went to the Alcazar café-concert, although no doubt apprehensive. He was there to see a performance by Thérésa (Emma Valadon, 1837–1913), a singer who had recently become wildly popular with her bawdy parodies of the sentimental ballad. Setting the stage, he writes of the crowded, smoky room, and of his difficulty in finding unoccupied seats. He is shocked to discover, for the first time, women smoking in a public place. With some misgiving, he describes Thérésa's entrance:

> SHE was about to appear, [and] a thunderous outbreak of applause announced her entry. I did not find her so hideous as I'd been told she was. She is rather a large girl, quite well built, without any charm besides her fame—which is charm of the first order, I admit. She has, I believe, some hair; her mouth appears to stretch right round her head; she has great fat lips like a negro; shark's teeth. . . . She knows how to sing. As for the song itself, it is indescribable, like its subject. You would need to be a Parisian to appreciate its qualities, a refined Frenchman to savor its profound and perfect ineptitude. It has nothing in common with any known language, or art, or truth.[1]

Veuillot's account renders Thérésa's appearance and her repertoire as something threatening, yet he is clearly fascinated, even seduced. The metaphors he uses convey an otherness; she has "negro lips" and "shark teeth," while Veuillot has only a begrudging recollection of her hair. Furthermore, her performance style lacks art; she acts out the song as much as she sings it, with bold use of her eyes, arms, shoulders, and hips.[2] Veuillot goes on to establish a connection between her music and the figure of the *voyou*, a masculine icon of the Parisian criminal class.

> The music has the same character as the words; they are both vulgar and corrupt caricatures, and moreover cheerless, like the sly face of the guttersnipe

27

[*voyou*]. The guttersnipe, the natural Parisian, does not cry, he blubs; he does not laugh, he cackles; he does not joke, he wisecracks, he does not dance, he does the *chahut;* he is not a lover, but a libertine. Art consists in assembling these ingredients in one song, and this the songwriters manage nine times out of ten, with the singer's help.[3]

Veuillot's description of Thérésa and her music is compelling, not only because it communicates his intense distaste, but also because it strives to relate Thérésa to a certain idea of Paris, or perhaps a way of inhabiting Paris that he deems "masculine." The *voyou*, he affirms, is a Parisian phenomenon. *Voyou* originally meant "tramp" or "vagabond"; then, around 1830, it referred to any "man of the middle or lower class with reprehensible morals." Around 1844, *voyou* took on the more specific meaning of a "gamin des rues, déluré et mal élevé [knowing and ill-mannered street urchin]."[4]

The figure of the *voyou*—the street urchin, the urban guttersnipe— recurs in various guises throughout French popular culture. He can be found in the *apaches* celebrated by Léger in his homage to the working-class dance hall,[5] in the *valse chaloupée* (literally, "swaying waltz"; also called the "apache dance") created in 1909 by Max Dearly and Mistinguett, in Louis Feuillade's serial films of the teens, and in 1930s cinema in the *mauvais garçons* (tough guys, hoods) played by Jean Gabin and Albert Préjean. Veuillot's incisive association of Thérésa and the *voyou* invites us to explore whether the realist singer—a concentrated "site" in which femininity, criminality, and Paris converge—is a kind of female incarnation of the *voyou*. Veuillot condemns Thérésa's performance specifically for lacking in feminine grace. He describes not only the shocking image of women in the audience smoking in public, but also the pathetic specter of defeated husbands dragged by their wives to witness this spectacle. The women are absorbed, scarcely sensing themselves out of place. "The presence of these 'proper' women lent the auditorium a special cachet of slovenliness: a social slovenliness!"[6]

Veuillot, perhaps in spite of himself, heralds an important shift in the social structure of popular entertainment, and more significantly, in its configuration of sexual comportment and roles. What is this space where women felt at liberty to smoke, where husbands bowed to their wives' tastes with apparent diffidence? To what extent can such cultural upheavals be attributed to the discourse of the performer: the ensemble of her persona, her interpretation, and the context in which she flourished?

This chapter lays out the lineage of the realist singer and the institutional contexts in which she functioned. Thérésa, the first modern popular (and populist) singing star, is the prototype of the realist singer. Let us look first to the institution of the café-concert itself to understand how the cultural context in which Thérésa performed contributed to her power to disturb conservative critics such as Veuillot. What sort of an audience frequented the Alcazar, for instance? How did the cultural determinations of the performance space affect that audience, or negotiate the vast distance between the performer and her heterogeneous public? More essential still, how are we to relate this particular mode of spectacle to performances in 1930s French cinema? It would be helpful, then, to begin with a rudimentary sketch of the popular culture from which this cinematic persona emerged, before embarking on a more thorough history of performance modes and performers.

THE CAFÉ-CONCERT

Long before Damia and Fréhel functioned as emissaries of the Paris gutter in 1930s cinema, Thérésa embodied *le peuple* and Paris itself in the mid-nineteenth-century café-concert. The café-concert was a boisterous entertainment space whose roots can be traced to Café des Aveugles, which opened in 1731 in the basement of the Café Italien at the Palais-Royal.[7] At the *café-chantant* (singing cafe), as it was usually called in the eighteenth century, singers and *musiciens ambulants* (strolling musicians) were offered a modest meal in exchange for their performances. The café-chantant proliferated in the aftermath of the Revolution, when the monopoly enjoyed by *théâtres de privilèges* (officially patronized theaters) ended. For the next fifteen years, what police surveillance reports interchangeably called the *café-chantant, café-concert, vocable musico, estaminet lyrique, salle lyrique, café-théâtre,* and *café-spectacle* flourished in Paris.[8] These establishments were clustered around the *barrières d'octroi* (tax collection points at the city gates), the Palais-Royal, the Tuileries, the main faubourgs, and the large boulevards of the city: Temple, Strasbourg, Ménilmontant, and Saint-Denis. The café-chantant was most often a modest affair. Songs were typically improvised at the back of a cafe or in its basement and the decor generally consisted of a simple painted backdrop. Most significantly, the cafés-chantants were accessible to those of all social categories.

The café-chantant was not allowed to flourish unfettered. Its history is marked with periods of restriction and censorship. After fifteen years of relatively unrestricted growth, the café-chantant was subjected to the control of Napoleon in a series of decrees in 1806 and 1807. The café-chantant, which had become the principal source of entertainment of the working-class population, was forbidden for reasons of "public security."[9] The theater monopoly was reestablished, while boundaries between the different kinds of entertainment were established and maintained. *Grands théâtres* were designated and included the Opéra, the Opéra-Comique, and the Théâtre-Français (the Comédie-Française); the *théâtres secondaires* included the Théâtre du Vaudeville and the Théâtre des Variétés.[10] In order to better control the distribution and performance of songs, the government also obliged each establishment to restrict itself to a specific repertoire or genre—pantomime, vaudeville, Italian opera, dance, melodrama, and so on.[11] From this period until 1830, then, cafés rarely featured attractions or singers. The accession to the throne of Louis-Philippe I in 1830 was followed by the reopening of some of the old cafés-chantants, but the monarchy was careful to maintain tight ideological surveillance over worker-poets who wrote and performed subversive songs. For about five months in 1848, censorship was lifted by Louis-Philippe, who wanted to placate republican opposition unhappy with the monarchy. The cafés-chantants, especially those in the Latin Quarter and the faubourgs, reopened and became centers of political life where students and workers met.

Following the events of 1848, tight control was again exercised. President Louis-Napoléon banned the public performance of political songs in the *goguettes*, the more militant of the cafés-chantants. It appears that it was at this point that the term *café-concert* came to be used more frequently, distinguishing between the political *goguette* and establishments more likely to feature romances and comic songs. The café-concert did not escape the watchful eye of the authorities, however. An elaborate apparatus of police surveillance and censorship was put in place for controlling the output of café-concert, which would persist throughout second half of nineteenth century.[12] The directors of cafés-concerts were required to go to the Prefecture of Police on a daily basis in order to have that evening's program approved. Nevertheless, the 1850s saw an increase in the number of establishments offering drinks and singing performances, especially in the northern and eastern sections of Paris. These establishments, however, were often short-lived and catered primarily to workers.

By the time Thérésa came on the scene in the early 1860s, the café-concert was enjoying another relaxation of rules and entering its thirty-year heyday. Larger, more monumental performance spaces were constructed, attracting both middle-class and working-class audiences. This new café-concert had its base in the Paris of Baron Haussmann, as T. J. Clark notes, inhabiting the *grands boulevards* constructed in the 1850s and 1860s.[13] The cafés-concerts, in fact, varied considerably in size, decor, and reputation in the mid nineteenth century. The most reputable houses were located on or near the

Champs-Élysées and the *grands boulevards*. On the Champs-Élysées were the outdoor, summertime cafés-concerts, among them the Ambassadeurs, the Pavillon de l'Horloge, and the Summer Alcazar, where Thérésa became famous in the mid 1860s. The ninth and tenth arrondissements contained the largest number of cafés-concerts in Paris. The luxurious Eldorado opened in 1858 on the boulevard de Strasbourg in the tenth arrondissement. The "Eldo" seated 1,500 people and boasted three balconies, elaborate decorations, and a large cafe. In 1860, the Winter Alcazar, designed to evoke a Moorish palace, opened on the rue du Faubourg-Poissonnière in the tenth arrondissement. The Bataclan, on the boulevard Voltaire in the eleventh arrondissement, opened in 1864. It resembled an immense Chinese pagoda and seated 2,500 people. Ten years later, the Scala, to which Fréhel refers in *Pépé le Moko*, opened on the boulevard de Strasbourg across from the Eldorado. The Eden-Concert, where Yvette Guilbert (1867–1944) began singing in 1889, and where she would ultimately hone her definitive look and performance, opened in 1881 on the boulevard de Sébastopol.

Not all cafés-concerts possessed the elaborate architecture and the comfort of the big halls. At the other end of the café-concert spectrum were the *beuglants* or *boui-bouis*, cafés-concerts that tended to attract an exclusively working-class or student clientele. The beuglant proliferated in the Latin Quarter, near the *barrières d'octroi*, and in the *faubourgs*. The Café de l'Annexion, for example, was located in La Chapelle; the Café de la Réunion was in Belleville, and the Concert de l'Abbaye was in Montmartre. The beuglant, often associated with prostitution and a general lack of hygiene, typically offered a modest performance space and a few singers, whose repertoires lagged behind those of the large cafés-concerts. The Chalet, located at the intersection of the boulevard Saint-Michel and the rue Auguste-Comte in the fifth arrondissement from 1880 to 1900, offered a particularly raucous atmosphere for its student clientele: "it's a wooden shack in the middle of a garden where the racket is such that it's not unusual to see the singer cease his vociferations and the overwhelmed musicians lay down their instruments without the slightest surprise on the part of the audience."[14] The Folies-Dauphine, perhaps the best-known beuglant in the Latin Quarter, was located on rue Mazet in the sixth arrondissement from 1850 to 1866 and served "students who did not study."[15]

The Ville Japonaise opened around 1890 on the boulevard de Strasbourg in the tenth arrondissement. The establishment was divided into two parts; on one side, humorous songs were performed; on the other, spectators could chat up the women singers until 11:00 P.M. At that time, the *caveau* opened on the lower level, and there were more singing performances until 2:00

A.M. Maurice Chevalier performed at the Ville Japonaise at the age of thirteen and describes it in his memoirs:

> The audience consisted for the most part of well-off old lechers accompanied by the young women they kept. . . . The rest of the hall was filled with a transitory audience, the *concert* being situated on the boulevard de Strasbourg, an exceedingly lively and raucous thoroughfare. Many business travelers awaited the hour of their train's departure from the gare de l'Est. A bad audience, indifferent to the efforts of the artists, who themselves had been hired from the lower ranks of the profession by musical agents of similar station. Quite often, an entire set of songs was performed without any applause whatsoever, so involved were these old perverts with their individual stories and pursuits. The whole establishment, from the management to the waiters, bore the imprint of this atmosphere, and if an artist, through some extraordinary chance, was talented enough to draw loud applause, I think he would have been dropped on the spot for disturbing the sweet tranquility of that blend of café-concert and *maison close* [brothel].[16]

Located on the café-concert spectrum somewhere between the beuglant and the glamorous Scala was the modest and more respectable *concert de quartier* (neighborhood café-concert). Like the beuglant, the neighborhood café-concert attracted people from the district in which it was located, but it was much larger (100–700 seats). It also tended to remain in business longer, and offered more variety in its programs.[17] Typically, the neighborhood café-concert offered a café, a dance space, and a terrace, in addition to the performance space itself. The Commerce, for example, opened on the rue du Faubourg-du-Temple in the eleventh arrondissement in 1879 and offered a solid program to its working-class patrons.[18] Maurice Chevalier reminisced about the Commerce.

> A big guy, supporter of all the cafes in the faubourg, performed as a monologist, and the workers liked it too. He stumbled, was forever between two glasses of wine . . . and joked in slang, having for the most part no time to work on his songs. He and the boss, Verner, always played together at the end of the show in a one-act play, of which, apparently, they had only learned the beginning and the end.[19]

The Commerce, and its attached brasserie, was the gathering place for all of the artists of the faubourg after midnight. It remained popular until 1919, when the rising popularity of the cinema forced it to close its doors.

Most historians estimate that between 1848 and 1914, there were, consistently, at least two hundred cafés-concerts in Paris. Concetta Condemi breaks down the location of the cafés-concerts for the period 1860–90. At this time, 37 percent of the cafés-concerts (approximately 121 establishments) were located in the ninth, tenth, and eleventh arrondissements; 25 percent of them (approximately 80) were located in the third, fourth, fifth, and eighteenth arrondissements, and the remaining 38 percent were scattered throughout Paris.[20] The popularity of the café-concert becomes even more apparent when one realizes that, in this same period, there were only around forty theaters in Paris.[21] The large cafés-concerts provided direct competition to luxurious theaters such as the Opéra, Comédie-Française, and Opéra Lyrique, as well as to the *bals publics* (dance halls), the Mabille, Bullier, and the Tivoli.

An evening at a café-concert differed in many ways from the experience at the theater or opera. There was no entrance fee, but one was expected to order drinks. Generally, between two *tours de chants* (singing turns), a sign would appear: "On est prié de renouveler" ("Please reorder") and one then ordered coffee, *limonade*, absinthe, wine, or champagne. Turnover was high; if one ran out of money or if the spectacle was uninteresting, one moved on, leaving an open seat for another spectator. The atmosphere was relaxed and boisterous; smoking was permitted and spectators laughed and talked amongst themselves, called out to the performers, sang along with them, and moved freely around the room. Adding to the sense of freedom at the café-concert was the open-ended nature of the entertainment. There was no clear beginning or end to the spectacle. Unlike at the theater or opera, customers could simply come and go as they pleased.

Up until 1867, the types of performances and costumes allowed in the café-concert were quite restricted. In order to protect the theaters, the authorities forbade costumes, spoken texts, pantomime, and dance in the café-concert. But in 1867, the director of the Eldorado defied the law by featuring a performance of passages from the works of Corneille and Racine by a *tragédienne*, a certain Mademoiselle Cornélie, involved at that time in a dispute with the Comédie-Française.[22] The audience approved, the press orchestrated a campaign, and the law was struck down, freeing the café-concert owners to expand their repertoires. Suddenly, singers could wear costumes and could borrow freely from other forms of entertainment, such as the circus, fair, theater, and ballet. By 1890, a troop of performers in a large café-concert included magicians, pantomimes, marionettes, acrobats, clowns, trained animals, dancers, and singers of all kinds. In a sense, it was precisely the liberation of the café-concert that encouraged the birth of the music hall by initiating more variety in the kinds of spectacles available.[23]

The café-concert program in the larger establishments changed every two weeks and was typically divided into three parts.[24] The first part of the evening was devoted to *spectacles de curiosité*—acrobatic and magic acts, animal acts, circus acts, and dance—acts borrowed largely from the country fair and the circus, which were both in decline in the second half of the nineteenth century. At the end of the first part of the evening's program, an orchestra of thirty or so played music for an hour. The second portion of the evening featured the singing of *romances* and *chansonnettes* (comic songs) performed by a group of beautiful, extravagantly dressed women arranged in a semi-circle on the stage. This was followed by the chief attraction of the program, the tour de chant, in which a star would typically perform three to five songs. Finally, the third portion of the program consisted of the performance of a portion of an opera, a vaudeville, or an operetta.

The tour de chant, more than any other type of act, defined the café-concert, and it was in this portion of the program that the realist singer performed. There were many other performance genres, as well.[25] The *comique troupier*, for example, sang comic songs about military life. The *diseur* or the *diseuse* (monologist), best exemplified by Yvette Guilbert, performed dramatic or comic songs in recitative. The *gambillard* or the *épileptique* sang comic tunes and used jerky, rhythmic body movements.[26] The best-known *gambillard*, Polin (1863–1927), "gamboled" about on stage, pretending to ride a horse in "En revenant de la revue" (While Coming Home from the Revue), his most famous creation.[27] The café-concert favored comic over vocal talent—the nonsense and wordplay of Fernandel (1903–71), for example, and the comic accents, physical grace, and humor of Paulus (1845–1908) or Maurice Chevalier (1888–1972). Some singers were associated exclusively with one genre, while other performers crossed easily from one genre to another in the course of their careers. Thérésa was classified as both a *chanteuse à voix* (a "singer with a voice," or one who relied heavily on vocal skills) and an *excentrique* (a burlesque character who mixed genres and used comic physique, body language, or costume). Mistinguett performed, at different stages in her career, as an *épileptique*, a *gommeuse* (a comic character of caricatural elegance who evoked the dandy or the prostitute), a *pierreuse* (an early version of the realist singer who sang songs about tragic subjects while dressed as a prostitute from the *barrière*), and finally, in the post–World War I era, as a *meneuse de revue* (star, or leader, of the revue).

The café-concert audience varied depending upon the type of establishment and the neighborhood in which it resided. The neighborhood café-concert and the beuglant tended to attract primarily people from the neighborhoods in which they were located. The Folies-Belleville and the Concert des Oiseaux in Ménilmontant attracted an exclusively working-class clientele, while the Folies-Dauphine in the sixth arrondissement primarily attracted students. Soldiers and domestics went to the Pépinière in the eighth arrondissement.[28] Bargemen and rowers went to the Grand Concert du Cadran and the Concert des Bateaux-Omnibus on the quai d'Auteuil, on the banks of the Seine near the fortifications in the southwest corner of Paris.[29] This is not to say that the bourgeoisie completely avoided the beuglant. On the contrary, an evening spent in a slightly menacing beuglant in the twentieth arrondissement held a great deal of attraction to the middle class, as well as to tourists, artists, and intellectuals. However, it was the large cafés-concerts that appear to have consistently attracted the most mixed audience. Guy de Maupassant's description of the Folies-Bergère in his novel *Bel-Ami* (1885) dwells on the mixed nature of the crowd.

> [B]ehind us, the most bizarre mixture in all of Paris. . . . They are of all types, of every profession and caste, but the scum predominates. Look at the clerks, the clerks from the banks, the stores, the ministries, look at the reporters, the pimps, the officers in mufti, the toffs in the evening dress, who have just eaten in some tavern and have slipped out of the Opéra on their way to the [boulevard des] Italiens, and then again a whole world of dubious men who defy analysis altogether.[30]

Edmond and Jules de Goncourt were equally struck, if not impressed, by the sights and smells at the Eldorado in 1865. They describe a dense fog of overhanging smoke in a gold-trimmed, faux-marble décor. The crowd is reduced to a sea of hats from all walks of life, under which, presumably, one would find shop assistants, camp followers, children, beribboned, bourgeois women at a safe distance in their stalls, soldiers, and whores. An account of the performance comes almost as an afterthought: "At the rear, a theater with a raked stage; on it, I saw a comic in black evening dress. He sang of things of no consequence, interspersed with chortling, barnyard cries, an epileptic gesticulation. . . . The house was enthusiastic, delirious. . . . I'm not certain, but it appears to me that we are nearing revolution."[31]

It was not unusual to see at the Pavillon de l'Horloge on the Champs-Élysées a mixture of people including wine merchants, journalists, bankers, peaceful bourgeois with their spouses, editors, tourists, couturiers, shop owners, modest industrial workers, soldiers, prostitutes, women alone, artists, and students.[32] Although the large cafés-concerts attracted a mixture of people, a class hierarchy was firmly in place within the establishments. The wealthiest and most elegant customers were seated on the ground floor, families and shopkeepers were on the second and third levels, and in *le paradis* (heaven), the highest level of all, were those at the lowest level of the socioeconomic spectrum.[33]

In her autobiographical novel *La Vagabonde* (1910), Colette offers an insider's view of the boisterous atmosphere that prevailed in café-concert audiences spanning the different social strata. She creates a portrait of apaches, in their sweaters and brightly colored collarless shirts, among the audience of a fictitious *concert du quartier* called the Empyrée Clichy.

> There he walks with silent steps, a cigarette-end sticking to his lips, and burying his hands in his coat pockets to outline his powerful back. [. . .] They are ready to knife each other in their eagerness to secure the cane-seated chairs nearer the stage, and procurable for two francs twenty-five. They are devotees and enthusiasts, who carry on a dialogue with the artists, hiss or applaud them, and have a special gift for throwing at them vulgar witticisms or scurrilous comments that set the whole audience laughing. Sometimes their success is intoxicating. The increasing uproar turns into a riot. From gallery to gallery remarks are bandied, highly flavoured with professional slang. [. . .] It is well for the artist who happens to be on the stage to wait, with impassive countenance and modest attitude, till the storm is over.[34]

Colette describes the café-concert with greater insight and appreciation than the Goncourt brothers, but the undercurrent of revolution nonetheless remains in her account. She sets the Empyrée Clichy somewhere along the boulevard de Clichy, separating the ninth and eighteenth arrondissements, the site of well-known cafés-concerts such as the Casino de Montmartre and the Casino de Paris. As in so many real establishments in that area of Paris, Colette's audience is composed, in part, of neighborhood toughs. *La Vagabonde* reflects the mixture of classes who attended the café-concert: along with the apaches, the wealthy suitor who pursues Colette's narrator frequents the café-concert, as does his bourgeois mother.

When her effort to work in the theater failed, Yvette Guilbert attended the café-concert every night for two weeks in 1889 in order to familiarize herself with its atmosphere and repertoire before embarking on a career as a singer. She found the song lyrics "idiotic" and was shocked at the audience's obvious enjoyment of them. Guilbert was terrified by her first appearance as a singer before an audience in Lyon. An obese singer preceded her on stage, to the delight of the university students who filled the house. Guilbert recounts with amazement the woman's vulgar gestures and songs, and the repeated calls for an encore that greeted the end of her act:

> Perspiring, panting, her fat body heaving with excitement, her arms red with the heat, she looked just like some great lobster. Her eyes were bulging out of her head; on her forehead she wore a fringe of black hair, crimped still like a horse's mane. Never for the life of me have I been able to recall her name; but I shall not easily forget the infinite sadness that descended on my soul at the

sight of her. I was aghast—dumbfounded—both at her personality and the effect she had on the audience.[35]

Mistinguett had a more positive view of the café-concert audience, characterizing the performer-spectator relationship as a kind of pact.

> Bataclan, the Eldorado, the Casino Montparnasse and the Casino Saint-Martin were the most popular *caf' conc'*s. In the cheap seats, there were hordes of women with their hair down sporting argyle caps. No one hesitated for an instant to tell the artists how to perform, and if someone's face didn't please the crowd, he was bombarded with cherry pits and orange peel. The house was not quick to applaud, and expected its money's worth. But once you won them over, they sang with you during the choruses. It was like a marriage proposal.[36]

Again, as in Veuillot's account of Thérésa's appearance at the Alcazar, the pact involves a particular understanding between the women in the house, who have in this case let their hair down, and their dynamic rapport with a singer. The combination of pleasure and anxiety produced by the café-concert, I contend, was in no small part due specifically to the role of women in this environment, both in the audience and on the stage. The journalist Veuillot, it will be recalled, was disconcerted, not only by the presence of women smoking in the café-concert, but by the appearance on stage of a particularly unruly woman. Who were these stars, so appealing to female spectators and equally threatening to male critics? Let us first consider the careers of three turn-of-the-century singing stars, Thérésa, Eugénie Buffet, and Yvette Guilbert.

THÉRÉSA AND THE LOCAL EXOTIC

Thérésa, whose performance at the Alcazar elicited a shocked response from Veuillot and other journalists, sang daring parodies of sentimental *romances*, eliciting an equally vivid, if less scornful, critique from the anarchist pamphleteer and poet Laurent Tailhade:

> When she appeared, with her lupine mask, her thin, hipless waist, her short arms, her lovely hands, which had not been gloved since a certain evening when the emperor had sung their praises, her biting voice, with its rich intonations, Thérésa instantly commanded an authority over the crowd usually reserved for kings of the stage, for sovereign artists.[37]

What was it, exactly, about Thérésa that inspired such a reaction? As Clark observes in his superb analysis of the widespread ambivalence in response to the mid-nineteenth-century café-concert, critics were offended both by the style of Thérésa's performance, the "vulgar, violent, proletarian songs, the slang, the obscene gestures, the lavatorial humour" and the frenzied relationship between Thérésa and her fans.[38] Thérésa represented the "assertive" culture of the café-concert we observed earlier, the rowdiness and potential violence of an evening at the café-concert. Crucially, Clark argues, the café-concert "interferes with the ordinary procedures for placing and containing the people and the 'popular.'"[39] As Clark and others have noted, because the café-concert attracted both bourgeois and working-class audiences, it was one of the few social spaces in nineteenth-century France in which class distinctions and identities could be "exchanged, blurred, momentarily forgotten."[40] The ambivalence toward Thérésa and the café-concert in general is also, I would argue, evidence of the discomfort, not only over the transgression of class boundaries, but also with the increasing visibility and social mobility of women. Thérésa's persona constitutes a profound rupture with the bourgeois codes of femininity of her era.

While the critical response to Thérésa was ambivalent, the public response was not.[41] For the first time, people attended the café-concert, not merely on the strength of the *salle* itself or to hear songs in general, but in order to hear and see a specific performer.[42] Thérésa's reign at the Alcazar was nothing less than the beginning of star-driven popular entertainment in France. The marketing efforts of music halls would henceforth center on the performer. The commodification of Thérésa flourished; between 1864 and 1870, there were a Thérésa liqueur, dress, soup, and cocktail.[43] Her performances were imitated by performers anxious to cash in on what was soon called the "Thérésa genre." Like Yvette Guilbert and Mistinguett after her, Thérésa conceived of herself as a businesswoman. "The success of one of my new songs preoccupies me as much, if not more, than the success of a large financial operation worries the Péreire brothers [prominent bankers, businessmen and politicians during the nineteenth century]."[44]

Within two years of her initial success, Thérésa published an autobiography, ghostwritten by three journalists, that chronicled her rise to success. It sold 60,000 copies within a few months.[45] The star autobiography would become a crucial way for performers to manage their images, and a fascinating source of information on the fantasies regarding class rise and female independence. The star discourses elaborated in the autobiographies of café-concert and music hall stars set the mold, in fact, for the discourse around cinema stars. All of the elements of star discourse present from the 1920s onward in mass circulation magazines devoted to film—"dramas of poverty and riches, of chance encounters, of being discovered, of trials and triumphs; sentimental romances involving love at first sight, impending tragedy, and reconciliation"[46]—are already present in the café-concert star discourse.

Raised by a dance hall fiddler, Thérésa knew popular songs by heart from the age of three. She began working as a milliner's assistant at the age of twelve, and, after being fired from eighteen different ateliers for singing on the job, she decided to attempt a singing career. She worked first as an extra at the Théâtre de la Porte-Saint-Martin, and, beginning in 1856, sang the *romance* at the Eldorado with limited success. Her "vigorous physique" and her simple, direct manners apparently didn't lend themselves to the genre.[47] In 1862, at a party for music hall artists, she sang a parody of the *romance* she had been singing without much success every night at the Eldorado, called "Fleur des Alpes." Arsène Goubert, the director of the rival café-concert, the Alcazar, found the performance so funny that he immediately hired her to sing comic songs at the Summer Alcazar on the Champs-Élysées and at the Winter Alcazar on the rue du Faubourg-Poissonnière. Forgoing the simpering style of *romance* singers, she adopted a vulgar, slangy style that enthralled audiences.

She became an immediate success, igniting a bidding war between the Eldorado and the Alcazar, the most prominent cafés-concerts in the 1860s. She assured the success of the winter and summer halls of the Alcazar and was invited to perform in the aristocratic salons of Faubourg Saint-Germain. She would remain successful until her retirement in 1893, singing both burlesque and sentimental songs. Her most popular tunes included "La Femme à la barbe" (The Bearded Woman), "Les Canards tyroliens" (Tyrolian ducks), "C'est dans l'nez qu'ça m'chatouille" (It Tickles My Nose), and "Rien n'est sacré pour un sapeur" (Nothing is Sacred to a Sapper). In addition to her café-concert singing, she performed in the Vaudeville, the Variétés, and the Bouffes-Parisiens Theaters in plays written around her persona.[48] Near the end of her forty-year career, she modified her repertoire somewhat, adopting more literary songs, such as "La Glu" (The Trap) and "La Terre" (The Land), written by the poet/songwriters Jean Richepin and Jules Jouy, respectively.

Although she differs in many important ways from the realist singers who succeeded her, especially in terms of her predominantly comic repertoire, a key parallel between Thérésa and singers such as Guilbert, Buffet, Damia, Fréhel, and Piaf must be emphasized: her self-conscious address to the working class. In her memoirs, dedicated to "the people of Paris," Thérésa discusses working-class audiences specifically:

> I attach great importance to the applause of the general public, but I confess that I have a weakness for the unfortunate portion of the population. Is this because I'm a girl of the people and that I was once unhappy like them? No! But it seems to me that they deserve all our attention. Against all odds, they

manage, for an evening, to free themselves from their lives of fatigue and work. We must entertain them at all costs, because they can't afford to return the following day.[49]

Thérésa not only sings to the people; she is a "girl of the people" and seeks to retain those ties. "This is how I find the means to remain with my family!"[50] Like so many singers that followed in the realist tradition, particularly Fréhel and Edith Piaf, Thérésa emphasizes her humble roots: a child of Paris, she claims the streets as her cradle. Her mother was a "woman of the people," while her father earned bread for the family as a "humble musician."[51]

Succinctly articulating the "rags-to-riches" scenario, she writes, "Only three years ago, I was a poor unknown girl; today my name is celebrated."[52] This "rags-to-riches" narrative is present in the discourse surrounding each and every singer discussed in this book and constitutes a key element of the realist singer persona. The notion that even a poor, uneducated woman could achieve financial and social success through a career in the café-concert provided a powerful fantasy of social mobility for women. The café-concert thus allowed women to play an active role in new modes of consumption, both as spectators and as performers, and gave the lucky few who became its stars an unprecedented visibility in French culture.

Veuillot was not alone in pointing out the specifically Parisian nature of Thérésa's brand of charm. Thérésa herself hints at her appeal to the capital's denizens in her memoir. She tells of how taxing it is to perform at the Alcazar's summer stage on the Champs-Élysées, not only because the singers had to rise above the sounds of traffic, but because the audience was not the typical Parisian one; it was full of visiting foreigners. "In order to appreciate these Parisian amusements, one must not only understand French, but also Parisian, which is a language apart, a language of conventions that never steps outside the city ramparts."[53] This link between Thérésa and the city of Paris would be played out in a number of ways by the realist singers who succeeded her.

Another element of Thérésa's persona that links her with future realist singers is the perception of her singing talent as "natural." Like Fréhel and Piaf after her, Thérésa emphasizes the "unschooled" nature of her singing abilities. "It seemed quite simple to me that one sang as one ate, to obey the call of nature."[54] Likewise, her description of her lack of education and "natural" instincts would echo in Fréhel's memoirs. "I had a feeling of independence, like all girls in my situation who grew up outdoors; my father taught me to read and write; I never attended school, no one had ever imposed his will on me; my character developed freely with the instincts of my somewhat wild nature."[55]

Yet another aspect of Thérésa's autobiography that would echo in the discourse surrounding future realist singers, especially Fréhel, is an emphasis on her chaotic love life and her tendency to discuss her sexuality frankly. "[I]'ve had my idyll, my pastoral moment full of poetry and pain. . . . Isn't love, finally, a religion with all women forever its apostles? I loved. I loved with frenzy, with delirium."[56] Although not a conventionally beautiful woman, Thérésa nevertheless positions herself as a sexual being, a paradox we can see also in the star personae of future realist singers.

EUGÉNIE BUFFET, THE *PIERREUSE,*
AND THE BELLE ÉPOQUE

Thérésa was the prototype, but Eugénie Buffet (1866–1934) was, strictly speaking, the first realist singer. Like Thérésa before her, Buffet published a memoir ghostwritten by a man. *Ma vie, mes amours, mes aventures* (My Life, My Loves, My Adventures) is nothing less than a combination melodrama, bildungsroman, and feminist treatise. Buffet was born in Algeria, the daughter of a seamstress and a soldier. Her father died in the military hospital in Oran when she was only six years old, leaving the family poor. Through all of her difficulties, one thing sustained her, "l'amour du théâtre, l'amour de la chanson [the love of the theater, the love of song]!"[57] Her autobiography emphasizes the force of her desires and her will. She has an epiphany while attending the theater for the first time.

> The music's charm, the magic of singing, the passion of the accolades, the curtain calls, all transported me, all drove me mad. . . . My dream took shape; my soul found its life; I was no longer an unconscious and disoriented child; I was already an artist, by the depth of my enthusiasm and the strength of my desire. I had made my decision, irrevocably. I would empty my heart of all the old sentimental preconceptions, so that my supreme will might triumph; to work in the theater.[58]

Buffet began acting at seventeen, but her career did not follow a straight road to success. During her early years, she often hovered near poverty and was forced to rely on male companions for financial help.

> All women who, like me, have suffered and struggled, all those who have carried the proud ideal of courage along with hatred for the harmful promiscuity of men, will understand the tortured anguish I experienced at the very idea that, in order to escape misery or the ultimate artistic failure, I might perhaps know a destiny even more shameful, joining the ranks of those destitute women forced to submit to degrading kisses, in exchange for a few coins on which they survive![59]

While it is true that the chronicling of trials and tribulations is, by the 1890s, a generic feature of the star autobiography, Buffet's memoirs, like those of Guilbert and Damia, are also a window, however mediated, onto the specific difficulties faced by young women in search of autonomy and artistic achievement. The need to prostitute oneself or seek support through a rich protector is not romanticized in memoirs of the realist singer.

Buffet, nevertheless, finds a kind man who offers to share his life with her, a man who treats her like an unfortunate *gamine.* She leaves him after a few months, however, and moves to Marseilles, where she tries to find work in the theater. Tired and poor, she returns to her boyfriend, who again offers her a calm life. Despite her promise to stay with him forever, she leaves him in the end, because her will to perform overcomes her. "Was it my fault if a greater will than my own pushed me toward the theater, toward song, toward art?"[60] She returns to Marseilles, where she nearly starves to death and is booed and hissed off the stage. Finally, tired of living in poverty in the "lower depths" of Marseilles, she becomes the mistress of a count and stages her entrance into Paris.

Buffet then describes the count's vanity when showing her off to his friends in Paris. "He was like those explorers, back from their travels in the steppes or the pampas, who trot out their bizarre insect collections with pride and ostentation, and lead their lovely tigresses, barely tamed, who frighten everyone."[61] This account curiously foreshadows the plot of *Princesse Tam Tam* (Edmond T. Gréville, 1935), in which the "exotic" Josephine Baker is brought to Paris from Africa by a Parisian novelist and paraded around the salons of his friends. Buffet then chronicles her life as a courtesan, peppering her account liberally with gossip about her contemporaries.

The turning point in Buffet's career comes with her association with Aristide Bruant in 1892. She sees him perform one night at the Chat noir and is profoundly moved: "I liked everything about him: his songs, full of suffering and rebellion, his simple and plaintive diction, his biting voice. It was a revelation. I went to hear him often, and one night I approached him and said: 'What if we were to stage one of these unfortunate girls, just as you portray them . . . ?' "[62]

Bruant granted his permission and Buffet learned three of his songs, "À Saint-Ouën" (In Saint-Ouën), "À Saint-Lazare" (In Saint-Lazare) and "La Fille à Poirier" (Poirier's Daughter). Wearing a tattered apron and red scarf just like those of the *barrière* prostitutes, she debuted at La Cigale in 1892. Fame and success followed. Buffet went on to perform at a number of large cafés-concerts, including the Gaîté-Rochechouart, the Gaîté-Montparnasse, and the Ambassadeurs. She sang one of Thérésa's creations, "La Terre" (The

Land), written by Jules Jouy.[63] Her biggest success was "La Sérénade du pavé" (Sidewalk Serenade), written by Jean Varney in 1895, the song that would be used by Jean Renoir in *La Chienne* (1931) and *French Cancan* (1955). In 1902, she briefly ran her own cabaret in Montmartre, the Cabaret de la Purée (Down-on-Your-Luck Cabaret), and then, in 1903, she opened a café-concert, the Folies-Pigalle, with little success. During World War I, she toured, performing for soldiers. In the early 1920s, she toured the United States, Morocco, and the Antilles, and she again performed in Paris music halls in 1924. Sick and poor by the late 1920s, she was the beneficiary of a fund-raiser organized by the arts magazine *Comoedia.* She died, penniless, in 1934.

Here, then, we have an element of the realist singer star image that would reach its apogee in Fréhel and Piaf: the life of the realist singer reflecting the same sad ironies and vertiginous shifts in fortune recounted in the melodramatic songs they performed. This link—real or fabricated—between the singer's life and the songs she performed is one of the key elements of the realist singer's fascination and power. The realist song, it will be recalled, was sometimes called the *chanson vécue:* the lived song. Buffet's story provides an extra plot twist, however, later repeated in the life stories of Fréhel and Josephine Baker. The "rags-to-riches" narrative is supplemented by a fall from "riches" back to "rags" story near the end of the singer's life. Buffet grew up poor and then adopted the exotic persona of the prostitute in order to boost her career in the café-concert. While successful, she often performed in the streets, as if she were an anonymous street singer, in order to raise money for the poor before, irony of ironies, falling back into poverty herself in the mid 1920s.

At least one aspect of Buffet's trajectory seems providential, both for her career and for the evolution of the realist singer's persona—her encounter with Aristide Bruant. As we shall see with her successors, Buffet had a highly specific notion of the performance style she wished to project, but lacked a coherent model around which to assemble the various elements of her stage persona. In Bruant's texts, she found the ideal focus for the different pieces of the puzzle—the pathos and misery of the gutter, the compromises and lessons of a life in the streets, the wistful familiarity with the city's working-class quarters, the abject self-denial of relationships with predatory men, the shrewd self-reliance of a lone survivor.

Bruant's songs are generally considered the most direct musical source of the realist song genre. In his cabarets in Montmartre, the Chat noir and the Mirliton, Bruant elaborated a geography of *Paris populaire* in slang-filled ballads. His 1889 two-volume collection *Dans les rues: Chansons et mono-*

logues compiles a lifelong output of mini-narratives centering on marginal figures. As the titles of the songs indicate, a strong sense of place pervades Bruant's songs: Montmartre, Montparnasse, boulevard de la Chapelle, rue de Grenelle, Saint-Ouën, the *fortifs* (the military ramparts constituting a second periphery beyond the *barrières*, or customs walls), or simply, the street, all of which were locations perceived to contain a potentially volatile mixture of poverty and crime. "À Montparnasse" offers a portrait of an alcoholic old woman:

Alle avait pus ses dix huit ans,	She was no longer eighteen,
All' 'tait pus jeune d'puis, longtemps	She hadn't been young for a while,
Mais a faisait encor' la place,	But still she hit the place,
À Montparnasse.	In Montparnasse.

"À la Chapelle" describes, in first-person narration, the lives of the homeless in La Chapelle:

Quand les heur' a tomb'nt comm' des glas,	When the hours fall like the tolling bell,
La nuit quand i'fait du verglas,	At night, when it freezes over,
Ou quand la neige a' s'amoncelle,	Or when the snow piles up,
À la Chapelle,	At La Chapelle.
On a frio, du haut en bas,	You're chilled, from top to bottom,
Car on n'a ni chaussett's, ni bas;	Since you've neither socks nor stockings;
On transpir' pas dans d'la flanelle,	You don't sweat in your flannels
À la Chapelle.	At La Chapelle.

In "Les Marcheuses," Bruant describes the lives of streetwalkers:

Les ch'veux frisés,	Permed hair,
Les seins blasés,	Sagging breasts,
Les reins brisés,	Ruined kidneys,
Les pieds usés.	Worn feet.
Pierreuses,	*Pierreuses,*
Trotteuses,	Streetwalkers,
A's marchent l'soir,	They walk at night,
Quand il fait noir,	When it's dark,
Sur le trottoir.	On the sidewalk.

The trajectory sketched in the song "Dans la rue" possesses a kind of inevitability; a sense that, once born as a foundling, a life on the street of pimping and thieving is impossible to avoid:

Moi, je n'sais pas si j'suis
   d'Grenelle,
De Montmartre ou de la Chapelle,
D'ici, d'ailleurs ou de là-bas;
Mais j'sais ben qu'la foule
   accourue,
Un matin, m'a trouvé su' l'tas
Dans la rue.

Y a ben des chanc's pour que
   mon père
Il ay' jamais connu ma mère
Qu'a jamais connu mon daron,
Mon daron qui doit l'avoir eue,
Un soir de noc', qu'il était rond,
Dans la rue.

J'n'ai jamais connu d'aut' famille
Que la p'tit' marmaill' qui
   fourmille,
Aussi quand je m'ai marida,
J'm'ai mis avec un "petit" grue
Qui truquait, le soir, à dada,
Dans la rue.

C'est ça qu' c'était ben mon affaire!
Mais un beau soir a s'a fait faite:
Les moeurs l'ont fourrée au ballon.
Et, depuis qu'alle est disparue,
J'sorgue à la paire et j'fais ballon
Dans la rue.

À présent, où qu'vous voulez
   qu'j'aille?
Vous voudreriez-t'y que j'travaille?
J'pourrais pas . . . j'ai jamais
   appris . . .
Va falloir que j'vole ou que j'tue . . .
Hardi! Joyeux, pas vu . . .
   pas pris . . .
Dans la rue.

Et pis zut! et viv'nt les aminches!

I don't know if I'm from Grenelle,
Or Montmartre or La Chapelle,
From here, or there, or way down
   there;
But I do know that the rushing
   crowd,
Found me one morning, on the job
In the street.

There's a decent chance that
   my father
Never even knew my mother
Who never knew my father,
My father who must have had her,
Some wedding night, when he was
   drunk,
In the street.

I never knew any other family
Than the small pack of kids in the
   streets,
So when I hitched up,
I got together with a little hooker,
Who tricked at night like a
   hobby-horse,
In the street.

That was a good deal for me!
But then one night she got nabbed:
The vice squad locked her away.
And, since she's disappeared,
I roam around, hungry
In the street.

Where am I supposed to go now?
Want me to work?
I couldn't . . . I never learned how . . .
I'll have to steal or kill . . .
Go on! If the cops don't see me,
   they can't get me, . . .
In the street.

To hell with it! Hurray for my
   buddies!

Viv'nt les escarp' et Viv'nt les grinches!	Hurray for the bandits and hurray for the thieves!
Un jour faudra que j'passe aussi	One day I'll be there too
D'vant la foule encore accourue	Before the ever-rushing crowd
Pour voir ma gueule en raccourci,	To see my mug in miniature
Dans la rue.	In the street.

The first verse is illustrated by a drawing of baby near a street lamp, while the last verse is illustrated by a sketch of a man on his way to the scaffold. This sense of circularity and inevitability are also present in "À Saint-Ouën," which describes a bleak trajectory: a child's birth is the result of furtive, semi-public copulation, followed by a short childhood lived near the periphery of Paris, working at the age of eight for a rag-and-bone man, hunger, crime, and, finally, the cemetery.

Buffet performed songs by Jules Jouy (1855–1897), as well, another Chat noir performer and composer. Jouy was well known for his biting *chansons d'actualité* (songs about current affairs) as well as his realist repertoire—he also wrote songs for Thérésa ("La Terre" [The Land] and "Les Enfants et les mères" [Children and Mothers]). His most famous song "La Veuve" (The Widow), which Damia later performed to great acclaim, offers a *"grand-guignolesque* vision of the guillotine as a bloody mistress 'hideously copulating' with her 'lovers.'"[64] Both Buffet and Yvette Guilbert would sing Jouy's "La Pierreuse" (The Streetwalker) with great success:

Y'a des fill's qu'ont la vie heureuse	There are girls who have a happy life
Et qu'occu'nt de bell's positions;	And who occupy a pretty station;
Moi, j'suis tout simplement pierreuse,	Me, I'm simply a *pierreuse*,
L'soir dans les fortifications.	At night at the fortifications.

The song, full of slang and onomatopoeia, comically depicts the ruses employed against bourgeois clients at the city ramparts, La Villette, and the exterior boulevards. It concludes with the guillotining of the prostitute's gigolo, Alphonse, at the place de la Roquette.

Buffet and other realist singers were associated not only with the song "La Pierreuse" but also the character of the *pierreuse*. The word *pierreuse* was used initially in the early nineteenth century by the police to designate "a prostitute who worked among the construction sites and building materials, particularly those of the Louvre in 1802."[65] By the late nineteenth century, the term *pierreuse*, or *fille à soldat* (soldier's girl or camp-follower), as she was sometimes called, referred to prostitutes working in the open air near the *barrière*. Alain Corbin provides a useful summary of her stereotype around the turn of the century:

> thin, ugly, "dirty, badly dressed, and badly combed," she was, it was said, usually over thirty-five or forty. She would often arrive in the wake of a regiment; abandoned by her lover, she was forced to live in a hovel, sometimes in a hut. She would sell herself to her clients for the derisory sum of two, four, or six sous, sometimes even for a hunk of bread, taking her client to a piece of waste ground, a thicket, a wood, a building site, or ruined ramparts.[66]

Prostitution in France in the Second Empire and into the Third Republic possessed a quite specific socioeconomic hierarchy.[67] Occupying the top level were the courtesans or *cocottes*, exemplified by Liane de Pougy or La Belle Otéro, women who also had careers in the music hall. Fictional courtesans in this category would include Zola's *Nana* or the Môme Crevette in Georges Feydeau's 1899 vaudeville *La Dame de Chez Maxim*. Just below the courtesan in this hierarchy were the elegant women who strolled on the *promenoir* at the Folies-Bergère or the women one could find at the Bal de l'Opéra. Next on the hierarchy were the shop girls who went to the popular dance halls such as the Bal Mabille looking for liaisons with the sons of the bourgeois. The scandalous cancan dancers of the Moulin Rouge, such as La Goulue, occupied the next level of the prostitution hierarchy, and finally, on the lowest rung of all, was the *pierreuse*. It was this character that Eugénie Buffet brought to the café-concert and the music hall.

Buffet was adept in imitating not only the *pierreuse* but another icon in the imaginary of *Paris populaire:* the street singer. In addition to performing in the café-concert and the music hall, Buffet performed the realist song in the streets of the poor neighborhoods of Paris in order to raise money for the poor and homeless. By taking on a street singer persona, Buffet was tapping into a tradition that thrived throughout the nineteenth century and was still going strong in the period between the wars. The music hall did not fulfill the needs or desires of every spectator, and not every spectator could afford the revues at the Casino de Paris. Thus, throughout the 1930s, street singing (and the *bal populaire,* another staple of working-class entertainment) maintained their popularity. Jean-Claude Klein describes the three tiers of the street-singing profession.[68] At the bottom of the spectrum was the singer, accordionist, or violinist who performed in courtyards of large buildings and then passed the hat. Generally accompanying this type of musician was an assistant whose job it was to gather up coins thrown from windows. A representation of this most modest type of street performance

can be seen in Clair's *Sous les toits de Paris*, in which Albert Préjean plays a
street singer, and in Renoir's *La Chienne*, in which a song is performed in
the street outside Lulu's apartment at the moment she is murdered. At the
next level was the cafe singer, guitarist, or accordionist who made a regular
circuit around specific cafes. An example of this can be seen in the opening
sequence of Duvivier's *La Tête d'un homme*, in which Simone Missia, a
well-known cabaret performer, sings in front of a Montparnasse cafe. At the
top of the hierarchy were the permanent outdoor musicians and singers
who enjoyed the best spots near metro entrances and markets. Typically,
these singers had loudspeakers and were accompanied by a violinist or guitarist and an accordionist and drummer. The musicians sold sheet music to
their audiences purchased from music publishers who catered specifically to
the street-singing market.

At the height of the vogue for the street singer, there were thousands of
professional and semi-professionals street singers all over France. Their
repertoire consisted primarily of *chansons sentimentales* that spoke of "love,
infidelity, betrayal, the comfort of a good home, the dishonor of a woman, in
short, that which connotes 'reality.'"[69] Crowds preferred emotional songs
with easily recognized cadences. Typically, street singers had nasal voices and
would draw out the final syllables of each line, a singing style that can be
heard in the songs recorded by Fréhel and Damia. Their repertoire often
traveled from the street to the café-concert and music hall, while songs that
originated in the music hall would often make their way to the streets. Some
of the most popular songs originating from the street singer repertoire,
"L'Hirondelle du faubourg" (The Swallow of the *Faubourg*)[70] and "Le Grand
Frisé" (Big Curly), for example, would become mainstays in Fréhel's career.

It is important to emphasize that Buffet *impersonated* a street singer, in
the same way that she quite self-consciously crafted the identity, habits, and
appearance of the *pierreuse*. In her memoir, Buffet emphasizes the research
necessary for the creation of her *pierreuse* character, likening herself to a
novelist:

> I was no longer sleeping, no longer eating. I lived only in the atmosphere of
> my songs. I lived the songs themselves, as a writer working on a novel plunges
> into the world in which his characters are evolving. At night, I followed the
> hookers prowling the boulevards at the edge of the city in every kind of
> weather. Huddled in the shadow of dark alleys, I espied their beckoning calls
> to passersby, followed them from afar, scraping invisibly along the walls, lis-
> tened to their words in the doorways of seedy hotels; sometimes, even, made
> up and dressed like them, I would slip among them, sitting at tables in their
> dives, and join in the conversation.[71]

Buffet writes of befriending one of these "cracked, re-plastered, suffering" women and borrowing her entire wardrobe. Crucially, although she dressed like the *pierreuse*—black dress, apron, a choker of ribbon worn around the neck—and wore the identical white makeup and red lipstick, Buffet never asserts that she is an actual *pierreuse*. Instead, she emphasizes her construction of the persona: "[I]t was no longer an individuality that I was showing, but the image of a generic type, and it was precisely in this that others were obliged to recognize the affirmation of my own personality! The livery of errant love that I wore, the tattered cast-offs of prostitution that I donned each night, this was the very image of the social misery of women."[72]

Searching in the "lower depths" for the raw materiel needed for her art, she positions herself as a kind of flâneuse. But Buffet accomplishes even more with this gesture: she emphasizes her construction of a generic image of women's poverty and, somewhat paradoxically, she asserts her "own personality" in this process. In a rather sophisticated gesture, she both asserts the value of chronicling poverty as it is experienced by women and celebrates female authorship (her own, that is). Although Bruant established the song genre that chronicled the lives of prostitutes in the streets of Paris, and Thérésa initiated the female singer's address to the peuple, Buffet was the initial "author" of the realist singer phenomenon in the fullest sense. Her research on the characters of the pierreuse and the street singer, her circulation and marketing of that persona in the music hall, the street, and her autobiography, and her awareness of creating a commentary on women's poverty, all the while managing to express "herself," reveal a sophistication we attribute more commonly to contemporary performers such as Madonna.

It is difficult to establish what Buffet's performances meant to her audiences at La Cigale and elsewhere. In his study of Aristide Bruant's songs, Dietmar Rieger claims that Bruant's bourgeois audience paid to "shudder" at the spectacle of the poor from the safety of their seats in a Montmartre cabaret: "[T]he fatalism of the misery allowed the distinguished bourgeois audience to take a particular delight in these songs that seemed to originate in an exotic, adventurous world. That lumpenproletariat of the *faubourgs*, which, lacking in any proletarian class consciousness, straddles the line between honesty and criminality, represented no great danger."[73]

One can imagine, too, the frisson produced by the voyeuristic scenario for the bourgeois spectators of Buffet's performances. However, it is likely that Buffet (and Bruant, for that matter) elicited a more nuanced response on the part of spectators than that which Rieger attributes to Bruant. Buffet's audiences at La Cigale, the Gaîté-Rochechouart, and the Gaîté-

Montparnasse, not to mention those of the streets, were far more diverse than those at the more intellectual Chat noir. Regardless of the location in which Buffet performed, we must keep in mind the possibility of cross-class identification among her public. It is far more likely that Buffet's spectators, regardless of their socioeconomic standing, suffered along with her pier-reuse, if only for the duration of a song. And what of the possibility that Buffet's underclass audience shared in the vicarious fantasy of her meteoric rise from the gutter?

Certainly, Buffet's own relationship to the working-class people and Paris neighborhoods, upon which her performances depended so heavily, is suspect, in some ways. She describes how one street-singing performance in 1895 came about:

> Georges Daniel, reporter for the *Journal* . . . wanted to do a story on *chanteurs ambulants,* the street singers, but he wanted, above all, for the décor and the characters to be picturesque, and, to be frank, his private intention was to fake the story in order to enliven the original. He wanted nothing less than real artists for the story. . . . Daniel's journalistic hoax seduced me; more than seduced me, it subjugated me. To sing like that for *le peuple,* among *le peuple,* was part of my dream realized.[74]

She thus acknowledges the element of fakery in the setup, but revels in the "authenticity" of *le peuple.* There is more than a hint of voyeurism and hypocrisy in her account of the "people's" relationship to song:

> The people love songs. They have always loved them. They especially loved them in my day, with a naïve, passionate fervor. You had to see, on summer nights, in the light of only a few gas lamps, those gatherings of working men and women who listened, on the popular boulevards, to the refrains of love, the sentimental or patriotic couplets that brought tears to quite a few eyes, provoking ardent frissons in their very being. What a simple, comforting sight! What a touching tableau![75]

For Buffet, then, an experience potentially compromised by its staging retains its power. She acknowledges the situation's artificiality, she admits that the intelligentsia needs a "picturesque" mise-en-scène of the working class, yet this does not prevent her from being moved by the emotion she detects in her audience. The staging of the event, for Buffet, does not negate the possibility of genuine experience and emotion.

It is more difficult to ascertain how the "people" themselves experienced Buffet's performances, of course. Buffet's costume and the songs she performed were highly codified representations of the marginalized people of Paris. The working-class spectators who saw Buffet perform were no doubt to a certain extent applauding caricatures of themselves. At the same time, we cannot rule out the possibility that the specter of a woman dressed exactly like the prostitute from the ramparts, singing of poverty, loss, and male brutality, touched the spectators, especially women, in new ways. Along with the fantasy of her celebrity, perhaps, women wanted to identify with the strength of her representation, her independence in choosing to portray this downtrodden figure of femininity, and the unexpected power of such a reversal.

Again, Buffet never claimed to *be* a *pierreuse* (she was too intent on establishing her artistry to make that argument) and, although she performed in the streets of Paris, she was not an authentic street singer, moving easily as she did between the café-concert, the cabaret, the literary salon, and the street. It is true that Buffet had experienced poverty and prostitution; this information was part of her public image. By the 1890s, she was "performing" these experiences in a gesture that all the realist singers who followed her would repeat. It was one thing to sing with feeling about the prostitute, as Bruant did, it was quite another to "assume" her mantle. Of course, both Buffet and Guilbert, as we shall see, were no more *pierreuses* than Bruant was. The distinction lies in actively seeking to identify themselves in this way, in choosing to identify *with* the figure of the *pierreuse*, only to transform it into something fit for public consumption, yet with the cachet of disrepute and the authority of truth. In this way, Buffet and Guilbert elaborate on the evolving template of the realist singer—the ensemble of her performances, her publicity, her autobiographies—that informs their stage personae, lending an aura of authenticity and emotion, thus generating a phenomenon quite different from that created by Bruant. Buffet and Guilbert occupy that uncertain terrain inhabited by all of the singers in this study: the shifting ground between evoking an experience and actually living it. This uneasy identification is, in fact, not necessarily "fit" for consumption, yet its appeal is undeniable. Before returning to the question of how, precisely, the figure of the realist singer may be consumed, let us first trace the career of another woman who charted its boundaries.

YVETTE GUILBERT: FROM MONTMARTRE BACK TO THE *FORTIFS*

The career of Yvette Guilbert, which flourished concurrently with that of Eugénie Buffet, constitutes the next important link in the realist singer trajectory. Guilbert experienced her first success in Paris at the Divan japonais cabaret in 1891. Dubbed the *fin-de-siècle diseuse*, she was known for her ability to inhabit comic and tragic characters and to sing their stories using a recitative delivery with precise diction. From 1892 to 1895, she sang slightly racy songs, narratives about adulterous lovers, prostitutes, pimps, and students, to full houses at the Scala, and later, at the Horloge, the Ambassadeurs, and in literary salons. Later, she grew tired of her risqué repertoire. Starting in 1913, Guilbert developed a new repertoire based on medieval songs. She performed works from the Old French Song tradition that she had meticulously researched at the Bibliothèque nationale and transposed.[76] She was thus not only able to modify her singing style and persona over time, in order to maintain the public's interest and to fulfill her own desires, but consistently imposed her own, unfamiliar style on the existing modes of entertainment.

Her autobiography, like those of Thérésa and Eugénie Buffet, is the story of a rise from poverty to wealth. She began working as a child. Abandoned by her father, she was obliged to work with her mother making hats. As a young woman, she worked as a seamstress, a model, and a clerk at the Printemps department store before her health gave out due to exhaustion. As is typical in star autobiographies, Guilbert recounts an anecdote that altered the course of her life: an encounter with a powerful man. One day the famous impresario Charles Zidler stopped her in the street and invited her to become an *équestrienne* at his circus. Her mother refused to allow Guilbert to embark on such a hazardous career, but Zidler's invitation provided Guilbert with the encouragement to attempt a career in the theater. Unlike Buffet's, however, Guilbert's career was launched without the help of a wealthy lover. Embittered by her father's abandonment, she resolved never to rely on men. Only at the relatively late age of thirty-two did she marry a doctor—a man who devoted himself exclusively to her career—and she maintained the public profile of an independent, even scholarly, woman. She published novels, several memoirs, and a singing manual. She ran an acting school in New York City from 1915 to 1922 and even maintained a correspondence with Sigmund Freud.

Guilbert's career also intersected with the cinema.[77] She had a major role, for example, in *Les Deux Gosses* (Louis Mercanton, 1924), an adaptation of a melodramatic novel by Pierre Decourcelle about a young boy sent by his father to live with a malevolent couple in order to punish the boy's mother for suspected infidelity. Guilbert played the role of shrewish Zéphyrine, one of the boy's caretakers. At the film's premier, held at the Gaumont-Palace on November 15, 1924, Guilbert performed a tour de chant.[78]

The most prestigious film on Guilbert's filmography is undoubtedly *Faust* (F. W. Murnau, 1926), in which she played the role of Marthe

Schwerdtlein. She appeared in a second film shot in Berlin in 1926, *Die lachende Grille* (Friedrich Zelnik). Back in France, Guilbert appeared in *L'Argent* (Marcel L'Herbier, 1928) and *Les Deux Orphelines* (Maurice Tourneur, 1932). She also performed in several short *chansons filmées* in the late 1920s and early 1930s produced by Tobis, the German production company, and Paramount. In her *chansons filmées*, she was able to bring her repertoire of songs from the seventeenth, eighteenth, and nineteenth centuries to the screen: *C'est le mai, La Lisette, Le Cycle du vin, La Mère Bontemps*, and *Voici le printemps*.[79]

In her autobiography, Guilbert emphasizes the precariousness of the Parisian working girl's existence. Her childhood working experiences among the young seamstresses in her mother's workshop, she says, taught her much about the cruelty of wealthy customers and the vulnerability of young women:

> I have always harbored a fondness for those who sew. I love them, they are so full of understanding! I owe the very basis of my talent to the Parisian working girl, yes, because it is from her that I learned about life, the life reserved for poor girls who have no one and nothing to defend them, except their Reason, their Decency and their Religion. . . . From the age of fourteen, I had heard it all! As soon as my mother left the workshop, they did not hesitate to discuss their loves, their joys, their heartaches. Ah, I heard more than a few stories of seduction, of dreams ending in hateful regrets! It was this milieu of girls who fought for bread and love that no doubt cultivated that exaggerated sensibility, that bitterness, that irony, from which my career as a singer would draw its most profound, most human and sincere effects.[80]

Adrian Rifkin points out that Guilbert's narrative of her days as a seamstress traces a discourse that is distinctly different in tone and uses from that of the flâneur, constituting nothing less than "an important and radical refusal of the contemporary clichés of easy virtue."[81] As we shall see in chapter 3, it is useful to map the realist singer onto the figure of the flâneur, if only to amplify the differences in their strategies and rapports vis-à-vis the audience.

Like Eugénie Buffet's memoirs, Guilbert's autobiography emphasizes the labor involved in constructing a stage persona, and her efforts to change her performance style when necessary in order to win over her audience. When attempts at a career in the theater failed, she turned to the café-concert, embarking first on a research trip through the world of Paris nightlife. Disgusted by the broad humor and vulgarity she found in these popular entertainments, she, like Eugénie Buffet, turned to the Chat noir cabaret in Montmartre for inspiration, engineering a meeting with the songwriter

Léon Xanrof (1867–1953) and then successfully adapting his songs to the café-concert. Finally, she managed to create a highly specialized stage persona for herself that combined the literary cabaret songs of Xanrof, Bruant, and Jean Lorrain with her unusual look: red hair, a chalk-white complexion, and vivid red lips. In an era in which plumpness and large busts were favored, Guilbert emphasized her long, thin neck and her flat chest. Fashion dictated voluminous silhouettes and light gloves, so she wore a green satin dress with simple lines and long black gloves.

Guilbert performed both witty and tragic songs in a small, dry, starchy voice. It didn't matter that she lacked a "big," or mellifluous voice, for Guilbert was a *diseuse*—a singer who relied less upon singing skill than on the ability to act out a song. Among her most famous songs were those written by Xanrof such as "Le Fiacre" (The Cab) (1892), which slyly mocks bourgeois hypocrisy in a tale of adulterous lovers cavorting in a horse-drawn carriage, using a jaunty polka rhythm and onomatopoeia for the sound of horses hooves ("Cahin, Caha, Hu', dia! Hop là!").

Guilbert's songs and performance style are more properly placed in the Montmartre cabaret tradition than in the traditional café-concert, although she traveled freely between these two performance spaces. She was not traditionally classified as a realist singer, but she performed songs from the genre, such as Jouy's "La Pierreuse." One of Guilbert's most successful songs was "À la Villette," by Aristide Bruant, a first-person narrative of a prostitute about her lover, Toto Laripette of La Villette. La Villette, a formerly outlying neighborhood incorporated into the city, adjoins the same locales popularized in other Bruant songs sung by Buffet: Saint-Ouën, Pantin, and La Chapelle:

Il avait pas encor' vingt ans,	He was not yet twenty,
I' connaissait pas ses parents.	He never knew his parents.
On l'app'lait Toto Laripette	They called him Toto Laripette
À la Villette.	At La Villette.

Toto is not a sharp dresser, but he knows how to talk to women:

Yen avait pas deux comm' lui pour	There was no one else like him for
Vous parler d'sentiment, d'amour;	Talking to you of feelings, of love;
Yavait qu'lui pour vous fair' risette,	Only he could make you laugh,
À la Villette.	At La Villette.

He slaps her around, but asks for forgiveness on his knees and calls her his "p'tit' gigolette." Sometimes, while she works the boulevards, Toto rolls drunkards. Their union might have lasted forever if the police hadn't nabbed him. As in "La Pierreuse," the prostitute's lover and "protector" ends up at the guillotine:

Qu' on l' prenn' grand ou p' tit,	Whether they get them big or small,
rouge ou brun,	red-haired or brown,
On peut pas en conserver un:	You can never hang on to one:
I's s'en vont tous à la Roquette,	They all head for la Roquette,
À la Villette.	At La Villette.
La dernièr' fois que je l'ai vu,	The last time I saw him,
Il avait l'torse à moitié nu,	He was stripped nearly to the waist,
Et l'cou pris dans la lunette,	And his neck locked in place,
À la Roquette.	At La Roquette.

It must be said that, while Guilbert's repertoire includes the realist song, her performance of songs such as "À la Villette" occurs in a different register than that which the interwar realist singer would use. Guilbert remains distant from her material and from any strong identification with the figure of the degraded woman, substituting a subtle wit and irony for the full-blown emotion present in later interpretations of the realist song by Fréhel, Damia, or Piaf.

Certainly, Guilbert's star persona drew upon the same mythologies regarding class rise and the romanticization of the working class. But even in terms of her autobiography, Guilbert provides a contrast to the realist singer of the period between the wars. Her life story contains the emotional upheaval and shifts in fortune typical of the realist singers' stories, but in the end, she was the witty, wily, knowing *parisienne*, not the beaten-down *môme* Piaf would incarnate. Rifkin observes:

> Guilbert does not offer herself for moral reproval, or enclose herself in the image of the "congenitally" degenerate strata of the urban poor. Nor does her life conform to the happy image of the little *midinette* [young dressmaker] as an archetypal Parisienne, mouselike but brave, even if *midinette* in part is what she was. The ambition and the decision to cross the borderline between the spectator and the performer, between the represented and their representative, immunises her from the unselfconscious animality of being a type.[82]

Here, again, is this notion of a boundary between the audience and performer that is transgressed, between identification *as* (representing) and identification *with* (representative). While it is true that Guilbert relied upon the songs of the *montmartrois* poets, it is she, Rifkin contends, who endows them with a voice and who creates a public for them across Europe and America. If she renders them more palatable through her distance, she nonetheless broadens their impact, allowing their stories to be told.

Whatever her differences with the realist singers who succeeded her, Guilbert shares once crucial tactic with them: she consciously gathers together the materials she needs for her art, using the mythologies specifically related to the geography of Paris. Eugénie Buffet, it will be recalled, went to the Parisian fortifications, the Montmartre cabaret, and the Paris street singer in order to create her persona and not, it must be emphasized, to her childhood in Algeria or her difficult years in Marseilles. Likewise, Rifkin points out, Guilbert constructs her particular version of *Paris populaire:*

> [I]n her autobiography, Yvette performs two quite distinct processes of self-realisation. One is the naturalistic, narrative account of her childhood and her emergence on the stages of the music hall. . . . The other is a re-appropriation of the people through the Montmartrois perspective, the truth according to Aristide Bruant. When, as a newly successful *diseuse,* she sets out to rediscover the meaning of popular Paris she goes back not to her own childhood, the workshops or her old music hall haunts, but to the worst *bouge* in the Rue Galande, a species of place sung as hell by Bruant. She speaks with the most decrepit, downfallen of the women, "a woman disfigured by a red stain that seems to cut her face in two," once the mistress of the criminal Gamahut. She reconstructs her Paris in the contrast between the scandal and misery of the ruined courtesan, who speaks of her lost love, and the space of entertainment.[83]

It is a gesture, the "reconstruction" of Paris, made by each of the realist singers across different venues and different eras. Of course, the reasons underpinning this reconstruction vary with time. The transformations in popular entertainment, and in the city itself, give rise to a new dimension in the connection between the realist singer and her audience.

The following chapter addresses one such transformation: the gradual waning of the café-concert and the growth of the music hall. Commercial entertainment began to evolve around the turn of the century from relatively modest forms that thrived on a sense of intimacy and community (the *bal,* the circus, and the neighborhood café-concert) to a more spectacular, technology-dependent form of entertainment found in the music halls. The café-concert slowly began to cede its place of centrality in Parisian commercial entertainment to the music hall beginning around 1890. The music hall itself underwent another metamorphosis and, by the end of World War I, the turn-of-the century music hall, sometimes called *music-hall de variétés,* had transformed itself into the *music-hall à grand revue.* With this shift from relatively participatory to spectacular entertainment came an increasing prominence of female stars in commercial entertainment culminating in the "reign" of the music hall queen Mistinguett in the *music-hall à grande revue* from the immediate post–World War I period throughout the 1920s. This shift from the more community-oriented, small-scale entertainment in the nineteenth century to the "Taylorized" music hall of the 1920s brought about unprecedented public visibility and social mobility for some women performers. Like the realist singers of the café-concert era, the queens of the modern music hall would "write" their own version of Paris.

2 · Music Hall Miss

In the thirty years separating the debut of Thérésa from those of Buffet and Guilbert, the café-concert underwent significant change. Several cafés-concerts were renovated and became even larger and more luxurious. By 1890, electricity had replaced gas in the café-concert, modifying the look of the spectacle. Gas lighting had illuminated the performers from below, producing a hardening effect on the artist's features and limiting the range of useful stage space.[1] Now, electric lighting flooded the stage, allowing the performers a greater liberty of movement and more variety in the mise-en-scène.[2] More important, ever since the 1867 decree authorizing costumes and a variety of acts, the café-concert had annexed increasingly diverse acts, borrowing attractions from the fair, the circus, pantomime, ballet, and theater. By the late 1890s, it was clear that a new form of entertainment, music hall, was eclipsing the café-concert.

"Variety" music hall had existed in Britain since the 1840s. The first music hall in Paris, the Folies-Bergère, opened in 1869 on Rue Richer in the ninth arrondissement. The Folies-Bergère differentiated itself from the café-concert by charging an entrance fee (from one to one and a half francs), but it still encouraged the audience to drink, smoke, and move about while waiting for the entertainment to begin.[3] This first incarnation of the Folies-Bergère was not successful. It was sold, renovated, and then reopened in 1872, when its combination of operettas, pantomime, gymnastics, ballets, and *tours de chant* finally won over the crowds.

Music hall not only eventually altered the nature of the spectacle but also changed the conditions of spectatorship. Whereas the café-concert had its roots in the *débit de boisson* (bar), the music hall was less likely to serve drinks or allow smoking. The tables of the café-concert gave way to rows of seats facing the stage. People came primarily for the show, not to drink and talk.[4] Moreover, the music hall attracted a more prosperous audience. The majority of cafés-concerts charged no admission fee,[5] while an evening at the Folies-Bergère or the Moulin Rouge was well beyond the means of the majority of Parisians.[6] In the late 1890s, the Olympia music hall charged five francs for men and two francs for women, while an unskilled worker in Paris earned around three francs per day.[7]

What differentiated music hall most from the café-concert was the nature of the entertainment. The music hall brought about not only an increase in variety but a new genre of spectacle: the revue. The revue, whose roots are in vaudeville and operetta, was initially a modest one-act sketch, typically a satire of current events, performed at the end of the evening. By the end of World War I, the revue had blossomed into a more spectacular, costly extravaganza, absorbing elements of the *féerie*, a nineteenth-century theatrical genre drawing on the marvelous.[8] As Jean-Claude Klein describes it: "The revue took the form of a series of 'tableaux' connected by a vague linking idea, enlivened by ballets, dances and choreography, by both individuals and groups, and interspersed with dialogues, comic sketches, songs and visual acts. The whole was given its rhythm, brisk and always quickening, by the star *(vedette* or *meneuse)* of the show, supported by the orchestra whose contributions, even in spoken scenes, were continuous."[9]

In October 1886, the Folies-Bergère devoted an entire show to the revue. In 1892, the impresario Joseph Oller opened the Olympia Music-Hall, an establishment designed specifically to offer this new form of entertainment, and the larger cafés-concerts increasingly began to use the fashionable English loanword music-hall to distinguish themselves. Eventually, music-hall came to mean both a physical location and the type of spectacle offered there. The programs were designed specifically to emulate British music hall, devoting the majority of acts to largely visual spectacles appealing to an international audience. In addition to the revues, there were tight-rope walkers, jugglers, magicians, clowns, mimes, strongmen, animal acts, and dance numbers of all kinds, including ballet. Notably, there were far fewer singers in this new style of entertainment. Increasingly, song was relegated to the level of one attraction among others. The tour de chant was in decline and, with it, the café-concert.

The café-concert tried to adapt to the new mode. Between 1900 and 1914, every café-concert of importance gradually incorporated the revue into its show. By World War I, the revue had definitively replaced the tour de chant as the centerpiece of the evening's entertainment. In the post–World War I era and throughout the 1920s, the revue maintained its prominence, becoming increasingly sophisticated and expensive. The revue now relied even more heavily on the register of the visual. A profusion of nudes, an increased richness in costume fabric and color, a new focus on dance, and a new reliance on complicated mise-en-scène were all part of this shift.[10]

This new emphasis on the visual coincided with an infusion of new musical influences. "Exotic" music and dance proliferated. On any given evening, from the late teens through the 1920s, one could experience in a revue the tango, flamenco, Russian music, Neapolitan music, Hawaiian dancers, Spanish dancers and singers, and a host of other national traditions. Even more significant in the development of the Parisian revue's increasingly "international" character was the arrival of jazz. The impresario Jacques-Charles mounted a phenomenally successful revue called "Laissez-les tomber!" (Let Them Drop) starring Gaby Deslys and the American dancer Harry Pilcer at the Casino de Paris in 1917. Deslys and Pilcer performed a ragtime and sang a blues duet before appearing in the final number, "Stars and Stripes." In addition to the explosion of individual jazz numbers in "Laissez-les tomber!" and the revelation of Josephine Baker and the Revue nègre a few years later (1925), the revue absorbed jazz in a more organic way. "Here it was the complete revue which was steeped in arrangements and rhythms inspired by this music, superimposed on tunes now composed by local musicians," Klein observes.[11] After importing American jazz, the Parisian revue synthesized it with European harmonic structures and modes of expression, thus adding to the revue's image of modernity.[12] The arrival of jazz in Paris music halls, it would seem, clinched the shift from the primacy of the tour de chant, with its emphasis on lyrics, to dance, with its appeal to the eye. A music hall critic observed in 1929:

> In France, the jazz which passed from the legs of Gaby Deslys into those of Mistinguett transformed the music hall and its revue. The décor, the artists, the nudes, the acrobats all yielded to its hegemony. A verse or a refrain are no longer anything in themselves unless the dance explains them. The word is today merely an adjunct of gesture; it is in the legs that one must have a voice.[13]

How did the French perceive this shift? Klein points out that, depending upon one's milieu, jazz was viewed in France as either " 'negro music,' fashionable dance music, or the very expression of modernity, canonized by the artistic avant-garde."[14] Jazz was also, obviously, "American." One aspect of this shift worth exploring (but beyond the scope of my research, unfortunately) is, precisely, the nature of this particular cultural exchange between America and France. Was the influx of jazz and other foreign music in the Parisian revue, combined with an increasingly international audience, composed in part of Allied soldiers on leave, perceived as a dilution of the "French" character of the music hall in some way? Without further research, it is difficult to say, but the subsequent deluge of revues insisting on the essentially Parisian nature of the music hall is striking indeed. Following "Laissez-les tomber," the Casino mounted "Pa-ri-ki-ri" (Paris qui rit [Laughing Paris]) (1918), "Paris qui danse" (Dancing Paris) (1919), and "Paris qui jazz" (Jazz Paris) (1920), "Paris en l'air" (Paris in the Air) (1921), "Bonjour Paris!" (1924), "Paris en fleurs" (Paris in Flowers) (1925), "Paris" (1926), "Paris–New York" (1927), "Les Ailes de Paris" (The Wings of Paris) (1927), "Tout Paris" (All of Paris) (1928), "Paris qui charme" (Charming Paris) (1929), and "Paris-Miss" (1929). The Moulin Rouge also built revues around the theme of "Paris," mounting "La Revue tricolore" (The Tri-Color Revue) (1915), "New York–Montmartre" (1924), "Ça c'est Paris" (That's Paris) (1926), and "Paris aux étoiles" (Paris in the Stars) (1927).

Critical reaction to the *music-hall à grand revue* was mixed. Pierre Bost had only contempt for this brand of spectacle, which he characterized as "nude women, sumptuous decor, millions wasted, revues without text authored by twenty people."[15] Nowadays, he lamented, it was the reign of the electrician, the machinist, the ballet master, the star, big machinery, forests in flames or steamships in a storm, disconnected and artificial spectacles. Bost went so far as to formulate his own "recipe" for a successful music hall program:

> Here is the recipe. Take two stars of ample fatness, or only one, if she is exceptionally fat (of the latter, there are scarcely four or five in the inhabited world); a pair of virtuoso dancers, a comic (indispensable); two venerable actors, a nude dancer, some huge set piece; a dancer (or actress) deemed "original"; a foreign orchestra and finally (obligatory) a troupe of well-trained dancing girls, which, as a rule, are the best of all these ingredients. If possible (more and more recommended) a troupe of dancing boys. Alternate dance sequences, historical tableaux, the comic sketch, the dramatic sketch (optional); garnish all this with a crowd of extras, lights, a pinch of ersatz poetry, a few grams of tragic heaviness (optional), a dash of sauciness, an English song, or one or two current jokes, preferably about Montmartre (a sure-fire miss), and serve. Two acts, forty tableaux, five hundred artists, three thousand costumes, get your program, eskimo bars, chocolate ices, surprise packets, coatroom, gallery. Orchestra seats eight francs, packed houses for six months.[16]

According to Bost, all of this plunged the spectator into a stupor, a numbing drunkenness.

Louis Léon-Martin, on the other hand, loved the revue, seeing it as utterly in step with modern times: "I come to the show a man of my time.

I like jazz; I like sports; I like speed; I like the streets, their faces and their fever; I like fashion. In short, I like life and all its seductive dynamism. At the music hall, I have never been obstructed in my fervor."[17]

The critic Legrand-Chabrier neither hated nor worshipped contempo-rary music hall, but he worried that it was stagnating. He argued in 1931 that something had been lost in the internationalization and standardization of music hall. A revitalization of the tour de chant, he suggested, might help bring back a kind of cultural specificity that had been missing. The tour de chant still existed in music hall, but it had been transformed into a more elaborate act. Whereas the tour de chant in the café-concert had existed to serve the song, it now served the singer in the music hall. Of course, Legrand-Chabrier forgets that the song certainly "served" Thérésa, Paulus, Polin, and other early café-concert stars, but his observation points to a regret felt by many critics in the 1920s with regard to the ever-increasing importance of the star in the world of spectacle. The real tour de chant, he says, would be one that comes from afar to offer us new songs and the "untranslatable je ne sais quoi of each country."[18]

The music hall critic Gustave Fréjaville initially held the imagination and ingenuity of the revue in some regard. His description of the format in 1919, however, conveys a discomfort with its new, anesthetizing function in the postwar atmosphere:

> The *revues à spectacle* adopted remarkable developments during the war. Tumult and lights, blinding colors, a profusion of decorative effects, little or no text: this is what we had come to by 1919. . . . A crowd fixed on the lights, drunk with uncertainty, eager for noise, movement and color. Only one thought haunted these brains, a poignant, hideous thought, that must be chased out for an hour or two. Any sedative would do for the task. We got drunk on jazz band, on lifted thighs, on big laughs, on ample foolishness, on coarse symbols, on standards brandished in a steady rhythm by half-naked women, on awkward jests, on plumes and on glitter. From the streets bathed in darkness, where the whispers of death rustled, we were delighted to cross into that blazing hell.[19]

Fréjaville also worried that the music hall had absorbed all that was valuable in the café-concert, especially the quality tour de chant. Song was not well suited to the music hall, he argued; the halls were too big and too noisy. Song needed the warm, intimate atmosphere once offered by the café-concert, where "hearts beat to a single rhythm and respond to each intona-tion by the singer."[20] The café-concert, he says, allowed its repertoire to degenerate, with third-rate singing turns followed by the "coarsest vaude-villes" and "trashy operettas." Renewal can only come about by improving the café-concert song repertoire and offering its spectators what they cannot find elsewhere: "the song, in its infinite variety, at each turn tender, enthusiastic, malicious, heroic, rebellious, ironic, libertine, and even Gallic."[21]

The revue, then, had both its ardent fans and its detractors. Even those who appreciated it worried that the revue had eclipsed the tour de chant, and with it, all of the positive connotations of community, cultural specificity, and intimacy associated with the café-concert by the 1920s. Fréjaville mourned a missing "Gallic" quality, while Legrand-Chabrier dreamed of the evolution of a tour de chant that transported the audience to exotic worlds with their own specific vernaculars. In some respect, the nostalgic world of the *faubourg* had become exotic to both, irreconcilable with the high-tech spectacle of the music hall.

In the period between the wars, one female performer was nearly synonymous with the music hall itself: Mistinguett. Whereas Thérésa had broken new ground by symbolizing one café-concert, the Alcazar, Mistinguett came to stand in for the entire institution of the music hall. "Le music-hall, c'est moi" (I am music hall), she was fond of saying. Exuding arrogance, ambition, and professionalism, she came to represent the positive and negative aspects of the shift from the café-concert to music hall. An examination of Mistinguett's career and performance style is thus essential for understanding contemporary French music hall itself.

MISTINGUETT

The performer who best incarnated the *music-hall à grand revue* must also be seen, somewhat paradoxically, as the next link in our realist singer lineage. Mistinguett drew from the realist singer tradition largely in the comic vein. Through her singing, dancing, and the careful management of her star discourse, Mistinguett elaborated an image of the *gosse de Paris,* the cheeky kid who made it to the top through sheer *culot* (nerve). She embodied the *parigote,* the streetwise Parisian, carefully balancing her image as both a woman of the people and the glamorous queen of post–World War I music hall.

At the height of her glory, Mistinguett was a *meneuse de revue* (revue star), sometimes called an *animatrice.* She dazzled audiences with her glorious costumes, but still managed to appear natural, warm, and joyous. The music hall critic Léon-Martin's description of Mistinguett's entrance captures both the glamour and the accessibility in her image:

> The orchestra, which had been playing with mutes, suddenly lets loose with full bows and brass; the [dancers'] canes are lifted with extended arms, and the

spotlights, focused on the top of the staircase, seek out a woman clothed in tulle and pearls, crowned with a pink feather headdress. The woman descends; she has ease and confidence, she is also ravishing. No affected pride, no imperiousness, no coldness, no pose, but rather a surprising natural air, an inimitable simplicity, the grace of a *parisienne* who likes tributes, and an immense joy, a new joy, as if given freely, a joy of the heart and of the face, a persuasive joy that wins over the entire house, hence the resounding ovation in tribute to the star whose smile, affected by such emotion, becomes tender. It is nothing, and it is a marvelous success. It is an instant, but this instant sums up music hall. It is a moment of sensitive charm, of panache, and of kindness. It is an entrance by Mistinguett.[22]

Leon-Martin's subsequent observations sum up the more positive, multifaceted view of Mistinguett: she is machinelike, yet joyous; dominating, yet sympathetic; she is the human face of the Taylorized music hall. Her revues are mechanical perfection, flawless in their locomotive rhythm, carefully engineered, and well-oiled.[23] Not everyone appreciated Mistinguett as much as Léon-Martin did. There are contradictions, not only in Mistinguett's image as both a woman of the *peuple* and a queen, but also in her status as a powerful, venerated star and as an object of derision for certain critics—tensions later reflected in films about music hall stars.

When Toulouse-Lautrec's posters of Yvette Guilbert adorned the walls of Paris, Mistinguett (Jeanne Bourgeois, 1875–1956) was still young and unknown. She grew up in Enghien-les-Bains, a town near Paris known for its elegant casino, racetrack, and hot springs. In contrast to all of the other singers in this study, Mistinguett seems to have experienced a stable, happy childhood. Her parents repaired mattresses for a living and supported Mistinguett in her desire to become a performer. In her autobiography *Toute ma vie*, the first volume of which was published in 1954, she lamented this unexceptional childhood. "I would like to be able to tell of my youth as though it were a music hall revue. I would say likeable, pleasant, extraordinary things about myself. I am unfortunately quite simple. I wasn't depraved. I was disobedient, but not every day.[24] Early on, Mistinguett demonstrated a passion for the theater. Her protective parents compromised, allowing her to take violin lessons in Paris at the age of twelve. She met a revue songwriter on the train who helped facilitate her debut at the Casino de Paris in 1893. Her real apprenticeship began in 1897 at the Eldorado, where she spent nine long years, primarily as a *gommeuse* (a comic singer in outlandish costume evoking the prostitute) slowly working her way up the music hall ladder. Like those of other realist singers, Mistinguett's trajectory was the antithesis of the overnight success story so common to Hollywood star discourse and, indeed, evoked in Mistinguett's one sound film, *Rigolboche*. In contrast, Mistinguett's story (with the exception of *Rigolboche*) emphasizes the years of hard work, the setbacks, and the steely determination crucial to her success.

Mistinguett's incarnation of both Parisian glamour and the plucky, street-wise *parigote* was built through decades of roles in music hall sketches, dances, and singing turns. At the Scala in 1908, for example, she created "La Môme Flora" (Kid Flora), a comic character for a revue sketch that contributed to her image as a Paris street kid. Dressed in rags, Mistinguett played a Montmartre street singer who tries to sing *Faust*, but forgets the words and must improvise in slang. In order to create her costume, Mistinguett recounts in her autobiography, she went to the owner of the Galeries Lafayette department store and requested a parade of his workshop employees.[25] The fashion designers and the seamstresses passed by, but Mistinguett did not find what she needed. Finally the lowly pin gatherer caught her eye—a small blond girl with hollow cheeks and cotton stockings, ruined boots and a dirty hair ribbon. Mistinguett bought her entire ensemble on the spot. Her tale of this creation process serves as a parallel to Buffet's trip to the *barrière* for her *pierreuse* costume, or to Guilbert's tour of seedy dives. Like Buffet and Guilbert, Mistinguett emphasizes the creative process in the construction of a character of *le peuple:*

> How one becomes the Môme Flora is difficult to say. You took at yourself in the mirror, but you look most of all in your memory. It's not about having been the Môme Flora, but about having seen her passing in the street, having heard her speak, having recognized her, having followed her. It's not a gift. It's memory, experience, imagination. And work. You must have seen, smelled, dreamed. Thought. To be a rag girl on the stage represents the fruit of considerable education. Not canned education, but that of the street.[26]

It is more difficult to be a member of the *peuple* than a snob on stage, Mistinguett wrote, grateful to have listened carefully to the accents of the merchants at Les Halles.

The turning point that would dramatically increase Mistinguett's visibility in the music hall world came in 1908 when Max Dearly (1874–1943), a more prominent music hall singer and actor, tapped Mistinguett to create a dance with him for a revue at the Moulin Rouge. The *valse chaloupée* was a wild, swaying, brutal waltz, in which Dearly hurled Mistinguett across the stage to the strains of Offenbach. The music hall critic Nozière describes the dance most vividly:

Suddenly, half-light, and the street prowler meets her pallid-faced boyfriend. They have come to the dance hall because they were weary of wandering the boulevard. Perhaps he's hiding out because he's just pulled something off. His hand is stained with blood. He needs to be dizzy. All at once, he seizes the woman. Imperious, brutal, he holds her. She trembles, but she is dominated by the power of his look, which shines in that face, livid as absinthe. Oh! How he looks at her. What a cruel expression contorts his mouth! She wants to break free. She manages; she seems to manage. With a movement of his arm, he pulls her back to him; he restrains her. Will he adore her or kill her? His mur- derer's fingers brush against the feminine neck, ruffle her mop of hair. The girl is no longer resisting, submissive, accepting love and death. He leans in towards her lips: a furied kiss that seems more like a bite. And with one rough shove, she is thrown far from him, like the peel of a fruit, like a flask of wine that intoxicates. And paler still, more formidable yet, he is on his way again— toward what acts?[27]

In choreographing the dance, Dearly was inspired by a "brutal and languid" dance that he saw performed by couples in a *bal musette* in Billancourt.[28] The dance was, more broadly, the result of the turn-of-the century fascination with the apache, a romantic criminal figure from the Parisian *faubourgs* who makes an appearance in serialized novels, in Louis Feuillade's film serials, and in Jacques Becker's late poetic realist film *Casque d'or* (1951).[29] The concept of the apache is said to have emerged from a bloody battle in 1902 between two rival groups of pimps from the Charonne neighborhood fighting over Casque d'or, a beautiful prostitute. Dubbed "apaches" by a journalist—a ref- erence to the native American Indian tribe—these were not viewed as ordi- nary thieves or pimps. They attempted to appropriate entire neighborhoods for themselves, to delimit their territory, sometimes in bloody battles.[30] They lived by a strong code of honor and devoted considerable energy to their wardrobes and physique.[31] In the apache dance, Dearly played the apache in his worker's cap and red scarf, while Mistinguett played the *pierreuse*, wear- ing a black dress and a red scarf. Like the realist song, the apache dance romanticized the imagined brutality and erotic obsession between the pros- titute and her pimp. In the early 1920s, Gustave Fréjaville wrote of the dance as a "somber and poignant masterpiece," a *poème-plastique* that "expresses in some simple and serious gestures the violence of desire, the charm of first embraces, the vertigo of the senses, the passionate submission of the woman, the tender and cruel pride of possession."[32] The apache dance would become important in the career of yet another realist singer: Damia's big career break came when she performed the dance, also with Max Dearly, in 1909.

Mistinguett's career is representative of the ease with which performers moved between the worlds of the music hall, the theater, and the cinema.

She is remembered primarily as the ultimate *meneuse de revue,* but she also performed many comic roles in the theater and she appeared in at least forty-six silent films, the majority of which were made between 1908 and 1917.[33] Many of Mistinguett's films were dramas and comedies made by the Société cinématographique des auteurs et gens de lettres (SCAGL), a Pathé affiliate that lured many music hall artists to the studio during the teens and was instrumental in redefining early French cinema through the attraction of a more bourgeois audience and the lengthening of films, which slowly led to the standard practice of including a feature film among a company's weekly releases.[34] Unfortunately, few of Mistinguett's silent short films survive, but the titles alone, listed in Martin Pénet's filmography, are suggestive. Titles such as *Fleur de pavé* (Flower of the Pavement), a *scène dramatique* co-directed by Michel Carée and Albert Capellani in 1909, and *La Ruse de Miss Plumcake,* a comedy directed by Georges Denola in 1911, indicate that her image as a cheeky urban sprite developed in the music hall was further elaborated in her film work.

Other titles indicate that Mistinguett specialized in active, even rebellious roles in comic films such as *La Fiancée récalcitrante* (The Recalcitrant Girlfriend) (1909) and *Une Femme tenace* (A Tenacious Woman) (Georges Monca, 1910). She may even have aspired to serial queen status à la Pearl White and Musidora. In *Mistinguett Détective I* and *Mistinguett Détective II* (André Hugon and Louis Paglieri, 1917), she plays a seamstress whose boyfriend works in counterespionage. When he becomes incapacitated, Mistinguett takes charge. Disguising herself as an English governess, a domestic, a chauffeur, a spy, and a detective, she prevents the spy from acquiring military secrets, exhibiting all the while a "stupefying sang froid."[35] The fact that the title invokes her name reveals the extent to which the line between Mistinguett as performer and Mistinguett as character had blurred. It also suggests how forceful the cinematic medium could be in disseminating a familiar, modest image concurrent with the larger-than-life persona of the stage diva.

L'Épouvante (1911), one of the few surviving films starring Mistinguett, further emphasizes the self-referential quality of her star text.[36] Mistinguett essentially plays herself in the role of a famous, but unnamed theater actress who returns to her apartment one evening to find a jewel thief in her bedroom. She manages to slip out and call the police. After a suspenseful chase sequence, the thief ends up hanging precariously from a gutter until the actress saves him. He returns her jewels, and she lets him go free. Richard Abel emphasizes the film's skillful use of suspense, generated by its framing and editing strategies. The film's basic scenario—famous actress encounters jewel thief in bedroom—would be repeated twenty years later in *Paris-Béguin,* a film featuring the music hall star Jane Marnac in the Mistinguett role and Jean Gabin as the jewel thief, which is discussed in more detail in chapter 4. *Paris-Béguin* develops the couple's encounter much further than *L'Épouvante;* in it, the tense standoff between star and thief resolves itself in bed. In the later film, the star's encounter with underworld virility results in the transformation of her music hall singing style, infusing it with "authenticity." Despite the differences between the two films, the repetition of *L'Épouvante*'s basic premise is striking and suggests that the power struggle between a female celebrity and a male underworld figure held considerable erotic fascination.

Fleur de Paris, directed by André Hugon in 1916, even more forcefully demonstrates the blurring of the line between Mistinguett's character and her star persona. Mistinguett plays two parts in the film: a famous actress named Mistinguett who accepts a contract to go to the United States, and Margot, a single working woman who is "discovered" by the actress's business partner and takes Mistinguett's place, with a possible marriage in the works.[37]

Mistinguett's silent film career was relatively short. The high point of her career occurred in the music hall near the end of the war and throughout the 1920s, when she starred in the revues at the Casino de Paris, the Folies-Bergère, and the Moulin Rouge. She created her most famous numbers at this stage of her career, "J'en ai marre" (I'm fed up) (1921), "En douce" (Quietly) (1922), "La Java" (1922), "Ça c'est Paris" (That's Paris) (1926) and "C'est vrai" (It's True) (1935). One of her most successful songs was the realist "Mon homme," written by Albert Willemetz and Maurice Yvain.[38] Based on a 1920 play by Francis Carco and André Picard, the song recounts the story, so typical of the realist song, of a woman under the thumb of her man:

Sur cette terr', ma seul' joie, mon
    seul bonheur
C'est mon homme.
J'ai donné tout c'que j'ai, mon
    amour et tout mon coeur
À mon homme
Et même la nuit,
Quand je rêve, c'est de lui
De mon homme.
Ce n'est pas qu'il est beau, qu'il est
    riche ni costaud

On this earth, my sole joy,
    my sole happiness,
Is my man.
I've given all I have, my love and all
    my heart,
To my man
And even at night
When I dream, it's of him
Of my man.
It's not because he's handsome,
    rich or brawny

Mais je l'aime, c'est idiot,	But I love him, it's stupid,
I'm'fout des coups,	He hits me,
I'm'prend mes sous,	Takes my dough,
Je suis à bout	I'm at my wit's end
Mais malgré tout	But despite everything
Que voulez-vous.	What would you have me do.
Je l'ai tell'ment dans la peau	He's so far under my skin
Qu' j'en d'viens marteau,	That I'm going mad,
Dès qu'ils s'approch' c'est fini	As soon as he comes here, it's over
Je suis à lui.	I'm his.
Quand ses yeux sur moi se posent	When his eyes are upon me
Ça me rend tout' chose.	I'm everything.
Je l'ai tell'ment dans la peau	He's so far under my skin
Qu'au moindre mot	That at the slightest slight
I'm'f'rait faire n'importe quoi	I'd do anything for him
J'tuerais, ma foi.	I'd kill, believe me.
J'sens qu'il me rendrait infâme	I know that he'd make me horrid
Mais je n'suis qu'un' femme.	But I'm just a woman.

Francis Carco's play tells the story of Clara, a former *pierreuse*, who is now the wealthy mistress of a Russian prince.[39] Longing to recapture her old life among the apaches, if only for one evening, Clara returns to the bal musette and falls into the arms of Fernand. They return to Clara's house, where Fernand is surprised at her wealth, but loves her for the woman she is. Suddenly, another man arrives, a presumed friend of the family, who is actually a jewel thief. Startled by Fernand's presence, the thief shoots and kills the apache. But before Fernand dies, he claims to have come to Clara's room to steal her jewels. He thus protects Clara's honor by deflecting suspicion that she had taken a lover and demonstrates the chivalry of the apache. The play draws on the realist universe stretching back to Buffet's *pierreuse*, as well as Mistinguett and Dearly's *valse chaloupée*. The songwriters Willemetz and Yvain drew on the themes of Carco's play for their song, which Mistinguett performed for the first time in the 1920 revue "Paris qui jazz" at the Casino de Paris. Mistinguett's "Mon homme" was a such a huge success that the actress playing the lead in Carco's play was ultimately obliged to incorporate the song into the play.[40]

That Mistinguett's singing performance of "Mon homme" could overwhelm and infiltrate the successful play on which it was based should not surprise us. Her star text possessed enormous power in French commercial entertainment during the period between the wars. Her persona was always "bigger" than any individual song or revue that showcased her talent. Even her flaws became fodder for her star text. "C'est vrai" (It's True)[41] comments directly on the legendary nasality of her voice, "this voice that is pleasing because it does not please."[42]

On dit que j'aime les aigrettes,	They say that I like plumes,
Les plumes et les toilettes,	Feathers and gowns,
C'est vrai.	It's true.
On dit que j'ai la voix qui traîne	They say I have a voice that trails,
En chantant mes rengaines	When singing my tired ditties
C'est vrai.	It's true.
Lorsque ça monte trop haut, moi je m'arrête	When it goes too high, I stop right there
Et d'ailleurs on n'est pas ici à l'Opéra.	And by the way, we're not at the opera.
On dit que j' ai l'nez en trompette,	They say that I sound like a trumpet
Mais j' s'rias pas Mistinguett	But I wouldn't be Mistinguett
Si j' étais pas comme ça.	If I weren't like that.

The self-referential quality of this song and others distances her somewhat from the other singers in this study. Mistinguett created gentle caricatures of the *pierreuse* that Buffet incarnated with utter sincerity. For example, two years after Mistinguett and Max Dearly danced the *valse chaloupée* at the Moulin Rouge, she and Maurice Chevalier created a parody of it called it—the *valse renversante* (knock-over waltz)—for the Folies-Bergère. Even her performance of the song "Mon homme" skirted the edge of parody. Although the song's lyrics are squarely in the tradition of the realist song, Mistinguett's performance of it occupied a different, more comic register than Buffet's performance of "La Sérénade du pavé" or Fréhel's "Où sont mes amants":

> When Mistinguett, no doubt tenderly, but above all tongue-in-cheek, belts out "I was born in the *faubourg* Saint-Denis" or "En douce," truth and social satire surface from under the teasing smile. When she sings "J'en ai marre" or "Mon homme," her voice, the tone, the stance give rise to a smile that steers clear of facile melodrama, and it is then perhaps that, more harshly but for the best, Mistinguett represents, as Mac Orlan thought, the "stylized expression in music hall of a profoundly tragic subconscious."[43]

One effect of this distanced relationship to her material and to the self-referential quality of her star image was that Mistinguett was able to project herself, not only into song lyrics, but into entire revues. A 1929 revue at the Casino entitled "Paris-Miss," starring Mistinguett, referred directly to her.

Mistinguett's larger-than-life presence extended to Paris itself. As we shall see in chapters 3 and 4, the realist singer was closely associated with the urban landscape of Paris. However, while Fréhel and Damia evoke certain neighborhoods—Montmartre, La Chapelle, La Villette, or the "street" more generally, Mistinguett manages to evoke the entire city of Paris. One of her most successful songs was "Ça c'est Paris" (That's Paris)[44] in which she defines Paris as a blonde with an upturned nose and laughing eyes:

Paris, reine du monde	Paris, queen of the world
Paris, c'est une blonde	Paris is a blonde
Le nez retroussé, l'air moqueur	The upturned nose, the mocking air
Des yeux toujours rieurs	The eyes always laughing
Tous ceux qui te connaissent	All who know you
Grisés par tes caresses	Intoxicated by your caresses
S'en vont mais revienn'nt toujours	Go away, but always return
Paris, à tes amours.	Paris, here's to your loves.

The blonde with the upturned nose, mocking air, laughing eyes, and unlimited resources for getting her way is a precise description of Mistinguett.

Mistinguett is linked with the city of Paris partly through her own assertions via her songs and revues that she "is" Paris in some essential way. Writers reinforced that association. For Cocteau, she was "that *tragédienne* who sums up our city because her poignant voice contains the cries of the newspaper vendor and the pushcart produce merchant."[45] According to the music hall critic Léon-Martin:

> She likes to handle fabric, ribbons, spangles, fashions, and silks. She brings to it the taste of a seamstress's apprentice and the eye of a *parisienne*. I say *parisienne* deliberately. Everyone knows the influence of the Parisian woman in the world. Mistinguett—in spite of her origins—personifies the *parisienne* with an astonishing joy, a striking accuracy, a joy and truthfulness that are at the roots of her universal renown.[46]

Pierre Mac Orlan elaborated, more vividly than any other writer of his era, an imaginary Paris that relied heavily on the realist singer. In the mid 1920s, in an essay entitled "Mademoiselle Mistinguett," he wrote:

> If, in the songs—which are very well done, incidentally—Miss Mistinguett evokes, most frequently, the silhouette of poverty, it's with hands stained violet from holding the first cuttings of lily of the valley and a voice hoarse from hawking issues of *l'Intran* [*L'Intransigeant,* a Paris daily] that she offers us the unspoilt heart of a young girl from Belleville for whom nothing stands in the way of a golden future.[47]

The poet and essayist Léon-Paul Fargue (1876–1947), writes of Mistinguett as the ultimate *parisienne:*

> She is *parisienne* by virtue of her prompt and often sharp repartee, by her wink, smile, the fleetness of her reactions, her sense of the ridiculous, the

botched, the whispered, she is *parisienne* in the sway of her shoulders, the ruse in her regard, the facility of her gestures, her skepticism, her incredulity, her ever-sharp grievances. . . . Through her, far from my apartment and my books, came the fragrant murmurs of the rue Lepic, the Bastille, la Cité, Batignolles, and Saint-Ouën. By means of a simple record or photo, I once again conjured up the porcelain dealers of the rue du Paradis, the trucks of les Halles, the canal de l'Ourcq, its clocks and its bricks, the men sitting on the sidewalk, the white wine of the boulevards, the flower-sellers, the kiosks, the taxis, the tobacconists. . . . Everywhere, Mistinguett's name, evoked, sung or pronounced, made me miss Paris, maternal and tragic Paris, Paris so necessary and so reassuring.[48]

Because Mistinguett's star image was synonymous with the music hall itself, she absorbed some of the criticism directed at it during at the beginning of its decline in the late 1920s. Pierre Bost's scathing critique of Mistingeutt, published in 1931, is revealing for a number of reasons:

I willingly recognize that she has had a considerable influence on the evolution of music hall in Paris for many years, that she is moreover the only French star capable of headlining a *revue à grand spectacle;* that she alone is capable (people have said it so often!) of descending a staircase followed by seven meters of feathers and with her head covered with fifteen pounds of plumes, that she is an acrobatic dancer of great strength, that she has a head for music hall, decor and mise-en-scène, that she is in a sense the author responsible for revues for which she has only been designated as a performer, that her whole life is work, research and love of the *métier,* that the public adores her and never tires of applauding her, that the songs she has launched, from "J'en ai marre" to "Mon homme" to "Valencia" have traveled around the world and back again thirteen times. . . . The question is whether it is sufficient to have the leverage to make a big music hall star, and whether the *faubourien* repertoire and the stories of the poor, lovable, heroic, beaten sparrow are bearable. . . . Ah! these sketches written so that Mistinguett, under a spotlight, can launch the song destined to cover, through sheet music and record sales, half the cost of the revue! Really, really, why are such spectacles still successful?[49]

Bost is tired of the scale of music hall, its excesses, and its arrogance. He laments the rise of stars in general and notes that the function of the French song has now changed because of the star phenomenon.[50] People now go see Damia or Mistinguett for themselves and not for the songs they will sing. In the past, the songs of the artist "made" his or her reputation; now, it is the artist who makes a song famous.

It is quite likely that the bitterness expressed by critics like Bost toward Mistinguett reflects, at least in part, a discomfort with the power wielded by a woman in French popular culture. Dudley Andrew rightly observes: "From 1910 to 1940 she was unquestionably France's dominant performing artist, 'a national treasure,' as Colette called her. A host of younger stars from Maurice Chevalier in 1912 to Fernandel in 1933 would be graced to trail behind her into the stage lights. One virtually needed her blessing to succeed."[51] Maurice Chevalier, Mistinguett's only equivalent in terms of star power and visibility in the entertainment industry between the wars, did not, it must be noted, elicit this same critical response from Bost and others. Starting out in the café-concert, Chevalier moved from one song genre to the next, first playing a *paysan* (country bumpkin), then a wily *parigot* (Paris street kid), and finally, in the post–World War I era, the affable, sophisticated, English-speaking international star clad in a tuxedo and a straw boater. Indeed, when one considers that Chevalier left Paris from 1928 to 1935 and became successful in Hollywood, it is surprising that more resentment was not directed toward him in the 1930s. He not only left music hall for the cinema, he left France as well, at a time when the French keenly felt the competition from the American film industry.

Why does Bost reserve his most venomous criticism of the music hall revue for Mistinguett? A consideration of the historical condition of women around 1930 sheds some light on this question. The early 1930s appear to have been a period of backlash against women after some years of improvement in their condition. World War I, in particular, brought about expanded job opportunities for women. Women who had never earned wages before had the opportunity to do so now; women who were already working gained access to better-paying jobs usually held by men. The working-class women who had embroidered, made lace, or worked as maids for low pay before the war were now working in explosives factories, the chemical or metal industries, or in transportation—the metro, the tramway, or the railway.[52] Options for white-collar female workers had also expanded beyond the traditional occupations of primary school teaching and secretarial work. Between 1906 and 1921, the number of women working in commercial jobs, the liberal professions, and public services nearly doubled.[53] The opening of business schools for women, such as the École de haut enseignement commercial, the École commerciale de jeunes filles, and the École hôtelière féminine, facilitated women's entry into accounting careers and hotel management.[54] Chemical and electrical engineering careers were also particularly accessible to women.[55]

Women's fashion underwent a huge shift around World War I, which contributed in no small way to the impression that women were in the midst of a large-scale transformation. Wartime work required more comfortable, practical clothing, and so stiff, confining corsets gave way to elastic girdles and silky *combinaisons;*[56] knee-length skirts replaced long skirts; the upswept hairdos requiring waist-length hair gave way to short, sleek styles. The innovations of Coco Chanel and Sonia Delaunay contributed to the representation of women as dynamic, mobile, and sporty.[57]

The impression that a new model of femininity was being elaborated was underscored by the phenomenal success of a controversial novel written in 1922 by Victor Margueritte, *La Garçonne* (The Tomboy). The novel's protagonist, Monique, rebels against bourgeois constraints by leaving the wealthy, but unfaithful fiancé chosen for her by her parents. She drives a sports car, listens to jazz, smokes opium, has lesbian love affairs, and achieves financial independence through a career before finally forming an egalitarian union with a man. Margueritte, an outspoken supporter of flexible divorce legislation, fair alimony, and legitimization of "illegitimate" children, lost his *Légion d'honneur* as a result of the novel's publication.[58] The novel scandalized and fascinated; it was read by 12–25 percent of the French and translated into twelve languages.[59]

The changes in job opportunities, fashion, and a compelling literary model of the "new woman" preceded somewhat the substantive legal changes granting women more control over their lives. The Civil Code treated married women like minors until 1938. But slowly, a series of laws altered husbands' control over everything from women's finances to their education.[60] By 1920, a woman could join a union without her spouse's authorization. In 1927, a Frenchwoman could finally keep her nationality after marrying a foreign man. By 1938, a Frenchwoman could finally open a bank account, obtain a passport, pursue higher education, and take competitive examinations without her husband's permission.

Despite these changes, a convincing argument has been made that women's lives did not actually change much during the period between the wars. Eugen Weber asserts: "One domain where change moved with positively glacial speed was the condition of women."[61] The same law of 1938 that allowed a woman to open a bank account also reaffirmed her husband's right to oppose her working outside the home,[62] and, despite numerous legislative battles throughout the 1920s and 1930s, women did not achieve the right to vote until 1944.[63] Moreover, due to fears of depopulation, authorities banned dissemination of information about contraception. Contraception itself was practically nonexistent until after World War II, leaving abortion as the principal method of birth control, which, in turn, began to be prosecuted vigorously by the courts.[64] James McMillan concludes that Frenchwomen were still largely constrained by ideologies of domesticity throughout the Third Republic, despite greater educational and job opportunities for both working-class and middle-class women living in an urban environment.[65] Women may have acquired industrial jobs, he argues, but working conditions were bad, and pay inequality remained. Women may have glimpsed a liberated feminist heroine in *La Garçonne*, but their roles in the family and in society remained stubbornly limited. Furthermore, McMillan argues, the massive influx of women in the chemical, metal, and electrical industries reflected, not an increase in the status of women as a result of their World War I experiences, but, instead, large-scale changes in the economy.[66]

McMillan may be right that women's legal and economic status had not changed significantly since World War I. Indeed, there is much evidence that in the 1930s, the inroads women had made in the job market during and after World War I had diminished. As the effects of the depression began to be felt, women were the first to be laid off from their jobs.[67] What seems clear, however, is that throughout the 1920s and the 1930s, women were *perceived* to be gaining more economic power and more public visibility in France. This perception may have helped generate ambivalence toward cultural symbols of female autonomy such as Mistinguett.

Thus, the ambivalence and outright resentment expressed with regard to the new, ever-more-powerful female star can be connected somewhat with the changes—or, at least, the perception of changes—in women's status in French society. Pierre Bost's rant against Mistinguett should also be seen as a manifestation of the rancor against the newly international, ever-more-expensive music hall itself, of regret for the loss of smaller-scale forms of entertainment that welcomed a cross-section of Paris and promised a community, of sorts. *Rigolboche*, Mistinguett's one and only sound film, exemplifies how earlier modes of entertainment were appropriated and reworked in the cinema.

RIGOLBOCHE

Rigolboche, which was written specifically for Mistinguett, was one of the six films made in 1936 by Christian-Jaque, one of France's most prolific and commercially successful directors from the 1930s through the 1960s. His *Un de la Légion* (1936), a vehicle for Fernandel made the same year as *Rigolboche*, was one of that year's most popular films.[68] Mistinguett was sixty-one at the time *Rigolboche* was made, and it is unclear why she consented to appear in it. She had been performing in music hall for forty years and certainly did not need the additional exposure. It is possible, however, that she may have prompted to make the film by her considerable jealousy of her rival Josephine Baker, who had just made *Zouzou* (Allégret, 1934) and *Princesse Tam-Tam* (Gréville, 1935).

In *Rigolboche*, Mistinguett plays Lina, an *entraîneuse* (dance-hall hostess, or taxi dancer) who works her way from a seedy bar in Dakar to music hall stardom as "Rigolboche" in Paris. The plot is a rather delirious potpourri of noir, melodrama, French boulevard theater, and the backstage musical. Lina flees noir-ish Dakar for Paris, mistakenly believing herself responsible for the death of a man. In Paris, she first visits her young son, whom she hasn't seen in six years, and who does not know that Lina is his mother. This "family romance" plot line, so common in melodrama, is not pursued at all in *Rigolboche*. We scarcely see the son again, and he never learns his mother's identity. His presence serves only to allow Mistinguett to sing a lullaby to him, thus revealing her softer, more "maternal" side. Next, she engages in sparkling, witty repartee typical of the boulevard comedy with Mr. Bobby, the slick con man who books acts for a nightclub and casino. Mr. Bobby is played by Jules Berry, whose performance as a smooth-talking, womanizing rogue here is quite similar to his Batala in Renoir's *Le Crime de Monsieur Lange* (1935). After a number of incidents involving mistaken identity, ruses in the casino, and bribery attempts, Lina ends up managing and performing in her own music hall, the Théâtre Rigolboche. The final ten minutes of the film consist of Lina's revue, the film's raison d'être.

The film is quite incoherent in its heterogeneous visual style, in its references to different film genres, and in its characterization of Lina. She is first a young, vulnerable dance hostess, then a mother, and finally a powerful music hall director. Mistinguett's role here can be explained, in part, by the contradictions in her star persona—contradictions savored by writers like Mac Orlan, Léon-Martin, and Fargue. Mobilizing a variety of elements from Mistinguett's autobiography and music hall performance history, the film shows us both the poor little singer with nothing but pluck and ambition and the powerful *meneuse de revue*. She is mother and star, just as she was in real life. She is both the "independent woman" and yet pragmatic enough to know when to accept the favors of men. She is both charming and generous, yet endowed with the steely determination and work ethic necessary to mount a revue. Above all, *Rigolboche* celebrates Mistinguett's persona as the ambitious star in total control of the show. In addition to running the Théâtre Rigolboche and starring in the revue, Lina oversees its choreography, set designs, and costumes. While wrapping yards of silk around a half-nude chorus girl, she barks out, Ziegfeld-style, "Find me a dozen more girls that look exactly like this one!" But she is not all steely nerves; she is just as comfortable, the film wants us to believe, singing a lullaby to her son ("Au fond de tes yeux") as she is performing for hundreds of people in an elegant nightclub, where she sings a decidedly nonrealist song called "Pour être heureux . . . chantez!" (To Be Happy, Sing!).[69]

The film builds to the opening night of the revue. *Rigolboche*'s final number combines Busby Berkeley–style expressionism and Parisian music hall glitz. A tracking shot reveals rows of dancing couples, creating a complex, nonrealist space that eschews Renaissance perspective. Columns and doorways jut out at strange angles, while the lighting is low-key. The dreamlike atmosphere leaves no room for the audience; there is no attempt to establish a viewing context or an audience response. As we shall see in *Zouzou* and in *Paris-Béguin* in chapter 4, the revue numbers in 1930s cinema generally celebrate an overtly artificial Paris *(Zouzou)* or an orientalist fantasy *(Paris-Béguin)*; vague "non-spaces" that transport us to a fantasy world instead of rooting us in the Parisian landscape. And yet Mistinguett wants to hang on to the *parisienne* connotation honed so carefully over the years, and does so through the lyrics of her song. Dressed in a white satin gown and a huge feather headdress, she appears at the top of a white staircase and descends, singing "Oui! Je suis d'Paris" (Yes! I'm from Paris) in her trademark nasal voice.[70]

Quand on m'voit	When people see me,
On trouv' que j'ai ce petit "je n' sais quoi"	They find that I have that little "je ne sais quoi"
Qui fait qu' souvent l'on me fait les yeux doux	Which makes them make eyes at me
Ce qui me flatt' beaucoup	And that flatters me a lot
J' l'avou'!	I must confess!
J'aim' flirter,	I like to flirt,
Quand on me plaît j' le dis sans hésiter.	When I like someone, I say so right away.
Dès que j'entends un refrain des faubourgs	The moment I hear a ditty from the *faubourgs*
Je m' attendris toujours.	I always soften up.
J' connais tous les mots d'argot	I know all the slang words
Mais j' sais m' tenir quand il faut.	But I know how to behave when I must.
Où donc suis-je né'?	Where was I born, then?
(Choeur: à Paris!)	(Chorus: in Paris!)
Vous l'avez definé!	You've got it!
Oui, je suis d' Paris.	Yes, I'm from Paris.
J'aim' tout c'qui sourit	I like everyone that smiles

Les Poulbots, les p'tits gavroch's à l'air mutin	The Poulbots, the little street urchins,
Les yeux de mes gentils béguins!	The eyes of my sweet crushes!
J'aim' me prom' ner tard	I like to stroll around late
Sur les grands boul' vards.	On the grand boulevards.
J'aim' Montmartre son entrain et son esprit.	I like Montmartre, its life and its mood.
Y a pas d'erreur, je suis d'Paris.	Make no mistake, I'm from Paris.

Just as in her music hall performances, Mistinguett aligns herself with Paris—the happy, smiling Paris, that is, in which the poverty, crime, and the brooding atmosphere of the realist song do not exist. Mistinguett, her song tells us, is just as comfortable in Montmartre as in *mondain* Paris. She knows all the slang, and her heart melts when she hears the refrains from the *faubourg*, but she can hold her own in any situation. She knows Paris inside out and just might be willing to give the slightly depraved male tourist a late-night tour of Paris:

Vous, monsieur,	You, sir,
Je crois qu' vous êtes un tantinet vicieux.	I think you're a wee bit naughty.
Vous cherchez quelqu'un, si j'ai bien compris	You're looking for someone, if I'm not mistaken
Qui vous fass' voir Paris la nuit!	Who will show you Paris at night!
Voulez-vous qu'après minuit je vous donn' rendz-vous	Shall we set a rendez-vous for after midnight
Pour aller danser dans un bar très bien	To go dancing in a very fine bar
Surtout très parisien.	Very Parisian anyway.
J' connais tous les bons endroits	I know all the right places
Ou l'on s'amus' comm' des rois	Where we can have a high time
Les biens cotés, les moins biens fréquentés.	With the right crowd, or with no crowd.

Once she reaches the bottom of the stairs, she continues to sing, surrounded by her adoring male chorus. The jolly march then gives way to a slow instrumental version of "Oui! Je suis d'Paris" to which Mistinguett and a male chorus dancer perform a ballet. This number reiterates the hybrid nature of the film as a whole: it combines her *gosse de Paris* image elaborated in the lyrics of the song with her familiar feather headdress, while the number shifts from a frisky march to a slow, dreamlike ballet.

The story the film tells about Rigolboche's rise to success is somewhat equivocal. On the one hand, the film makes it clear that she needs men in order to succeed. Mr. Bobby introduces her to the music hall director; her admirer, the Count, buys the Théâtre Rigolboche for her. Yet the film wants to disavow the "casting couch" and "sugar daddy" connotations here. The film avoids any hint that Rigolboche is the Count's lover. On the night she finally consents to dine at his house, she disappoints him by scurrying away to the music hall to rehearse after dinner. At the end of the film, the Count proposes marriage, asking her to trade in her stage name "Rigolboche" for "Comtesse." She gestures toward a series of posters lining a wall that feature her face and huge letters spelling out "Rigolboche." "Jamais!" she says, implying that her place is in the music hall.[71]

Rigolboche appears to have been neither a popular nor a critical success. An offhand remark by Georges Sadoul in the review of another film leaves little doubt about *Rigolboche*'s failure: "Some have reproached *Jenny* [Carné, 1936] for its subject and undoubtedly they're not wrong. . . . Yet no one, despite a certain family resemblance in subject and milieu, would dream of comparing *Jenny* to *Rigolboche*, a pitiful balloon inflated for an old hag like Mistinguett."[72] The experience must not have been a pleasurable one for Mistinguett, for she scarcely mentions the film in her autobiography, and she never attempted to make another.

In the context of an astute comparison between *Le Crime de Monsieur Lange* and *Rigolboche*, Dudley Andrew writes of the two different modes of entertainment represented in the two films: the "Arizona Jim" *photo-roman* serial in *Lange* and the music hall in *Rigolboche*.[73] *Le Crime de Monsieur Lange*, Andrew notes, more authentically celebrates popular entertainment:

> *Arizona Jim* is closer to the pleasures offered by the circus, the *bal populaire* and the *café-concert*, while *Rigolboche* celebrates more modern practices of entertainment like music halls and, implicitly, extravagant sound films. While the former mode features variety, satisfying interaction between audience and performer, and a strong sense of community, the music hall relies on hidden technology, continual novelty, and the female body.[74]

Andrew identifies an irony in casting the powerful Mistinguett, who incarnates the resolutely twentieth-century *revue*, with all its glamour and spectacle, to play a music hall star named after the genuinely popular nineteenth-century café-concert star Rigolboche.[75]

Mistinguett, like *Rigolboche* and the *music-hall à grand revue*, wants to "be everything to everyone," in a sense. The heterogeneity of *Rigolboche*'s style recalls music hall's wholesale absorption of other kinds of popular entertainment: the circus acts, the tour de chant, operetta, dance, and so on. Likewise, this pirating of other performance traditions corresponds with

Mistinguett's own adoption of certain elements of the realist singer tradition. She absorbs from the realist singer the aura of working-class "authenticity," the rags-to-riches trajectory, and the plucky, street-smart quality, then places these in the context of a grand, factorylike music hall managed by an imperious director in the Ziegfeld mold. It should hardly surprise us that the one sound film in which Mistinguett appeared bears little resemblance to the kinds of films that would feature realist singers like Fréhel, Damia, and Odette Barencey. Most of the films in which the latter group appear are poetic realist films or films that are keener to capture the texture of the working class and the underworld than to convey the glitter of music hall.

Ironically, Mac Orlan and Léon-Martin seem not to have understood the qualitative difference between a Mistinguett and a Fréhel. They flatten out the differences between them, rhapsodizing about the ability of both to evoke Paris. But it is nevertheless worthwhile constructing a distinction between the realist singer proper and her transmutation at the hands of music hall stars, and through the rise of spectacle more generally. Mistinguett seems to be a strange exception to the rule, emblemizing perfectly, in a sense, the damage the cinema did to music hall, reprising the demise of the café-concert. In fact, Mistinguett seems literally to have hurt herself by starring in the unfortunate, amorphous *Rigolboche*. Unlike Fréhel's, as we shall see in the next chapter, Mistinguett's persona evoked nothing but ridicule in the context of a talking picture. Even so, we cannot discount her centrality to the tradition of the populist French *chanteuse:* for better or worse, she is firmly inscribed in the history of popular entertainment in Paris. More important, she cues the cultural importance of various other manifestations of the realist performer by attempting to appropriate elements of their singing styles, multiple class identifications, and mobilization of autobiography. She is also an undeniable constellation in the music hall "firmament" that figures so strongly in the films discussed in chapters 4 and 5. Finally, she is the embodiment of the strong, self-determining woman who creates or redefines herself as necessary in order, not only to succeed, but to express something she claims she was "born" to express. This latter characteristic aligns her irrevocably with the other subjects of this study. Before moving on to more concrete analyses of how these figures operate in the cinema, though, let us examine more closely how, exactly, the cinema spelled the end of the music hall era.

I have only mentioned in passing how the café-concert's demise following the advent of music hall produced a certain kind of nostalgia. Contemporary critics differed on exactly how much music hall was to blame. Some rejected the extravagant spectacle of music hall outright, longing wistfully for the days of Thérèsa and Eugénie Buffet. Others channeled their nostalgia into a newfound, if slightly distorted, appreciation of music hall, as we can see in the following music hall critic's 1928 review of a show at the Bobino that revived the café-concert style:

> The staging of a super-revue of a grand music hall offers us, at this time, the evocation of the old *caf'-conc'*. It is charming, delicate, and slightly nostalgic. How we knew how to laugh and smile then, how the joy resonated, honest, fresh, and frank! How much the war and the jazz band have destroyed in the ring and on the stages! Yet, we can still breathe in that atmosphere, which has perished everywhere else, save between the repainted walls of that old Bobino. . . . Yvette Guilbert regales us with her repertoire of long ago. She has abandoned her long silk gloves and her tight sheath dress. The queen of French song now appears on stage in a spectacular flowing costume. Comic or tender, sly or pitiful, she speaks, sings, lives. . . . [A]nd from the orchestra seats, where chic people have traveled from distant quarters, to the gallery, where the regulars, standing, munch on fritters and French fries, the silence is total, perfect. This silence that is, to the artist, the most precious, most delicate tribute, and that ends, suddenly, in a thunder of applause when "le Fiacre" . . . clip-clop . . . has come to a joyful end.[76]

Music hall supplanted the café-concert as a far-reaching form of popular entertainment and, eventually, music hall too would give way to yet another innovation, cinema. Some music halls addressed the threat by showing films in between live acts. Others looked to the past by focusing on the tour de chant, the mainstay of the café-concert. The experience of the Gaîté-Rochechouart is illustrative of this tendency.[77]

This venerable café-concert opened in 1865 on Boulevard Rochechouart in the ninth arrondissement. Beginning in 1892, the café-concert began mounting elaborate revues. Fréhel sang there in 1910, early in her career; Colette performed a pantomime act there around the same time. Facing competition from the cinema in the late 1920s, the Gaîté-Rochechouart switched gears. The director's new plan: "No more costly stars, which incidentally, in these difficult times are no guarantee of box office receipts, but a solid troupe of faithful and disciplined artists. No more ruinous sets, few costumes. No longer aim for the snobs, but for the general public, without offering that same public any vulgar concessions, making it laugh without making it blush." The results were encouraging, and so the artistic director decided to focus even more on the tour de chant and thus "restore honor in the French song."[78] The Gaîté-Rochechaouart turned to the publisher André Danerty, the organizer of the "Galas André Danerty," a series of programs devoted exclusively to song that featured old favorites from the café-concert as well as new faces. In an attempt to respond to the nostalgia felt by many for this bygone form of popular entertainment, Danerty programs were added to the Gaîté's lineup in 1930. Among the performers were Eugénie Buffet; Paulette Darty, who had retired in 1908 after a successful career singing the waltz; Gaby Montbreuse, famous for her vulgarity in performances of realist and burlesque songs at the cabaret Chez Fysher; Lucienne Boyer, singer of intimate songs at the Cabaret Fysher and best known for her "Parlez-moi d'amour," which won the first Grand Prix du Disque in 1930; the tenor Jean Lumière, the *chanteur du charme*, and Fréhel. This strategy of turning to the café-concert repertoire and performers seems to have worked only for a short while; the Gaîté-Rochechouart floundered and became a cinema in 1933. Nonetheless, it anticipated a practice that would be taken up by the cinema, as we shall see: the evocation of nostalgia and community through the figure of the realist singer.

Other establishments also participated in this return to the tour de chant. The Casino-Montparnasse, a modern, comfortable café-concert with 1,200 seats, two balconies, box seats, a *promenoir*, a large terrace, a bar, and an immense hall, located on the rue de la Gaîté in the fourteenth arrondissement, had opened in 1910.[79] Owned by Georges and Léon Comte, the brothers responsible for the success of the Casino Saint-Martin, an important café-concert in operation from 1907 to 1920, the Casino-Montparnasse was a worthy competitor to the other large establishments in Montparnasse, the Gaîté-Montparnasse and Bobino. Most singers of renown passed through the Casino-Montparnasse between 1910 and the mid 1920s, including Fréhel, Damia, Mistinguett, Maurice Chevalier, and Georges Milton. With its modern equipment, the Casino-Montparnasse was able to mount the revues that the Comte brothers had originally produced at the Casino Saint-Martin. The revues weren't as elaborate as those of the Scala or the Ambassadeurs; they rarely exceeded one act. But they were written specifically for the neighborhood audience, echoing the communal resonance of the old café-concert experience. After 1920, the decline of the café-concert encouraged the Comte brothers to focus exclusively on the revue. A 1929 restoration of the café-concert and the appearance of nude women on stage could not compensate for the competition offered by the talkies. For the 1931–32 season, then, the artistic director booked the Galas André Danerty.

The Galas took place also at the Concordia in 1933. Located on the rue du Faubourg-Saint-Martin in the tenth arrondissement, the Concordia had been "one of the most joyous and characteristic of the working-class and *faubourien* cafés-concerts" around the turn of the century.[80] Nevertheless, just as the Galas André Danerty could not save the Gaîté-Rochechouart, they could not save the Casino-Montparnasse, the Casino Saint-Martin, the Concordia, or the Printania, all of which closed their doors in the early 1930s and became cinemas.

This was the institutional context, then, in which the realist singer was performing by the early 1930s. She represented the past, in the sense that the café-concert era, which had engendered her, was long dead. The music hall, now the primary performance venue of both realist singers and *meneuses de revue*, was in decline, even as it prompted a certain nostalgia for the days of the intimate caf'-conc' that it had supplanted. This nostalgia was no doubt exacerbated by many other factors of the dawning modern era, both political and economic as well as technological. With the concurrent evolution of mass industry, popular entertainment, communism, fascism, syndicalism, feminism, psychoanalysis, sexual liberation, and so on, it is hardly surprising that audiences longed to inscribe themselves in a relationship with certain performers who evoked an imaginary community sharing a common geography and class identity. That this community no longer existed, if it ever *had* existed, was all the more reason to seek out a locus, the realist singer, around which to organize that imagined past. The fact that the realist singer looked toward the future by inserting herself into the medium of sound cinema, the very medium that was responsible for music hall's demise, had no bearing on this. Notwithstanding the nostalgic *passéisme* involved, there was nothing conservative about this phenomenon, which sought a fulcrum from which to up-end social and sexual norms. The real community, as we shall see, was radical, comprising those who recognized and shared in the excitement of the transgressive undercurrent of the old café-concert, where class and gender boundaries had been crossed, and who hoped to rewrite that transgression in the new era.

3 · Voices from the Past

As we have seen, the realist singer emerged from a very specific entertainment context—the raucous nineteenth-century café-concert—but persisted in the more sedate and regimented music hall, despite the gradual replacement of the tour de chant by the revue as the mainstay of live performance. The realist singer, we have also seen, was the product of discourses that emerged from two main sources: the writings of male music hall critics, novelists, and poet-flâneurs; and the authorial gestures of the singers themselves, such as the "rag-picking" activities of Eugénie Buffet and Mistinguett and their self-presentation more generally via interviews, autobiographies, and performance.

In this chapter, I address two main issues, focusing more directly on the realist singer's film roles: how these two main sources of discourse (those of the male author/flâneur and the realist singer herself) about the realist singer persist and mutate; and how the importance of the realist singer as a symbol of working-class femininity and of Parisian urban space more generally intensifies in French cinema of the 1930s.

THE INTERWAR FLÂNEUR AND THE REALIST SINGER: PIERRE MAC ORLAN

During the interwar period, the male music hall critic and the flâneur (who were often one and the same) continued to be intrigued by the realist singer. However, the assessments of Gustave Fréjaville and Léon-Paul Fargue are substantially more positive than the acerbic mid-nineteenth-century commentary by Louis Veuillot, who was horrified by the audacity of Thérésa and her female spectators alike. Even if, in the 1920s and the 1930s, the occasional commentator, such as Pierre Bost, expressed resentment about the star power of the *meneuse de revue* and perceived the music hall experience as increasingly formulaic, the discourse generated by men of letters about the realist singer during the interwar period evinces an intensified fascination with her evocative powers. The writings of Pierre Mac Orlan (1882–1970), poet, novelist, journalist, and flâneur of the period between the wars, provide a particularly good example of this preoccupation.

In a essay written in 1923 entitled "La Seine et les ponts de Paris" (The Seine and the Bridges of Paris), Mac Orlan describes a tall, thin, blonde prostitute who works underneath the bridges of the Seine from Billancourt to Bagatelle.[1] He has always felt drawn to this *belle* apache, he writes, and he regrets that he does not know her name. Mac Orlan, well known to film historians as the author of the novels from which the poetic realist films *La Bandera* (Duvivier, 1935) and *Quai des brumes* (Carné, 1938) were adapted, also contributed to a tradition going back at least to Baudelaire of writing about the city of Paris as a text to be interpreted, savored, and celebrated. In contrast to his contemporary Walter Benjamin's more theoretical and historiographic *Passagen-Werk* (translated as *The Arcades Project*), Mac Orlan, along with other interwar literary figures such as Francis Carco, Eugène Dabit, and Léon-Paul Fargue, unabashedly celebrates specific neighborhoods, streets, and popular entertainment in Paris. Many of their works were published in deluxe, limited editions that included pen-and-ink drawings, watercolors, or photographs of street scenes and the people of Paris.[2] Mac Orlan's essay "La Seine et les ponts de Paris" was originally published in a book of essays entitled *Aux lumières de Paris* (In the Lights of Paris) in 1925, a collection of short, poetic homages to the street life of nocturnal Paris. In the essay, Mac Orlan evokes the violence, sordidness, and allure of this Paris prostitute's world.

> It is ordinarily in the shadow of a bridge at the edge of the bank, where the waves lap, that one finds fragmentary pieces of dismembered women. These past few years have been especially notable for this type of assassination, which gives a perverse tint to the Seine's shadows, and especially to locales whose walls have witnessed this type of operation. This image, when applied to any one of the thousand houses, interspersed with the *guinguettes* [open-air taverns], that one finds along the Seine on the outskirts of the city, gives a singularly literary quality to these lodgings, which are terrorized, after all, by bedbugs. In these parts, one encounters Latin faces whose dark stubble, badly shaven against skin gone green from sleeping under the stars, makes them marvelously responsible for anything that solitary strollers from a different milieu can imagine. But what is there to say about the girls, young girls relegated to such distress without remedy?[3]

In response to his own question, "What is there to say about the girls?" Mac Orlan writes a kind of history of them In his lyrical, dreamy testament, he invokes none other than Fréhel, who, he notes, sang of such girls in her recent performances at the Olympia:

> The girls sung about by Fréhel were born under bridges. It is under a bridge, perhaps a more nuptial bridge, because of the richness of its ornamentation, that their secret flesh is moved for the first time. . . . [T]hese girls, born on the humid stone, participat[e] in urban landscapes of the Seine and [are] familiar with, perhaps, the ferocious pleasure of being goddesses of the sewer, those of the black smoke of the tugboats, and of the somber silence that welcomes the farewell to life of those frail suicides.[4]

He thus enlists Fréhel, whom he calls "one of the true interpreters of misery," in his project—without her, he cannot "interpret" the prostitute's life.

Mac Orlan is fascinated, in fact, not only by the prostitute, but by her surroundings: the bridges, the Seine, the *guingettes*, and Paris more generally. This attention to "atmosphere," a defining element of poetic realist cinema, is already present in the writings of Mac Orlan, Dabit, Carco, and the other writers of the teens, the 1920s, and the 1930s, whose work would form the literary sources of poetic realist cinema.[5] Mac Orlan's linkage of the realist singer and the geography of Paris is quite explicit in his essay. He proposes that the city of Paris organize a celebration of the bridges of Paris in which the realist singer will play a key role. In his fantasy orchestration, Mistinguett will sing under the Pont Mirabeau (in the southwestern corner of the bourgeois fifteenth arrondissement, where the *quais* are bleaker and more industrial than in the city center) for the girls born on the banks of the river. Fréhel, "pale and desperate," will sing under the Pont de Grenelle (also in the fifteenth arrondissement). Damia and Andrée Turcy[6] will sing beneath the Pont au Change in front of the Palais de Justice, where the "well-to-do" legal prostitutes go to register. Mac Orlan concludes with the image of a prostitute's dead body floating down the Seine, wryly noting that it is only decent to remember her in the midst of this public festivity.

How can we untangle this juncture of the realist singer, Parisian urban space, and the interwar flâneur? Setting aside Mac Orlan's own peculiar brand of wistful morbidity when musing about the fate of the "girls," we should not discount the coincidence of so many of the elements that characterize the *réaliste* performance. Mac Orlan's role in the elaboration of a realist, populist universe in 1930s cinema lends him considerable authority.

Although he wrote the dialogue for only one sound film (*Choc en retour*, 1937), his novels' visual qualities, with their emphasis on foggy, desolate spaces in Paris and elsewhere, and his fascination with the underworld tie him intimately to the poetic realist film movement.[7] Likewise, Mac Orlan's "cinematic" prose and his passion for nocturnal Paris and its inhabitants link him with the work of the photographers Eugène Atget and Brassaï.[8]

Less known is Mac Orlan's love of popular song and realist singers. In the early 1930s, he wrote a column and reviewed records for a magazine published by the Columbia record label. Moreover, several of Mac Orlan's poems were set to music by the well-known composers Georges Van Parys and Philippe-Gérard.[9] He actually wrote and published realist songs, becoming a member of SACEM (the French equivalent of ASCAP) in 1936.[10] Mac Orlan's "Ça n'a pas d'importance" (It's Not Important) and "La Fille de Londres" (The Girl from London) were performed and recorded in the 1950s by Germaine Montero, his favorite performer.[11] Monique Morelli, a realist singer of the 1950s, also performed the songs of Mac Orlan, as did Juliette Greco, the "muse of Saint-Germain-des-Prés," who debuted in 1949.[12]

Mac Orlan was thus intensely invested in popular song and in the realist singers, in particular. But his investment in the music and in the realist singer constitutes more than simply another outlet for his literary production. To Mac Orlan, his favored singer Germaine Montero was not so much an independent presence as a projection of his consciousness. Adrian Rifkin observes:

> As late as 1965 the elder surviving master of bohemian Parisianism, Mac Orlan, was insistent that the status of woman in his work could achieve a substantial value only in so far as she could voice his feelings. Of all his modes of writing, and of all the types of women, the song and the singer alone were able to complete this transference, this realisation of self in sexual and social alterity.[13]

When Mac Orlan invokes the realist singer in "La Seine et les ponts de Paris," he uses her not as mere shorthand for the Paris prostitute, but as a go-between to a world he knows, but to which, as a comfortably well-off literary personage, he does not belong. That he recognizes this more marginal figure suggests once again that she represents, in an unaccountable, or at least unexpected, fashion, a bridge between complicated layers of longing, identification, and even Parisian authenticity. In fact, the realist singer is also, for Mac Orlan, a site for the projection of his own desires. He needs the connotative powers of Fréhel, Mistinguett, and Damia in order to create the affective landscape into which he can place his prostitute, a landscape that will, in turn, nourish his fantasies of the prostitute.

Mac Orlan's contemporary and fellow flâneur Francis Carco wrote himself even more directly into the fantasy landscape inhabited by the realist singer. Carco wrote poetry, nonfiction, and crime novels set in the Paris underworld, such as *Jésus la Caille* (1914). He also wrote realist songs. His most famous song, "Le Doux Caboulot" (The Darling Dive) was performed by the realist singer Marie Dubas in the early 1930s.[14] It will also be recalled that Carco wrote the 1920 hit play *Mon homme,* which served as the inspiration for Mistinguett's song "Mon homme." The confrontation between upper-class women and the underworld explored by Carco underscores the contradictions, but also the rapports, inherent in the café-concert tradition of heterogeneous audiences of bohemians and bourgeois, "liberated" (at least for the span of an evening) women and disconcerted men. This confrontation still preoccupied Carco in the 1930s, when he wrote the script for *Paris-Béguin* (Genina, 1931) and *Paris la nuit* (Diamant-Berger, 1930), films about wealthy women attracted to the virility and mystery of the underworld.[15]

PRISONS DE FEMMES

Carco's most sustained injection of his own persona into the realist imaginary occurs in the film *Prisons de femmes* (Women's Prison), eleventh at the box office in 1938.[16] The film's director, Roger Richebé, is best known to historians of 1930s French cinema as the business partner of Pierre Braunberger, with whom he formed one of the most important production companies of the decade. Etablissements Braunberger–Richebé purchased and modernized Billancourt studios at the coming of sound, produced Renoir's *La Chienne* (1931) and *Fanny* (1932) and launched the film career of the music hall performer Jules Raimu.[17] Richebé is not at all remembered for the seventeen films he directed between 1933 and 1957, and *Prisons de femmes* is thus usually associated with Francis Carco, who wrote its script. The film is based on Carco's nonfiction book *Prisons de femmes* (1931), in which he chronicles his visits to women's prisons around France and his encounters with notorious inmates such as Dédée-la-folle (Crazy Dédée) and Lulu-petit-poisse (Bad Luck Lulu).[18] Carco actually plays himself in the film, a writer with links to both the underworld and the *haute bourgeoisie.*

Prisons de femmes opens with a scene of an elegant party at the home of Juliette (Renée St.-Cyr) and her husband, an industrialist. Late in the evening, she receives a mysterious phone call and then slips away, unseen by her husband. She enters the Montmartre hotel room of a pimp named Dédé, played by Georges Flamant. (Flamant played a pimp, also named Dédé, in Renoir's *La Chienne*.) Dédé has been blackmailing Juliette and now makes an unwanted sexual advance, which is interrupted by his girlfriend Régine (Viviane Romance). Régine, believing that Juliette is trying to steal her man, shoots her. Later that night, half-conscious in her hospital bed, Juliette whispers to her concerned and mystified husband, "Carco will explain everything." Carco, our bourgeois tour guide through Paris's criminal underworld, then narrates Juliette's life to her husband (and to us) in a series of flashbacks.

We learn that Juliette met Régine in prison, when Juliette was serving time for having stabbed a man in self-defense. Juliette, the film is careful to make clear through flashback and Carco's voiceover narration, was born into a well-to-do family and orphaned at age eleven. She was taken in by a greedy couple who later attempted to exploit her by marrying her off to an unsavory character. Juliette resisted the suitor's advances, defending herself with a knife, and was sentenced to three years in prison. Régine, a jovial café-concert singer, is serving time for a crime committed by her boyfriend Dédé. She befriends the innocent Juliette, and it is through Régine's friendship and protection that Juliette survives her prison term.[19] Released from prison, Juliette explicitly rejects prostitution as a means of support, finding work instead in a department store. There, she meets, and later marries, a wealthy man, keeping her past a secret. Later, Régine too is released from prison; she willingly returns to her old life with Dédé. Juliette encounters Régine and Dédé one day by chance and, soon thereafter, Dédé begins to blackmail Juliette, unbeknownst to Régine.

Prisons de femmes, like Mac Orlan's nonfiction writings on the *milieu*, or Paris underworld, despite the pretext of its being a simplistic morality tale, seeks nothing more than to expose viewers to the city's underclass. This "slumming" is played out in a number of ways. The film comments directly on the bourgeois predilection for visiting the milieu when Juliette's husband chastises Carco for exposing his wife to the city's seamier side. Unaware of her prison experience, he assumes that the only way Juliette would have become associated with a character like Dédé is through Carco's frequentations. (Carco's research for novels and his taste for the characters and ambience of the underworld presumably take him to places to which most bourgeois never venture.) He denies having exposed Juliette to the dangers of the underworld, however, and explains that her current predicament is, in fact, her husband's fault, because wealthy people view others as either "good" or "bad," and are thus blind to subtler shades of the human predicament. Carco then begins his defense of Juliette, implicitly promising a more nuanced narrative (one that does not preclude a voyeuristic thrill or two) set among the underclass and its fallen women.

It is not surprising, therefore, that there is an apparently gratuitous scene in this carefully plotted and ultimately rather conservative film. When Régine is released from prison, she and Dédé go to Le Paradis, the picturesque café-concert (a seedy beuglant) where she used to sing before going to prison. She greets old friends and, later, performs a song called "Je n'ai pas le temps d'aimer" (I don't have time to love), a comic tune about the need to unionize prostitution.[20] In response, the audience of hustlers and their women erupts with applause; a series of shot/countershots establishes a connection between Régine and her appreciative audience. Viviane Romance, a former music hall performer with a reputation as an unruly woman both in films and in life, brings her usual bawdiness and effervescence to this role. Romance provides a stark contrast to the passive, frail, victimized Renée St.-Cyr as Juliette, who here plays an ingénue similar to those played by Danielle Darrieux in 1930s films, complete with shiny black raincoat and beret. The sequence breathes some much-needed fresh air into an otherwise stilted film and communicates above all that these marginalized people—petty criminals and the poor—constitute a community. This community has its own rules, its own forms of entertainment, and its own kind of emotional power. Carco wants to celebrate this community, and he does so, interestingly, by offering a glimpse of female audacity in Romance's singing performance.

This moment of celebration is only a short scene in a film that concludes by returning Régine to prison for shooting Juliette and by securing Juliette's place in the bourgeoisie alongside her newly understanding husband. The film exposes, but does not challenge, the class determinants in the lives of these women. Juliette is returned to her "rightful" class, and Régine, despite her goodwill, generosity, and vivacity, is "fated" to return to prison. However, *Prisons de femmes* also explicitly identifies the constraints and injustices of patriarchy as a force in the women's lives, showing that the greed and lechery of men (on the part of both Juliette's adoptive father and Régine's boyfriend/pimp) are responsible not only for the women's woes, but also for destroying the strong cross-class friendship between them that propels the narrative. Paradoxically, Carco's narration, his attempt to acquit Juliette in the eyes of her husband, functions at the expense of Régine, the other basically "good" woman caught up in unfortunate circumstances. Given the sympathy and fascination that *Prisons de femmes* generates for

Régine, the narrative's resolution seems to work against its own logic. What drives Régine to sacrifice her friendship in defense of a man who has so conspicuously and repeatedly betrayed her? Petty jealousy seems a weak argument, given the film's focus on the force behind the solidarity of women. The scene in the beuglant, brief as it is, calls on the realist singer to convey the powerful emotion and sense of community in the milieu, just as Mac Orlan turns to Fréhel's songs to explicate and translate the prostitute who intrigues him. Whether Régine's condemnation is a correction for this autonomy or merely a sad acquiescence to the primacy of the pimp-prostitute coupling, the narrative reinforces the inalienable martyrdom so essential to the realist performer. She is doomed to love her man, whatever the circumstances or the level of his own commitment (recall the apache dance described by a music hall critic in chapter 2), and to suffer as a result. She simultaneously celebrates this fatalism and begs for the audience's sympathetic identification by evoking a recognizable myth, steeped in nostalgia and pathos.

The realist singer is, without a doubt, an essential character in the realist literary and cinematic fantasies authored by men like Mac Orlan, Carco, and Richebé, and revolving around prostitution, murder, poverty, and the cityscape. But clearly there is a tension between what she represents to men and what she evokes in women, or represents of herself, as illustrated in the ambivalent, uncomfortable responses in the café-concert described in chapter 1. Let us explore this tension further through analysis of the interwar realist singer's self-presentation and her roles in 1930s French cinema, for the realist singer is much more than the voice of the male flâneur's feelings and fantasies. In her creation of "texts" from the material of her own life and from the now well established imaginary of the realist song, the realist singer played a large role in the authorship of her own public persona. This had been true of the fin-de-siècle realist singer, but the interwar realist singer relies even more heavily than a Buffet or a Guilbert on one specific intertext: the story of her own life. Fréhel, the best-known realist singer of the 1930s, will provide a good starting point, for her "authorship" of her star persona demonstrates most clearly the intensification of the use of autobiography as intertext characteristic of this period.

THE REALIST SINGER'S SELF-PRESENTATION: FRÉHEL

Biographical and autobiographical information about Fréhel, much of which consists of recycled anecdotes published over the years in newspaper reviews and magazine profiles, reveals a distinct self-consciousness on her part. In her serialized autobiography, published in the tabloid *Point de vue—Images du monde* in 1949, she begins by comparing her life to a song genre: the *complainte*, a ballad.

> The ballad of my life, the ballad of my life. . . . And how would I not call my life a ballad, me, who since the age of five have never ceased pushing romance, me who at age five, it seems, without knowing anything of existence, conveyed in my songs all the misery of the human heart, all the frenzy of love and all of its sadness?
>
> Tough blows, the blues, joys, triumphs and downfalls, my life rushed through all that pell-mell. A single moment each night finds me myself again, that moment when, before the lights, everything is silent in me; when for the tumultuous being that I am is substituted the image that public has built around me: Fréhel, the ballad of Paris.
>
> I had some good moments and others that were atrocious, I was poor, I was rich, I had my follies and my foolishness, I loved with passion and hated with force, I hauled my ass here and there and saw a lot of things. In other words, it doesn't make a bad ballad.[21]

This passage's repetition ("coups durs, coups de cafard" [tough blows, the blues]), its parallelism ("I was poor, I was rich . . ."), and its oppositions ("I loved with passion and hated with force") indicate a carefully crafted presentation of the self and an awareness of her story's generic characteristics. Whereas the fin-de-siècle realist singers Eugénie Buffet and Yvette Guilbert had constructed their star personae primarily from material appropriated from the Montmartre cabaret and from their encounters with prostitutes and seamstresses, Fréhel's star image relied most heavily on its autobiographical and biographical intertext.

Born Marguerite Boulc'h in Paris on July 13, 1891, Fréhel spent her early years living with her alcoholic grandmother in Primel-Trégastel, a small Breton town.[22] Her father was a sailor in the French Navy and later a railroad employee, while her mother worked as a maid. Shuttled back and forth between her grandmother and her parents in Paris, Fréhel suffered from neglect. She often had fleas and nearly died of croup at the age of three. By the age of five, she was singing with a blind man who performed in the streets and in bars. Her mother, delighted with the unexpected income, often sent her out to sing until 2:00 A.M. Like Buffet and Guilbert, Fréhel gives a vivid description of the perils facing young girls raised in situations of neglect. Sent out of the apartment one evening so that her mother could be with a lover, Fréhel was attacked by an old man, whose roving hands she escaped by biting.

The family troubles multiplied. Fréhel's grandmother was killed by a cow, a cyclone hit their house in Courbevoie, a fire destroyed the house, nearly killing Fréhel, and then her father was hit by a train and killed. Her childhood ended, she says, at the age of eight, when her mother forced her to contribute regularly to the family's income. Echoing Thérésa's early work history, Fréhel recounts how she worked as an errand girl for a salt company in the courtyard of their apartment building but was fired because she sang all day and the workers listened to her instead of working. She worked, also, for a pharmacy delivering beauty products, where she met La Belle Otéro, the dancer and courtesan. In her free time, she hung around Labbé, a music publisher, where she met many singers. Amused by her audacity, they taught her such songs as "Mam'zelle Pervenche,"[23] and the realist repertoire of Montéhus (Gaston Brunschwig [1872–1952]), one of the last of the worker/anarchist songwriters of the nineteenth-century *chansonnier* tradition."[24]

Fréhel made her debut in 1906 at the Brasserie de l'Univers, a medium-sized café-concert on Avenue Wagram in the seventeenth arrondissement seating five hundred people. She was sixteen years old and had not eaten in two days. Her account of her audition at the Univers reveals a common theme in descriptions of the realist singer: the mining of painful past experiences to add power and verisimilitude to her performances. The realist singer had often lived the pain she sang of and relived it as she performed: "I sang the repertoire of Montéhus, ballads about poverty and pain. While singing, I saw again all the hard knocks of my childhood, the dark stairway, the old man's attack in the vacant lot, the beatings, the lack of tenderness around me, the abandonment, and from that day on, I put my soul into those ballads."[25] In addition to Fréhel's sheer vocal power and stage presence, then, it is precisely the "performance" of these experiences—the perception that Fréhel knew firsthand the experiences she sang about—that permitted her to function as a credible "performer of poverty."

Fréhel quickly became a notorious figure in the music halls and cabarets, whose wealthy patrons she insulted in the manner of Aristide Bruant at the Chat noir. The novelist Colette, whose music hall career as a dancer coincided with the early period of Fréhel's career, includes a particularly vivid profile of her in her novel *La Vagabonde*:

> Jadin is a *petite chanteuse*, and such a novice on the halls that she has not had time yet to dye her chestnut hair golden. She has, so to speak, jumped from the *boulevard exterieur* on to the stage, and she cannot get over the fact that she is earning, with her voice, two hundred and ten francs a month. She is eighteen. The suddenness of her luck seems to have frightened her, and her elbows, for ever on the defensive, and all her stubborn little body bent like a

gargoyle, seem intent on parrying the jokes of the brutal Fates. She sings like a seamstress at her work, or like a street urchin, and it never occurs to her that it might be possible to sing otherwise. Quite ingenuously she strains her voice, which is a rasping, fascinating contralto that suits admirably the pink and sulky face of a young Apache. Her dress, purchased haphazard, is far too long; her chestnut hair is innocent of "waves," her slanting shoulder seems dragged downwards by the heavy laundry basket; the down on her upper lip is white with cheap powder. And the public worship her.[26]

The early period of Fréhel's career culminates in her love affair with her fellow up-and-coming café-concert star Maurice Chevalier. The Chevalier love affair is, structurally, the marker that divides the two portions of Fréhel's life as it is usually narrated. First there is the young, beautiful, wild singer who performed in cafés-concerts and at the cabaret Chez Fysher and who partied at Magic-City with the grand duchess Anastasia (aunt of the czar) and the prizefighter Jack Johnson. Then there is the overweight, alcoholic cocaine addict who spent eleven years in exile before returning to Paris and mounting her comeback. Between these two periods, her love affair with Chevalier took place. The relationship developed quickly, was volatile, and "made her a woman." But despair was just around the corner. "[A]t the height of my beauty, at the height of my popularity, at the height of my happiness, I burned up my life. How could I have guessed that the dark days were so close, the days of anger, the days of despair?"[27] Chevalier reportedly betrayed her by entering into a liaison with Mistinguett. Fréhel, crazy with grief, carried a knife around town for a time, ready to strike at Chevalier or Mistinguett if the opportunity arose. She consumed more and more alcohol, ether, and cocaine in an attempt to forget Chevalier, and eventually attempted suicide. She then left for what was intended to be a two-month tour in eastern Europe, but that stretched into a self-imposed exile lasting eleven years. She lived in Constantinople for five years, and then in Russia and Romania for several more. The loss of another lover to the war, followed by depression and serious financial setbacks, added to her misery. Fréhel would not return to Paris until 1923, at which time she experienced a spectacular comeback, performing in the music hall and, in the 1930s, the cinema. Her life would come full circle, however, like that of Eugénie Buffet. By the late 1940s, Fréhel was living in a home for the destitute in Le Vésinet, a suburb near Paris. The first installment of her memoirs was, in fact, published on the occasion of a fundraiser on her behalf at the Européen, the music hall where she had performed so often in the 1920s and 1930s. She eventually moved back to a shabby hotel on the rue Pigalle, where she lived in poverty until her death in 1951.

Fréhel, then, brought to her 1930s film roles a palimpsest of images: the strikingly beautiful, self-destructive singer of the prewar years; the years of heartbreak, drugs, depression, and exile; and, finally, resurrection, perseverance, and nostalgia. More than any other realist singer before her, Fréhel was adept at drawing on public knowledge of her poverty-stricken childhood, ties to the underworld, drug abuse, and failed romances. The music hall critic Maurice Verne said, "It was quite simple, these women brought their lives to the stage."[28] But it was not, of course, simply a question of just "being themselves"; the realist singers transformed autobiographical experience into performance material, manipulating in a very self-conscious way the codes of realism and melodrama already circulating in literature, film, and the music hall.

Like every realist singer, Fréhel possessed a keen sense of marketing, a self-consciousness about her persona as a brand name. Her 1949 description of her pre–World War I self resembles, in its distanced character and its use of the third person, a discussion of a product logo.

> Red scarf worn haphazardly, crumpled skirt, hand on her hips and a *goualante* [popular song sung on the streets] on her lips, that's me, Fréhel, just as you saw me on the stages of the Parisian music hall, in the era when old man Poincaré put his nose in the business of France. Oh! Certainly, I had changed. The "Pervanche" of the sweet life, thin as one of Carmen's cigarette girls, had been replaced by a fat old granny, heavy-jowled and truculent, with arms as big as the Republic. But what remained was my vitality and my outspokenness, these essential weapons for those who want to try for the floodlit glory of the *caf'-conc'* where the audience is the most difficult in the world.[29]

It was this ability to market herself and her past that made Fréhel's 1923 comeback at the Olympia music hall possible. Overweight and unrecognizable, she was promoted as "Fréhel, the unforgettable unforgotten." She was, in fact, quite forgotten by the Parisian public at that point and had to rebuild her career entirely.[30]

Fréhel constantly evokes her own past in her songs, films, and interviews. She carries with her into every performance the terrible childhood, the golden memories of her early stardom, the break with Maurice Chevalier, and the years of exile in eastern Europe in which Paris was lost to her. This autobiographical intertext is most evident in Fréhel's performance in *Pépé le Moko* (Duvivier, 1936).

PÉPÉ LE MOKO

In *Pépé le Moko*, Fréhel plays a small, but important role as Tania, the companion of a Paris gangster who is confined to the Casbah, the Arab quarter of Algiers. The proletarian icon Jean Gabin stars in the film as Pépé, the notorious head of the criminal gang to which Fréhel's lover ("Carlo," played by Gabriel Gabrio) belongs. Pépé rules over his world in the exotic and lawless Casbah but cannot leave it for fear of arrest in the French-governed city beyond. His nostalgia for Paris and his desire for Gaby (Mireille Balin), a glamorous *parisienne*, prompt him to try to escape. Ultimately, Pépé is betrayed to the police by his Arab lover Inès (Line Noro) and then commits suicide at the harbor as the ship taking Gaby back to France pulls away.

Fréhel had appeared with Jean Gabin in another 1930s film, *Coeur de Lilas* (Litvak, 1931), which we shall explore later in this chapter. Gabin had had only a secondary role as a *mauvais garçon* in *Coeur de Lilas*, but his career had taken a dramatic turn since then. By 1936, he was a full-fledged star at the height of his powers, the hero-protagonist of some of the most important films of the decade. Through his roles in *Paris-Béguin* (Genina, 1931), *Coeur de Lilas*, *Zouzou* (Allégret, 1934), and especially *La Bandera* (Duvivier, 1935) and *La Belle Équipe* (Duvivier, 1936), Gabin's star persona had come together into the sympathetic, alluring proletarian or gangster figure who embodied 1930s working-class Frenchness and masculinity.[31] After *Pépé le Moko* (1936), Gabin continued building on this image, starring in a string of some of the most commercially and critically successful films of the 1930s: *La Grande Illusion* (Renoir, 1937), *Gueule d'amour* (Grémillon, 1937), *Le Quai des brumes* (Carné, 1938), *La Bête humaine* (Renoir, 1938), and *Le Jour se lève* (Carné, 1939). A key element of the melancholic poetic realist sensibility, Gabin is inevitably brought down in the end by a woman and by larger social and economic forces.

While Fréhel, who by the 1930s was a frumpy ruin of her legendary youth, never became a cinema star on the level of a Jean Gabin or a Michèle Morgan, she nevertheless had many important, critically acclaimed roles before performing in *Pépé le Moko*. In 1933, she had a substantial role in Pierre Chenal's *La Rue sans nom* (The Street without a Name), "the first film baptized 'poetic realist' for its naturalistic acting, its mobile camera work, and its setting—a poverty-ridden, dead-end street in Paris."[32] Here, Fréhel sings a song called "C'est la rue sans nom" (It's the Street with No Name) and plays the wife of a reformed criminal in this atmospheric narrative, which resembles a realist song in its moodiness and its themes: betrayal, erotic obsession, sickness, child mortality, and the impending demolition of the neighborhood by the authorities. Fréhel's performance was praised for its "discretion," its "truth," and its "emotion."[33]

Next, Fréhel had a cameo role in *Amok* (Ozep, 1934), an adaptation of a short story by Stefan Zweig about a debauched Parisian doctor living in the

Malaysian jungle. A beautiful society woman (Marcelle Chantal) comes to the doctor seeking an abortion after an affair with a young officer conducted in her husband's absence. He refuses but later has a change of heart. It's too late; she has died of a botched abortion performed by a villager. Determined to make amends any way he can, the doctor goes to the harbor and cuts her casket loose from the ship that is carrying her body back to France for the autopsy demanded by her husband. He thus manages to save her honor, but becomes entangled in the rope attached to the casket and drowns. The film's emphasis on atmosphere (its sets were designed by Lazare Meerson) and obsession, and its tragic ending, mark it as an early poetic realist effort.[34] Fréhel appears in only one scene. When the doctor, crazy with grief and remorse, enters a seedy cabaret/brothel, Fréhel is there, singing a mournful tune entitled "J'attends quelqu'un" (I'm Waiting for Someone). An aging prostitute/chanteuse, she is grieving for Paris and her youth.

In Sacha Guitry's 1936 *Le Roman d'un tricheur* (The Story of a Cheat), Fréhel appears in one of the many flashbacks that structure this picaresque social comedy—a film quite different from the poetic realist films in which Fréhel was more likely to appear. Guitry, the hero-narrator in this ironic and self-conscious work, writes his memoirs in a café. In a flashback to the years of his military service, Fréhel sings "Et v'la pourquoi" (And That's Why), written by Guitry for her. The soldiers in the audience sing along with Fréhel during the song's chorus: "That's why/Each Sunday/I no longer put on my white dress/To walk in the forest/With the one I adored."[35] Although the sequence as a whole is meant to be comic, Fréhel's appearance connotes lost sexuality, intense emotion, a generalized nostalgia, and a sense of community.

Given her prior film roles alone, Fréhel is thus right at home in *Pépé le Moko*, a film about despair, impossible desire, the implacable workings of fate, and a longing for the sense of community available in the "good old days" back in Paris. Both Fréhel and Gabin, in fact, symbolized a disappearing or unavailable Paris at this point. Not only had Fréhel "lost" Paris during her self-imposed exile to eastern Europe in the teens, but her film roles tie her intimately to a decaying, soon-to-be-razed Paris *(Coeur de Lilas, La Rue sans nom)*, to exile from Paris *(Amok, La Maison du Maltais)*, and to "the past" in general *(Le Roman d'un tricheur)*. *Pépé le Moko*, likewise, demonstrates a deep affection for a Paris beyond reach. The film takes place in Algeria, but Paris lurks constantly in the memories and fantasies of the displaced Parisians who are trapped there. A conversation between Pépé and his love-object, Gaby—one of the dialogue writer Henri Jeanson's best-loved creations—demonstrates this best. Discovering that they are both from Paris, Pépé and Gaby take turns recalling street names, mentally traveling through the city, until they "arrive" simultaneously at Place Blanche. As Ginette Vincendeau points out:

> The scene is a brilliant condensation of the touristic appeal of Paris with precise social topography, which moreover reflects the stars' images. Gaby's itinerary is that of luxury shopping and commodified entertainment: it starts at the Champs-Elysées and takes in Opéra, Boulevard des Capucines, Rue Montmartre and Rue Fontaine to end up at place Blanche, while Pépé reaches the same destination via working-class Rue Saint-Martin, Gare du Nord, Barbès, La Chapelle, and Boulevard Rochechouart. Place Blanche is the meeting point of working-class and criminal Montmartre with seedy night-club land Pigalle.[36]

Urban space, class, and character are intimately linked in *Pépé le Moko*, and indeed, in much of French populist cinema of the 1930s. Gaby, the sophisticated *demi-mondaine*, forever out of reach,[37] and Pépé, the gangster with a heart of gold, take very different trajectories through Paris. Tellingly, their trajectories meet precisely at the Moulin Rouge, located on Place Blanche, a space where the intermingling of classes was permitted. "Though not actually mentioned in this particular exchange, the Moulin Rouge acts as a mythical reference point for Gaby and Pépé, connecting them with the French café-concert and music hall traditions explicitly represented in *Pépé le Moko* by Gabin's and Fréhel's songs."[38] This site is also associated with loss as well as connection and community, however. Jean Gabin had made his debut at the Moulin Rouge in a revue starring Mistinguett, it will be recalled; and the Moulin Rouge was forced to close in 1929, before reopening as a cinema.

This paradox of the cinema memorializing the live entertainment forms it displaced is played out even more directly in Fréhel's singing turn in *Pépé le Moko*. Until her singing performance, Fréhel appears only a few times onscreen. As Tania, the companion of the most violent member of Pépé's entourage, she is characterized quite explicitly as a physically abused woman. The first time we see her, she has a swollen eye. She explains that Carlo beats her, like all the other men she has known, including a *chanteur de charme* (crooner) she once knew. Here, two identities merge: the familiar female character of the realist song, beaten, yet faithful to her man, and the identity of Fréhel, the singer, who loved and lost another singer (Maurice Chevalier). This merging of the historical Fréhel and the character in the realist song intensifies when she sings to Pépé a bit later in the film.

Pépé reclines in Tania's room, increasingly depressed by his inability to leave the Casbah. Tania comforts him, explaining what she does when she's depressed. "I think of my youth, I look at my old photo and I tell myself I'm in front of a mirror; I put on one of my old records from the time when I was so successful at the Scala on the Boulevard de Strasbourg." Next, Tania puts on a record and hand-cranks an old phonograph. The song is "Où est-il donc?" (Where Is It, Then?), a hymn to a disappearing Paris.[39] She listens to it pensively for a time, then sings along with her own recorded voice.

Où est-il mon Moulin d' la plac' Blanche	Where is my Moulin de la Place Blanche
Mon tabac, mon bistrot du coin?	My tobacconist, my corner bistro?
Tous les jours étaient pour moi dimanche.	Every day was Sunday for me.
Où sont-ils les amis, les copains?	Where are my friends, my pals?
Où sont-ils tous mes vieux bals musettes	Where are all my old dance halls Their *javas* to the sound of the
Leurs javas au son de l'accordéon?	accordion?

Fréhel's tear-stained face fills the frame in this static, lengthy take. Her performance halts the narrative, inviting us to ruminate along with her about all she has lost. The performance expresses a "double nostalgia," as Vincendeau calls it,[40] a longing for a Paris that is beyond reach altogether, or quickly disappearing, and an intense melancholy for all that Fréhel, personally, has lost in her tumultuous life.

Fréhel's persona was linked quite specifically to the *peuple* and landscape of Paris. Like Mistinguett's, Fréhel's name evokes specific areas in and around Paris, but the places she is associated with are even less affluent than the neighborhoods with which Mistinguett is associated. The journalist Maurice Verne, writing in the 1930s, sums up Fréhel's image during the 1920s:

The aggressive passion of this almost masculine face with its large cheeks, the fleshy silhouette of a nervous hulk, the insulting laugh, and this broken voice carry us toward the landscapes of the Zone *[des paysages de la zone]*, to these shacks that overlook continually burning furnaces, the smoking chimneys of Saint-Denis or of muddy Aubervilliers, work, the fleabags of the unlucky and their women, *Mesdames* the streetwalkers. It is Fréhel, the realist singer, a misbegotten daughter of Aristide Bruant and Yvettte Guilbert at her debut. But she, she is of the people.[41]

Fréhel's personal history and losses are condensed with the larger phenomenon of a changing Paris and, specifically, the disappearance of Montmartois popular culture. In his 1980 history of Montmartre, the social historian Louis Chevalier discusses this sequence in *Pépé le Moko* at length. Fréhel functions for Chevalier as a summary of his own memory of Montmartre in the 1930s, contemporary with the film's release. "For us, she expressed a certain working class sentimentality, a certain joking or mocking tone [*gouaille*], with the physique to match. She was Montmartre and then some."[42] Fréhel, a symbol of nostalgia in the 1930s for the café-concert, and for the pre–World War I era more generally, becomes for a contemporary historian, a symbol of his own nostalgia for the late 1930s. Chevalier uses the very lyrics of Fréhel's song ("où sont-ils les amis, les copains?" [where are my friends, my pals?]) as a springboard for his other investigations of Montmartre in the era between the wars. "Where are they, or rather who are they, the friends, the pals. Who are this crowd that come here for amusement? It is Fréhel again who will help us to see it clearly."[43] Chevalier's investigation of Montmartre proceeds, then, relying on anecdotes about Fréhel, relayed to him by Montmartre locals, as a window onto that culture. Chevalier's tribute attests to Fréhel's evocative powers as a performer and to the persistence of her ability to symbolize both the pre–World War I era and the interwar period.

The song Fréhel sings in *Pépé le Moko* also mourns the changes occurring in the landscape of Paris. The song's lyrics are quite explicit, for example, about the disappearance of old Montmartre. The following verse is not actually performed in the film, but was perhaps known to spectators, since the song predates the film.[44]

Car hélas de saison en saison	Because, alas, from season to season
Des Abbesses à la place du Tertre	From Abbesses to the place du Tertre
On démolit nos vieilles maisons.	They're demolishing our old houses.
Sur les terrains vagues de la butte	On the empty lots of the Butte
De grandes banques naîtront bientôt.	Large banks will soon go up.
Où ferez-vous alors vos culbutes	Where will you do your somersaults then
Vous, les pauvres gosses à Poulbot?	You, Poulbot's poor kids?[45]
En regrettant le temps jadis	While missing the olden days
Nous chant'rons, songeant à Salis,	We'll sing, dreaming of Salis,[46]
Montmartre, ton "De Profundis."	Montmartre, your "De Profundis."

Here again, Fréhel is associated with areas in Paris slated for demolition. In *Coeur de Lilas,* as we shall see, it is a question of the fortifications; in *La Rue sans nom*, it is the houses on either side of the "nameless" street. In *Pépé le Moko*, her song speaks of the "demolition of old houses" on the butte Montmartre, which would have resonated with viewers experiencing a project of slum clearance initiated by the municipal authorities before World War I.[47]

Fréhel's song in *Pepe le Moko* is also, specifically, an indictment of the transformations in popular entertainment ("Where are the dance halls?"; "Where is the Moulin [Rouge] of the place Blanche?"). As we have already observed, the teens, 1920s, and 1930s were marked by shifts in technology that changed the nature of popular entertainment. The high-tech revue, the radio, the phonograph, and the sound cinema all altered the traditional relationship between spectacle and spectator. The proximity between audience and performers and the identification it no doubt facilitated was mourned. Fréhel stands in for the bygone café-concert era and the *tour de chant*, and she stubbornly clings to the (by then) old-fashioned genre of the realist song. The Scala, the café-concert mentioned in Fréhel's dialogue, closed in 1933, only three years before *Pépé le Moko* was made.

Popular music itself underwent significant change in the 1930s. New performers emerged, such as Charles Trenet, influenced by jazz and Tin Pan Alley, and Tino Rossi, a heartthrob "crooner" from Corsica who was among the first singers to establish a career through records, radio, and cinema rather than through live performance.[48] Fréhel, for her part, resisted changes in her repertoire and even resisted the microphone, whose use brought about a whole new style of singing in the early 1930s. The intimate "murmuring" of Jean Sablon, Lucienne Boyer, and Tino Rossi was quite at odds with the realist singer's style of "singing from the gut." Fréhel preferred to express herself *à nu* (naked, exposed), as one biographer puts it, usually accompanied only by an accordion.[49]

Pépé le Moko's use of Fréhel, then, offers us the richest, most layered vision of the realist singer in 1930s French film. She is, first and foremost, a prostitute, or at least a former prostitute. Her status as the beaten woman and the companion of a gangster is straight out of the realist song narrative stretching back to Eugénie Buffet. Fréhel, as we saw, represents in her purest form "the past." This "past" has a number of components: (1) her own personal history, including the memories of childhood poverty, early stardom, her vertiginous fall, and, finally, her partial recovery; (2) the shifts in the urban landscape of Paris that brought about a loss of community; and (3) the changing landscape of French popular entertainment (from café-concert to music hall). Fréhel's functions in *Pépé le Moko* serve as a useful template from which to consider other performances of the realist singer in 1930s French film.

COEUR DE LILAS

Pépé le Moko was not, in fact, the first 1930s film to bring together Fréhel, Jean Gabin, and the ambience of the café-concert and the underworld. *Coeur de Lilas* (Anatol Litvak, 1931) is one of the most intriguing examples of the hybrid nature of early 1930s French film. A harbinger of poetic realism in its visual style and in its evocation of the Paris underworld, the film also invokes a number of entertainment contexts: the café-concert, the music hall, and even, indirectly, the boulevard theater. *Coeur de Lilas* is yet another "nonmusical" 1930s French film in which songs play a key role. The film's three songs, all written by the veteran music hall and operetta composer Maurice Yvain and the songwriter Serge Veber, are performed by Fréhel, Jean Gabin, and Fernandel. By highlighting popular singers and the social spaces in which they perform, the film mobilizes the layers of nostalgia surrounding Fréhel and live performance more generally, in the process providing a commentary on the intransigence of class and gender boundaries.

When the dead body of a bourgeois factory manager is found on the fortifications of Paris, Detective Lucot (André Luguet) sets out to investigate Lilas (Marcelle Romée), a prostitute who may be guilty of the murder. Lucot infiltrates the prostitute's neighborhood disguised as a working-class man in order to gather information on the crime. He collides with La Martousse (Jean Gabin), Lilas's protector. The detective and Lilas fall in love, but just when happiness seems within their reach, Lilas discovers the detective's true identity, and, devastated, turns herself in for the crime.

Coeur de Lilas appears relatively unconcerned with the motives and identity of the criminal or with police procedure, unlike other *policiers* of the early 1930s, such as *Le Chien jaune* (Jean Tarride, 1932). Moreover, the importance of the film's central love relationship between the detective and the prostitute, ostensibly the narrative focus of the film, is minimized. Instead, *Coeur de Lilas* invests most of its energy in the representation of urban and aural space found in the city of Paris. This space belongs, specifically, to the working class and coincides (in the film and, often, in the popular imagination) with the space of the underworld, and consequently with spaces of popular entertainment frequented by or located within the milieu. Even the protagonist's name, Lilas, French for lilac, evokes Les Lilas, the name of a working-class commune just beyond Belleville and Menilmontant. This emphasis is made evident in the film by the specificity and variety of urban spaces that are explored and, especially, by the linking of specific spaces with singing performances by three prominent music hall performers of the period: Fréhel, Jean Gabin, and Fernandel.

The film's insistence on the specificity of place is tied to song early on. Lilas lives in a working-class neighborhood, presumably La Chapelle or La Villette. (The murder, a newspaper headline informs us, was committed in La Chapelle.) The neighborhood, with its tiny, winding streets, looks distinctly pre-Haussmann. In a series of striking tracking shots, the camera deftly weaves around the neighborhood, exploring a café and bal musette, and moving in and out of cheap hotel rooms. This space is constructed in such a way that it appears both intriguing and confusing to outsiders.

The first tracking shot is remarkable for its attention to detail and its obsession with the evocation of a particular social space. A hand cranks a barrel organ, then we hear the music for "Dans la rue" (In the Street).[50] A café shutter rises, revealing steamed windows and lace curtains. On the soundtrack is Fréhel's voice singing the words to "Dans la rue." True to the genre of the realist song, the song is a bittersweet narrative about the lives of prostitutes on the streets of Paris.

Dès qu'on a vu se barrer l'soleil	As soon as we see the sun clear out
Tous les jours, c'est pareil.	Everyday, it's the same.
Sans hâte, on descend sur le trottoir	Taking our time, we go down to the sidewalk
Pour chercher les coins noirs.	To look for dark corners.
Fuyant le regard du flic	Fleeing the cop's eye
On a des espoirs de fric	Hoping for cash,
Princess' de la boue,	Princess of the mud,
Rein' de la gadoue	Queen of the slime
Fleur de bitum' qui s'enroue.	Flower of the asphalt with a hoarse voice.

The tracking shot continues through the neighborhood streets, pausing on prostitutes, their clients, and policemen. A fade provides a bridge to Fréhel, who washes laundry as she sings, "But if the client isn't happy/And if he grumbles on his way out/We say to him, little one, next time, I'll put on silk stockings." She makes a sarcastic face: these streetwalkers can't afford silk stockings. Fréhel's song, along with the active camera, functions to illustrate and exemplify this urban world and its inhabitants, and in particular, the lives of the anonymous prostitutes we see on the street.

It is particularly meaningful that Fréhel sings a song called "In the Street." The street was a dominant trope of the realist song and in the discourse surrounding the singers themselves. Both Fréhel and Piaf were street singers as children, and Piaf's legend included the apocryphal story that she was found on a doorstep in the rue de Belleville. Piaf's mother was also a street singer, and her father performed as an acrobat in the street. One of the most evocative films of the early 1930s containing the performance of a realist song is entitled *Dans les rues* (In the Streets) (Trivas, 1933).[51] The very titles of realist songs (e.g., "La Rue sans nom" [The Street with No

Name] and "La Rue de nôtre amour" [The Street of Our Love])[52] emphasize
this fascination with the street. Bruant, it will be recalled, entitled his collection of realist songs *Dans les rues*.

In Fréhel's serialized autobiography, she inserts herself directly into this
mythology around the urban landscape when she insists that the street not
only raised her but taught her to sing:

> It was the street that raised me, the street that made me as I am, with my
> qualities and my faults. It was the street that taught me to sing. While pass-
> ing by the bistros, the first phonographs sent me the fashionable refrains in
> their nasal voices, amplified by enormous loudspeakers. I would stop short, I
> would stay out under a freezing rain sometimes for hours, my little skirts
> lifted by a gust of wind, in ecstasy for hours. The song recorded itself in me,
> music and words. I never forgot a song I heard.[53]

The street "produced" Fréhel, and, in turn, Fréhel brings the street to *Coeur
de Lilas* and to the spectators through her songs and her persona.

The film opens on the fortifications. After the dead body is discovered,
onlookers are shown racing up and down the steep slopes of the fortification
in a series of pans. There is a great deal of attention to the graphic qualities
in this sequence, such as the pattern of a bridge's iron bars, and the angles
of the landscape itself. Sound is emphasized immediately; just before the
body is discovered, the camera lingers on a blind man playing a plaintive
tune on his barrel organ. The insistent shrieks of a train whistle punctuate
the sequence, reminding us of the proximity of the gare du Nord.
Onlookers, residents of the Zone, gather, and the camera pans slowly around
the circle, taking in the details of their idiosyncratic faces. An onlooker calls
the police and specifies that the body has been found near the boulevard de
la Villette. A newspaper headline reads "A Crime in La Chapelle: A Cadaver
on the Fortifications."

The locations of *Coeur de Lilas* were carefully chosen for their ability to
connote a very particular space of urban poverty. La Chapelle, a neighborhood located immediately to the east of Montmartre, is in the eighteenth
arrondissement in the northeastern corner of Paris. Directly to the east of La
Chapelle in the nineteenth arrondissement is La Villette, the location of the
dead man's factory in the film. Both La Chapelle and La Villette are
working-class neighborhoods steeped in urban lore. "À la Villette" and "À
la Chapelle," it will be recalled, are the titles of two of Aristide Bruant's
songs. Léon-Paul Fargue—like Mac Orlan and Carco, a connoisseur of marginal Parisian sites—claims La Chapelle as his own in a 1932 essay entitled
"Mon Quartier" (My Neighborhood): "[T]his swarming and sonorous cir-

cus where iron mixes with man, the train with the taxi, and cattle with soldiers. A country, more than a district, formed by canals, factories, the Buttes-
Chaumont, the port of La Villette."[54] This neighborhood of train stations,
slaughterhouses, chemical factories, the canal de l'Ourcq, the aerial metro
line Porte Dauphine–Nation, and workers' cafes is a "pure neighborhood,
both rich and dense, enemy of God and snobbism."[55] Tourists who traipse up
and down the streets of La Chapelle during the day looking for a restaurant
or who stop to look at the charming church at the place de Joinville earn the
contemptuous smile of its indigenous people. Fargue prefers the neighborhood at night, when it takes on its sordid and fantastic qualities: "The
evening La Chapelle really is this country of marvelous and fascinating
lugubriousness, this paradise of lost souls, street urchins, and tough guys
who have honor on the tips of their tongues and are loyal down to their fin-
gertips. Also, it is nocturnal La Chapelle that I know the best and that I pre-
fer. It has more glamour *[elle a plus de chien]*, has more soul and more resonance."[56] La Chapelle was thus no ordinary poor neighborhood. Its sense of
melancholy, its texture, and its décor fascinated writers like Fargue, Mac
Orlan, and Carco.

Louis Chevalier also devotes a chapter to La Chapelle in *Montmartre du
plaisir et du crime*.[57] He traces the lineage of this area of Paris (and includes
with it La Villette and the canal Saint-Martin) from the songs of Bruant to
Carco and Mac Orlan and, finally, to the films of Carné and Prévert. It is the
pont de La Chapelle, and the noise and the smoke from the nearby trains,
that provide the backdrop for the lovers in *Hôtel du Nord* (Carné, 1938).[58]
This urban space, he says, has nourished succeeding generations of artists,
oscillating between "image" and "reality" for the artists who incorporate its
props, locations, and characters in their work and lives. "[J]ust as the images
of Zola and Bruant became the reality of Carco and Mac Orlan, the images
of Carco and Mac Orlan would become the reality of Prévert and Carné,
whose images, in turn, would be the daily bread of young people who came
after them."[59]

Critics were struck by the representation of urban space in *Coeur de Lilas*.
La Cinématographie française observed that *Coeur de Lilas* is "obviously a
special film" and praised its images of the fortifications, of the working-class
suburb, and of the street with dance halls.[60] The film's evocation of the
"Zone," in particular, was seen as one of its strengths. Short for *zone non-
aedificandi* (no-construction zone), the Zone refers to the officially unin-
habited ring of land just beyond the military fortifications constructed in the
1840s around the city of Paris.[61] Permanent buildings were prohibited in the
Zone to ensure a clear view of enemy approaches, but low, temporary struc-

tures were allowed. The area was a center for illegal prostitution and shantytowns inhabited by the poorest Parisians, pushed to the margins of the city as a result of high rents and demolitions. The Zone not only "set off the sumptuousness of Paris with a frame of filth and squalor,"[62] it served as the repository of intense mythologies, from the turn of the century to World War II, around the underworld, illicit sexuality, marginality, and nostalgia for a Paris that was disappearing. Proposals for the demolition of the fortifications and the shantytowns in the Zone had been discussed since the 1880s, when the obsolescence of the fortifications was made evident by their ineffectiveness during the Franco-Prussian War.[63] The legal acquisition of the fortifications from the Army took place in 1919, but their demolition was not completed until 1932, a year after *Coeur de Lilas* was made. The redevelopment of the Zone itself would take much longer, until well after World War II. But the disappearance of the Zone, with its connotations of working-class sexuality and criminality, but also community, was mourned in the music hall, the nightclub, and films long before its actual demise.[64] The realist song mourned the disappearance of the Zone with particular intensity. *Coeur de Lilas*, through its setting, its visual style, and its use of the realist song, participates in this process of mourning and celebration.[65]

Of the three singers who perform musical numbers in *Coeur de Lilas*, Fréhel brings the best-defined public image to the film, since she had been performing in French music halls much longer than Gabin and Fernandel. Fréhel was enormously popular in the early 1930s, while Gabin and Fernandel were not yet the cinema stars they would become a bit later in the decade. *Coeur de Lilas* was Fréhel's first sound feature film. She plays a character named, simply, La Douleur (Pain), one of the underworld cohorts of Jean Gabin's character. The film does not tell us directly why she is called "Pain," but spectators would have understood instantly that Fréhel's La Douleur is a character straight out of the realist song: a broken-down, disappointed prostitute who has loved and lost, but who still possesses considerable verve. Spectators would also have understood La Douleur as a direct reference, of course, to Fréhel's personal pain.

The emotional losses and the physical changes Fréhel experienced do not seem to have diminished her ability to express her sexuality with boldness. One such performance of robust female sexuality occurs in *Coeur de Lilas*'s second song, "La Môme Caoutchouc" (The Rubber Kid). The neighborhood people have gathered at a dance hall. The film's camera work, once again, helps emphasize the importance of space in *Coeur de Lilas*. This sequence actually begins in the hotel across the street from the dance hall. Another lengthy, elaborate tracking shot follows Lilas and Lucot as they leave her room. The camera, instead of following them down the stairs, reverses direction and travels across Lilas's room and out on her balcony, picks up the couple as they exit the hotel, and follows them into the dance hall across the street. Instead of simply cutting to the dance hall, then, the film takes the time to reveal the neighborhood's layout.

The bal musette (a working-class dance hall with an accordion band), like the fortifications in the film's opening sequence, carried very specific connotations for 1930s audiences. The bal musette thrived in the period between the wars and embodied the opposite of the values of the *music-hall à grand revue*. Here, far from the fashionable music halls and the elegant dance halls, people were not yet dancing the Charleston, the blackbottom, or the shimmy; they were still dancing the waltz, the polka, the marche, the tango, and the java.[66] Dance hall culture was a source of intense fascination for artists, writers, and the bourgeoisie in the 1920s and 1930s. Eugène Dabit, author of the novel *Hôtel du Nord*, celebrated the *bal* in an essay he published in 1935 in the *Nouvelle Revue française*.[67] The photographer Brassaï devoted a section of his *Le Paris secret des années 30* to the *bal*.[68] In a 1925 essay, Fernand Léger writes a kind of domestic ethnography that links the popular dance hall with the working class and with Frenchness itself:

> Dance, like all the other national qualities, is exclusively the domain of the masses. Paris and the provinces are its original source, but you must go out and look for it to find it. It is quite difficult. Since it is scattered in the four corners of France and in the Paris dance halls, you must have perseverance and a particular taste for those things. All these places are very closed, hostile to strangers and spectators, often dangerous. . . . So go to one of their dance halls. The door opens, you are immediately the target of every eye. The man who is entering is watched, weighed with infinite subtlety. Once as far as the door, you gauge whether the situation is feasible or not. In spite of my great familiarity with these places, I sometimes come to a standstill and I have to leave. No word or gesture is exchanged, but by the looks alone or the pause in the conversations, it's clear that "things won't jell," and you go away. Not that the situation would be dangerous (it can be), but your aim is frustrated; the spectacle stops, is changed; you break the fragile atmosphere that makes it worth seeing. But once you are inside without a scratch, you will have the very distinct feeling of being with very pure Frenchmen, absolutely unalloyed, where all the traditions are preserved. These places have a beautiful and tragic atmosphere, charged with intrigues of passion that are veiled or break out into the open with incredible swiftness.[69]

The dance hall then, houses a kind of culture that is specifically French, endowed with an atmosphere both "beautiful and tragic," a world essentially closed to outsiders. Léger's respect and even reverence for this space correspond with Litvak's representation of the *bal*, and the underworld in general, in *Coeur de Lilas*.

Lilas and the detective enter the dance hall, where an accordion band plays a waltz. The couple have a drink together, while La Martousse (Gabin) looks on from the bar with jealousy. Wearing a wrinkled scarf at his neck and a fedora perched rakishly on his head, he's a slightly rumpled gangster. He tosses his glass on the floor and begins singing along to the accordion music we've been hearing since the beginning of the sequence, "La Môme Caoutchouc," a witty, slightly vulgar tune. He drifts through the crowd on the dance floor, playfully shoving the dancing couples out of his way.

J'ai une petite gosse extra [inaudible]	I have an extra-special kid [inaudible]
Et la fille est vraiment fantastique.	And the girl is truly fantastic.
Elle se met la tête sous les pieds	She puts her head under her feet
Et les doigts de pieds dans le nez.	And her toes in her nose.
Brusquement au plumard elle fait le grand écart	Suddenly she does a split on the bed
Elle se met en vrille,	She spins,
Elle vous fait la chenille.	She does the caterpillar.
Tout à coup les jambes à son cou	All at once, her legs are at her neck
Elle s'enroule, se met en boule	She winds herself up into a ball
Et se vrille ses genoux.	And spins around on her knees.
La môm' caoutchouc	The rubber kid
Avec elle, c' qu'on peut faire	What one can do with her
Ah! C'est fou.	Ah! It's crazy.
Elle vous prend et toc et toc!	She takes you and [that's it]!
On n'est plus qu'un' loqu',	You're only a rag, worn out
Ah c'est pas du toc.	It's no sham.
Ell' vous disloque	She dislocates you.
La môme caoutchouc.	The rubber kid
C'est un lot c'est un drôl' de p'tit bout.	She's a beautiful prize, a funny little thing.
On la cherche par dessus	One looks for her underneath
Mais on la trouve en dessous	But one finds her on top;
La môm' caoutchouc.	The rubber kid.

Notably, Gabin is not marked through the visual style as a star performer in this sequence. He is not emphasized via backlighting or placed in the center of a static frame. Instead, tracking shots follow him as he weaves through the crowd, apparently just as likely to throw a punch as sing another verse.

The crowd joins in on the chorus, further underscoring Gabin's status as "insider" in this community of underworld marginals.[70] He performs, also, for the sake of entertaining the habitués of the dance hall—and the film's spectators, of course. The number is integrated into the narrative; La Martousse performs it in order to get the attention of Lilas and to show Detective Lucot his supremacy in this space. The number is not at all self-contained; he stops singing in order to whisper an instruction to a fellow gangster, to dance with another woman, to warn Lilas about taking up with another man and to confront Lucot.

It is not surprising that Gabin sings in the film. Like so many 1930s film actors, Gabin got his start in music hall. Only two years before making *Coeur de Lilas,* he performed in a revue at the Moulin Rouge. The year before he made *Coeur de Lilas,* he sang in an operetta at the Bouffes-Parisiens. The son of a café-concert singer, he performed in revues, and had bit parts in operettas and musical comedies beginning in 1923. His big break came in 1928, when Mistinguett hired him as a chorus singer and dancer for a Moulin Rouge revue called *Paris qui tourne.* Gabin's film career began in 1930 with the French version of *Chacun sa chance* (Hans Steinhoff), a German vaudeville comedy. He appeared in another film that year, *Méphisto* (Henri Debain), and, just as he was mulling over the music hall director Henri Varna's offer of a three-year contract at the Palace and at the Casino de Paris, he acted in *Paris-Béguin* (Augusto Genina, 1931), in which he played his first *mauvais garçon* role. *Coeur de Lilas,* made in 1931, was his fifth film.

Midway through the number "La Môme Caoutchouc," Gabin is joined on the dance floor by Fréhel. Overweight, dressed in a shapeless knit dress and cardigan, she belts out the lyrics, giving a lusty, humorous performance that could scarcely be further from Mistinguett's compliant woman in the apache dance. When Gabin sings the words of the song, it's a question of a man bragging about his sexual exploits with a certain Môme Caoutchouc while trying to win back his girlfriend. But when Fréhel declares that, "just between us, the Rubber Kid is yours truly" she takes possession of the song and exceeds Gabin's audacity and sexual verve. It's one thing to have loved the Rubber Kid; it's quite another to *be* the Rubber Kid.

Je peux bien vous dire entre nous	I can tell you, just between us
Et bien la môme caoutchouc, c'est ma pomme	The rubber kid is yours truly
	Oh yes, that's what they call me.
Et oui, c'est comme ça qu'on me nomme.	Compared to me, taffy
	Is as stiff as a board.
La guimauve à côté de moi	When we beat the snake, my man,

C'est un vrai morceau de bois.
Quand on bat le serpent, mon petit,
  qu'est-ce que je leurs rends!
Je te ferai la roue
Je me tirerai les joues
Je bondis comme un ouistiti
Le ménage, je te le gâte,
Mais je veux qu'on en rire.

how I give it back!
I fan my feathers for you
I pinch my cheeks
I jump like a marmoset
I ruin your household,
But I want us to laugh about it.

La môme caoutchouc
C'est . . . nous.
Quand tu prends mes deux
  roplopos,
Mes deux gros lolos, ça c'est
  du boulot.
La môme caoutchouc
Quand il m'attrape par l'un de vous
Ça lui fait les biceps
Ça l'aiguise . . .
La môme caoutchouc.

The rubber kid
That's . . . us.
When you take hold of my two
  bazooms,
My two big boobs, that's a chore.
The rubber kid
When he gets hold of one of you
It gives him biceps
It turns him on
The rubber kid.

This is a highly unusual performance for 1930s film, not only because women were rarely positioned in such a sexually aggressive fashion, but also because Fréhel departs significantly from the norms of 1930s beauty because of her large size. In combination, Fréhel's two performances in *Coeur de Lilas*, "Dans la rue," and "La Môme Caoutchouc," rely for their fullest meaning upon the spectators' knowledge of the two sides of Fréhel's persona, both formed by her music hall performances and her autobiography: the depressed but still plucky streetwalker and the ribald, sexually aggressive "comeback" woman.

Both in its representation of the sexually aggressive woman and in its willingness to take seriously the allure and the cultural specificity of the working-class dance hall, this sequence marks the opposite end of the spectrum from Mistinguett's *valse chaloupée*. The apache dance, it will be recalled, was inspired by Max Dearly's trip to a bal musette in Billancourt, performed in a revue at the Moulin Rouge in 1909, and parodied by Mistinguett herself two years later in another revue at the Folies-Bergère. The music hall translated the "closed," "hostile," and "purely French" experience Léger relished at the bal musette into something easily parodied and appealing to an increasingly international crowd. *Coeur de Lilas*, on the other hand, wants to retain the authenticity and the cultural specificity of the bal musette experience.

"La Môme Caoutchouc" is, on an obvious level, about a woman's physical agility, her mobility. As the additional verses of the song tell us, she can thread her way through small places and she can puff up her pectorals in the metro in order to stand her ground. However, as exhilarating as Fréhel's performance of "La Môme Caoutchouc" is, and as suggestive as these lyrics are, it must be noted that her character's mobility and prowess are limited in the film as a whole. Despite the distinctiveness of her presence in this number, she remains outside the intrigue unfolding on the dance floor (the Lilas–Lucot–Martousse triangle). Moreover, La Douleur never achieves a larger mobility in the film as a whole; she is never shown outside of the café or the dance hall. Fréhel may be the Môme Caoutchouc, but Gabin's character is more mobile, both in his singing performance (he moves across the dance floor while she remains at the margins of it) and in the fact that he leaves the milieu to search for Lilas after the detective takes her away. Of course, the bourgeois detective is the most mobile character of all, for he can slip undetected into a working-class (and thus "foreign" community) and then escape when he needs to, unlike Lilas, who does not possess the ability to manipulate the signs of class and thus lacks mobility. Though she will put on bourgeois clothing, Lilas cannot escape her working-class/criminal origins. All this serves to reinforce the "commodification" of this underclass culture for the film audience: the bourgeoisie's access to its thrills and charms (although, in contrast to *Prisons de femmes*, the detective has a professional "pretext" for penetrating this realm—he is not merely "slumming"), the audacious, frank sexuality expressed by its denizens, and the reassurance that this dangerous, unruly world is ultimately contained by social and urban boundaries. None of this, however, diminishes the residual strength of these performances or of the identification that takes place, however momentary, between performers and the audiences inscribed both within the film and by its production.

Other locations and characters in *Coeur de Lilas* bring the sordidness and visual texture of the criminal milieu into relief. When the bal musette is raided by police, Lucot and Lilas flee the working-class neighborhood, embarking on a kind of tour of Paris. The film's first half contains a veritable compendium of locations and characters from the symbolic universe of the realist song, while the second half ventures out into a different Paris. First, Lilas and Lucot board a bus. In a magical sequence, with the lights of the city flashing across their faces, they discover their love for each other. They ride the bus all night, Lilas dozing in Lucot's arms. The next morning, they visit Les Halles, the wholesale market in central Paris, where Lilas gazes with longing at flowers and food. They enter an elegant boutique, where Lucot buys clothes for Lilas. They row down the Marne river and dine in a restaurant on the "Île de l'amour." These "travelogue" sequences contrast two very different urban spaces: the enclosed, dangerous exotic milieu, which is materially poor, but rich in visual texture and community, and the spaces of abundance: the sunny, open market, the boutique, and wedding celebration.

The contrast occurs not only visually, but musically. The final singing performance, featuring the music hall comic singer Fernandel, occurs at a wedding celebration on the island. Lilas and Lucot dine in a private room, while the wedding party enters the hall next door, the bride dressed in an elaborate satin gown. Lucot hums along as the orchestra plays "Tu ne plains pas qu'la mariée soit trop belle" (Don't Complain That the Bride Is Too Beautiful), and he sings a few bars to Lilas in a joyous, spontaneous fashion. It seems for a moment that the sort of life represented by the wedding party is within their reach.

The number gradually becomes a production number featuring Fernandel, who is the best man in the wedding party. Fernandel (1903–71) began his career in the music halls of Marseilles launching his Parisian music hall career in the late 1920s. When he started making films in 1930, he was already quite well known and would go on to enjoy an immensely successful film career. Fernandel appeared in several of Marcel Pagnol's films, but he was primarily known as a *comique-troupier*, a singer of comic songs about military life in films such as *Ignace* (Colombier, 1937). His performance style, which we can locate at the opposite end of the spectrum from that of the restrained, naturalistic Gabin, has been described as "a conception of acting founded on grimaces, tics, and effects."[71] When Fernandel takes up the song, he is centered in the frame, static, and shot head on. He sings alone, and, although the crowd joins him at the refrain, his performance connotes a more staged, artificial sense of community than that of the bal musette. The lyrics of "Ne te plains pas que la mariée soit trop belle" contrast sharply with those of "Dans la rue," which, it will be recalled, sympathetically sketch out the lives of streetwalkers. Fernandel exhorts the wedding party not to complain about the bride being too beautiful. "Don't complain if we paw your woman/Don't complain if we take her from you [. . .]/ You shouldn't have chosen a woman so beautiful that she excites our desires./If she had an ugly face we'd leave her for you alone."[72] Here, the woman is an object of exchange in the bourgeois ceremony of marriage, valued solely for her appearance. The positioning of the woman here differs also from that of Fréhel singing "La Môme Caoutchouc" back at the bal musette. Here, in sharp contrast to Fréhel's enunciation of the sexually aggressive woman, we have a passive, unsmiling bride who does not sing. Despite the film's conservative containment of the underworld, it does not refrain from an incisive portrayal of the dismal conventions of bourgeois marriage.

The dissonance in the relationships between men and women and the dysfunction of community outside the Zone are further emphasized by the fact that it is here that the relationship between Lucot and Lilas unravels. Lilas discovers Lucot's real identity during Fernandel's song. She flees, and the happy wedding music metamorphoses into "La Môme Caoutchouc" in a minor key. The music of the two different cultural spaces thus melds together, becoming distorted and dissonant, reflecting the impossibility of their union.[73]

In *Coeur de Lilas,* characters are defined in part by the style and location in which songs are performed. The couple's relationship cannot be sustained once Lucot takes Lilas away from her milieu. In the end, Lucot and Lilas cannot be together, because Lilas is from the world of the *bal populaire* and Lucot belongs to the world represented in the Île de l'amour sequence: bourgeois matrimony, music hall, and the law.

Gabin, Fréhel, and Fernandel all performed in the glamorous music halls of the 1920s and 1930s, but in *Coeur de Lilas,* their performance styles are wedded to specific places and to specific classes. Gabin and Fréhel represent the working-class entertainment milieu by performing in a bal musette, and they also evoke the café-concert, the smaller-scale neighborhood performance spaces that preceded music halls. Fréhel's star text, in particular, signifies the same nostalgic, affectionate vision of *Paris populaire* we saw in *Pépé le Moko.* Here, however, is an added emphasis on Fréhel's sexual audacity through the performance of "La Môme Caoutchouc." Fernandel and Luguet stand in for the large-scale music hall and the bourgeois *boulevard* theater, respectively, and represent an existence that is well beyond the reach of La Martousse, La Douleur, and Lilas.[74] But the film does not mourn the impossibility of bourgeois respectability for its marginalized characters. On the contrary, *Coeur de Lilas* celebrates that which is marginal in the Paris landscape through its visual style and its use of Fréhel and Jean Gabin, the key emblems of underworld sexuality and criminality in 1930s French film.

L'ENTRAÎNEUSE

With the help of Fréhel, *Coeur de Lilas* evokes a world felt to be quickly disappearing, including certain modes of prostitution. The prostitute who solicited clients on the fortifications was being replaced by the more discreet, upscale, dance hall hostess. The legal brothel—the shuttered *maisons de tolérance* or *maisons closes* bearing large house numbers—were giving way to discreet encounters in regular apartments, the unregulated *maisons de rendez vous*. While the image of the streetwalker still held an attraction for 1930s film audiences and for the fans of the realist singers, "the *fille des remparts* and the *pierreuse* were disappearing, while the apache, or Parisian tough, did not survive his time in the trenches."[75] Albert Valentin's 1938 film *L'Entraîneuse* (loosely, "dance hall hostess," "taxi dancer," or, more literally, "woman who leads one astray") contains representations of both the old and the new forms of prostitution, old and new forms of sociability, and old and new models of femininity.

The film was made at the UFA studios in Berlin in 1938—one of many French-German co-productions of the 1930s. Its director, René Clair's former assistant Albert Valentin, is perhaps best remembered for his contributions to the screenplays for Jean Renoir's *Boudu sauvé des eaux* and Jean Grémillon's *L'Étrange Monsieur Victor* and *Le Ciel est à vous*. The screenplay of *L'Entraîneuse* was, however, written by Charles Spaak, with whom Valentin had worked on the screenplay of *L'Etrange Monsieur Victor*. Spaak was, along with Jacques Prévert and Henri Jeanson, a key screenwriter of the 1930s; he also assisted in the writing of *Pension Mimosas, La Bandera, La Kermesse héroïque, La Belle Équipe, Les Bas-fonds, La Grande Illusion,* and *Le Grand Jeu*.

Suzy (Michèle Morgan) works at a Montmartre nightclub, La Dame de Coeur. Her job at the club is, as she puts it, "to dance with sweaty people and listen to their stories." In such establishments, clients could dance and talk with the *entraîneuses* for the price of an expensive bottle of champagne, as well as make plans for a more intimate encounter elsewhere. With the financial help of a benevolent dance hall client, Suzy manages to vacation on the French Riviera. There, she makes friends her own age, picnics, swims, and generally metamorphoses into a "modern," athletic woman. Fréhel's character, called "la chanteuse" in the credits, performs at the Dame de Coeur and stands in for the closed universe of the old-fashioned prostitute in the realist song.

The film opens with a dinner party honoring the president of a prosperous company, Monsieur Noblet (Félicien Tramel). It's a muggy July evening in Montmartre. The window is open, revealing the nightclub across the street. A poster of Fréhel decorates the front window of La Dame de Coeur. Inside, Suzy and the other women discuss vacation plans in the dressing room. The restroom attendant invites Suzy to her vacation rental, where she could be sure to make some money. Fréhel chides the attendant to stop acting like a pimp, reminding her that Suzy needs to relax. Noblet, the company president honored at the dinner, then enters La Dame de Coeur with two colleagues. Noblet tries to play on Suzy's sympathy by characterizing himself as a lonely widower. Fréhel then sings "Sans lendemain" (With No Tomorrows).[76]

Jamais l'espoir d'un autre soir	Never the hope of another evening
Bonjour, bonsoir	Hello, good-night
Adieu l'amour	Farewell to love
Sans lendemain, sans rien qui dure	With no tomorrows, with nothing
Voilà ma vie depuis toujour.	that lasts
	This has always been my life.

After a close-up of Fréhel's face wearing an expression of pain, the song ends. Soon after, Noblet dismisses Suzy rudely when it becomes clear that she will not consent to a rendezvous later that night.

Later, Suzy enjoys her modest vacation in the south of France. There, she hides her identity as an *entraîneuse*, calling herself "Suzanne," bicycling with wealthy people her own age and dating a young man, Pierre. One day, Pierre's uncle arrives at the pension; he is none other than Noblet, the client Suzy rejected on her last evening at La Dame de Coeur. At first, it appears that Noblet will generously keep Suzy's past a secret, but that night he confronts her in her bedroom, demanding his "reward." She begs him to leave her alone, and he agrees after she promises to accommodate him the following evening. Early the next morning, she flees to Paris and, brokenhearted, returns to La Dame de Coeur. Her old friend, the kindhearted client, offers to take her on a tour of the world and introduce her to a younger man in another country who "doesn't know what she is." Noblet comes to the nightclub and offers to set Suzy up in an apartment where he can visit her several times per week. Deeply offended, she throws her drink in his face and is promptly fired by the nightclub manager. Fréhel reassures her that she did the right thing and then sings "Sans lendemain" again. Left without any other options, Suzy agrees to go on the trip with her protector. The film's last shot, lit in dramatic low-key style, is a slow track ending in an extreme close-up of Fréhel's face. The camera moves closer and closer until Fréhel's face is out of focus, unrecognizable, and thus "generalized." "Voilà ma vie, depuis toujours" (This has always been my life), sings Fréhel, concluding the film.

In *L'Entraîneuse*, the *pierreuse* from the realist song and from films earlier in the decade, such as *Coeur de Lilas* and *Faubourg Montmartre*, has given way to the *entraîneuse*, but no substantial change has occurred in terms of the woman's trajectory through the narrative. Suzy may have been able to masquerade as a "modern," athletic woman on the Côte d'Azur, but the film offers no exit from her life as a kept woman, *L'Entraîneuse* criticizes this trajectory, exhibiting, according to Noël Burch and Geneviève Sellier, a "lucidity on the inextricable character of patriarchal oppression."[77] In its negative portrayal of Noblet, the film offers "one of the most realistic portraits of the hypocrisy in the character of the rich executive, debonair autocrat at home, exploiter of girls in town."[78]

As Vincendeau observes, *L'Entraîneuse* is structured by a series of oppositions that lay out competing images of the condition of women: Paris and the South of France; interiors and exteriors; and Suzy and Fréhel.[79] The sequences in Paris all take place at night and nearly always indoors. They are characterized by a feeling of claustrophobia, which connotes the closed world of the *entraîneuse*. The one exterior scene in Paris, in which Suzy and her gangster boyfriend break up, takes place near a train station. The scene's steam, fog, and rain, and high-contrast lighting constitute the classic vision of Montmartre at night seen in any number of poetic realist films. The scene contrasts sharply with the sunny exteriors on the Côte d'Azur.

Generally speaking, in *L'Entraîneuse*, Fréhel evokes the same things she stands for in *Pépé le Moko*. She connotes geographical stasis (just as she is confined to the Casbah in the latter film, she is forever relegated to the Montmartre nightclub in the former) and loss and depression, as well as the past. Her song's title even, "With No Tomorrows," emphasizes this focus on the past. Crucially, Fréhel's appearance, age, and autobiographical intertext are deployed against those of Michèle Morgan. Fréhel belongs to the interior, nocturnal, Paris world, of course, while Morgan is associated with the exteriors of the south of France. Fréhel and Morgan are contrasted in yet another way; Fréhel is a large, decrepit woman, while Michèle Morgan is slim and athletic, well-suited to outdoor activities. While in the south, she replaces the upswept hairdo and floral gown she wears at La Dame de Coeur with a simple hairstyle and a plain white dress, a bathing suit, or shorts. Morgan, in fact, epitomized a new model of femininity, which began to emerge in the late 1930s in France. The image of this new, athletic woman was created, in part, in the pages of new women's magazines such as *Marie-Claire*, on whose cover Morgan appeared in 1938.[80]

The film's oppositions between north and south, between the "old-fashioned" and "modern" women, indeed, between the star images of Fréhel and Morgan, are ultimately shown to be false oppositions. Although the film can imagine a "way out" for Suzy, it does not succeed in realizing such an escape from "the life." Despite her "modern" desires and the apparent opportunity to construct a new life that the film holds out to her, Suzy is, ultimately, stuck in her role as a prostitute or, at least, as a "kept" woman. The only compensation the film can offer Suzy is a benevolent father/lover figure (the trip around the world). The film does, however, offer that now familiar brand of female solidarity characteristic of these films and the imaginary of the café-concert world in the relationship between Suzy and Fréhel—a bond between women that we shall see repeatedly in other films featuring the realist singer.

THE REALIST SONG WITHOUT THE REALIST SINGER

Thus far, we have examined the realist singer in her "purest" form in 1930s film in the sense that *Pépé le Moko, Coeur de Lilas,* and *L'Entraîneuse* cast Fréhel, an actual realist singer (and one who is most representative of the interwar realist singer's mobilization of the autobiographical intertext), for the performance of the realist song. Given the way in which the realist singer's star image depended upon the perceived correspondence between her persona in performance and her autobiography, one might question whether the realist song could ever be performed convincingly by a nonrealist singer. In fact, many films in 1930s French cinema call on the tradition of the realist song without actually casting a realist singer in this role. The realist singer was so recognizable a category in French popular culture that she became a "type" in her own right, whose bundle of qualities could be separated, with more or less success, from the "real" realist singers.

In *Un Soir de rafle* (The Night of the Police Raid) (Carmine Gallone, 1931), Annabella, best remembered as the ingénue in *Hôtel du Nord* (Carné, 1938), plays a realist singer in love with a boxer played by Albert Préjean. Dressed in a black velvet sheath exactly like those worn by Damia, she sings "Ce n'est pas drôle" (It's Not Funny), a song about the tough lives of prostitutes. The waiflike, girlish Annabella, however, fails to convey the physical strength and aura of world-weariness of a realist singer like Damia. Moreover, Annabella is overshadowed by her co-star, Albert Préjean, who had played the lead in *Sous les toits de Paris* (René Clair, 1930). It is Préjean's singing performances in *Un Soir de rafle* that move and unite the diegetic working-class audiences.

The café-concert *chanteuse,* realist and otherwise, makes her appearance as a character in French cinema even before sound cinema. As early as 1912, *Dancing Girl* (Jean Durand) features a *gommeuse* (a female comic "dandy" character meant to evoke the prostitute) based on the singer Polaire. Musidora's Irma Vep is a singer in a beuglant in Feuillade's *Les Vampires* (1915–16). *Sa gosse* (Desfontaines, 1919) features a realist singer played by Elmire Vautier, whose memories of the unwanted child she left in the country are invoked by the lyrics of a realist song brought to her by a songwriter. Though silent, *Sa gosse* attempts to render visually the experience of hearing a realist song by juxtaposing close-ups of sheet music with nostalgic flashbacks of the singer's life in the country. All of these examples of the realist singer *character* highlight the currency of the authentic realist singer herself; her familiarity and desirability as a category of female performance in French culture.

As a conclusion to this chapter and as a bridge to the next, which concerns the apparent antithesis of the realist singer, the music hall queen, let us examine in detail a film that draws on the realist universe through the use of the realist song without depicting the realist singer. In Renoir's *Le Crime de Monsieur Lange* (1936), revue star Florelle performs a realist song written for the film. Florelle, whose career I shall analyze in some detail, manages to evoke many of the same qualities Fréhel conveyed, while also connoting a "healthy" working-class femininity absent from the image of the realist singer. Chapter 4, in contrast, features female singers—revue stars— who lack the working-class or underworld associations of the realist singer but nevertheless attempt to appropriate her connotations.

LE CRIME DE MONSIEUR LANGE

For many film historians and critics, this film is one of the most politically appealing and aesthetically accomplished films made in 1930s France. Consequently, the film's place in Jean Renoir's oeuvre and within Popular Front culture has been discussed at length.[81] Much of the commentary on this political allegory set in a workers' cooperative has, quite rightly, focused on its political meanings. Little has been said about the presence of a realist song in *Le Crime de Monsieur Lange* and the film's highly unusual construction of working-class femininity.

Approximately halfway through the film, Valentine, the laundress, sings a realist song to Lange, the distracted creator of the popular *Arizona Jim* serial. Valentine is played by Florelle (Odette Rousseau, 1898–1974), an important music hall singer and cinema actress known especially for her revue performances at the Moulin Rouge and the Folies-Bergère, as well as for her starring role in *L'Opéra de quat' sous* (1930), G. W. Pabst's French version of his *Die Dreigroschenoper,* in which she performs Kurt Weill songs. Florelle's primary star identity was thus not that of a realist singer. Indeed, Florelle brings to *Le Crime de Monsieur Lange* a wide range of meanings from her other performances. But she nonetheless intersects with the realist singer persona in many of her cinema roles. She played Fantine in

Raymond Bernard's adaptation of Hugo's *Les Misérables* (1933), a literary antecedent to the realist song and to poetic realism. She slipped easily into the murky world of the milieu as the capricious, unfaithful girlfriend of the gangster played by Charles Boyer in *Tumultes* (Siodmak, 1932). Her performance of the realist song, along with the multifaceted star image she brings to *Le Crime de Monsieur Lange* works to amplify other elements of female characterization in the film, creating a film that is rather startling in its progressive representation of femininity.

Le Crime de Monsieur Lange takes place in the courtyard of a building in working-class Paris and tells the story of a group of workers in a publishing concern managed by a nefarious embezzler, Batala (Jules Berry). A brief shot of Sacré Coeur early on indicates that the film takes place in Montmartre. But the majority of the action in *Le Crime de Monsieur Lange* centers not on the larger social topography of Montmartre, with its more familiar connotations of the underworld and the music hall, but on the modest building and courtyard that house the print shop, the laundry, and apartments. While first and foremost a working-class space, the courtyard functions also as a microcosm of society, in which printers and laundresses cross paths with the swindler Batala and his various creditors, who come looking for money. Renoir's roving camera and deep compositions construct a pliable, multilayered space in which these encounters take place. As Alexander Sesonske argues:

> Being Renoir's primary instrument for establishing the social focus of the film, the court becomes a structural element within the action itself. The people in the film have an essentially topographical relation to each other; their encounters depend not upon class or profession or even preference, but upon the fact that they work and love around the court. In all of Renoir's films no locale is more firmly identified nor more clearly linked to the lives of his characters.[82]

Batala eventually leaves Paris, fleeing his creditors, and appears to die in a train crash. Freed from Batala's mismanagement and deceit, the print shop employees form a cooperative and produce a wildly popular serial about the exploits of a cowboy, "Arizona Jim." Batala then reemerges, disguised as the priest, whose identity he assumed after the train wreck, and threatens to take over the operation. The appealing dreamer Lange (René Lefebvre) shoots him dead in the courtyard.

The film opens in the hotel near the Belgian border where Lange and Valentine take refuge after the murder of Batala. The café's patrons recognize Lange from a newspaper photograph and consider whether or not to turn him in to the police. Valentine enters the room and defends Lange before this makeshift jury of his peers.[83] The overt framing device is somewhat like that of *Prisons de femmes,* in which Francis Carco functions as our narrator and interpreter. Here, however, the working-class Valentine is our storyteller. Her defense of Lange takes the form of a flashback and constitutes the bulk of the narrative. The film is marked as "her" story. In *Le Crime de Monsieur Lange,* Florelle represents "a public that has a voice of it own, that can sing its life in its own style," Dudley Andrew observes.[84] As in *Prisons de femmes,* the use of flashback positions both the story and the idealized community it recounts within a nostalgic framework of loss, irretrievable whatever the narrative outcome (will Lange be handed over to the police, or will he escape? In *Prisons de femmes,* the question of the framing narrative centers on whether Juliette will survive and be forgiven by her husband, while the friendship she shared with Régine in the marginal underworld, as well as her access to that world, are immutably closed to her).

As she begins her defense of Lange, Valentine enters through a door in the middle of the frame, walks straight toward the camera and directly addresses the men seated before her, and us, the audience. The high-key lighting, the framing of Florelle in the center of the image, and her engaging way of addressing the people combine to give the sense that she has just walked onto a stage and is addressing an audience seated on all sides. Florelle's parallel career in the music hall reveals itself here and, as a result, her performance has seemed artificial and mannered to historians such as Alexander Sesonske: "Perhaps her theatrical style ill-befits the naturalistic scene of this film, but her laughter seems forced, the toss of her head exaggerated, her movements sometimes calculated rather than spontaneous. She is most incredible when she sings to Lange; here Renoir's penchant for inserting a song into the texture of his film has gone awry."[85]

In contrast, contemporary critics of *Le Crime de Monsieur Lange* did not object to Florelle's performance. In fact, 1930s film audiences were quite used to Florelle's style of address and, indeed, to the mix of acting styles contained in the film. As Ginette Vincendeau has revealed so expertly, French cinema of the 1930s is permeated with references to the theater and music hall on the level of performance style.[86] Florelle's hybrid performance style in *Le Crime de Monsieur Lange* and her star image more generally offer us the opportunity to consider how the realist singer's connotations begin to be absorbed by nonrealist singers in the 1930s.

Florelle brings to *Le Crime de Monsieur Lange* a range of images from her other film and music hall performances, which, taken together, have been seen to constitute a kind of composite portrait of 1930s femininity. The film critic Jacques Siclier devotes a full chapter to her in his 1957 *La Femme dans le cinéma français*. "The smile, the eyes, the physique of Florelle, her way of walking, of speaking, of dressing are the perfect hallmark of this era. . . . [She is] the personification of 1935 femininity."[87] Indeed, Florelle's appearance, unlike that of Damia and Fréhel, places her squarely in the mainstream of the canons of female beauty in the 1930s. For this reason and due to the multifaceted nature of her star image, Florelle cannot, strictly speaking, be classified as a realist singer. But, as in the case of Mistinguett and other "queens" of the music hall revue, Florelle's star persona nevertheless absorbs elements of the realist singer persona.

Florelle was born in 1898 in Sables-d'Olonne, but her family moved to Paris when she was six years old.[88] Her mother worked as a cashier at La Cigale, an important café-concert in Montmartre, where, it will be recalled, Eugénie Buffet debuted with the realist song in 1892. Florelle began performing at the age of ten, and, by the time she was only thirteen years old, she was appearing in sketches with Raimu, a prominent film actor and music hall performer. In the late teens, she performed at the Européen and the Bataclan music halls, where she was noticed by Maurice Chevalier. She appeared with Chevalier in *Gonzague* (Henri Diamant-Berger, 1923), in her first film role. She continued working primarily in the music hall, serving as Mistinguett's replacement in the traveling Casino revues. In 1926, she starred in "Ça c'est Paris" (That's Paris) on its tour of South America and enjoyed her first taste of real fame in Argentina. Back in Paris in 1927, she performed at the Casino de Paris, the Folies-Bergère, and the Moulin Rouge.

On one of her European tours, in 1929, Florelle met the German film director G. W. Pabst, who was preparing a film adaptation of Bertolt Brecht and Kurt Weill's *Die Dreigroschenoper*, which had been hugely successful on stage in Berlin since 1928. He offered Florelle a role in the French film version, *L'Opéra de quat' sous*. Here, Florelle plays Polly Peachum, the daughter of the king of the beggars, who metamorphoses from ingénue to hardened *habituée* of the underworld. Shot in 1930 and released in 1931, the film marked the real beginning of her film career. She made five films in 1930, nine in 1931, and seven in 1932, all the while performing at the Folies-Bergères. The most active years of her film career were between 1930 and 1935, when she made a total of thirty-three films.

Florelle's encounter with Pabst led to another role in a "multiple-language" film for UFA shot in Berlin. In the French version of *Tumultes* (Siodmak, 1931), Florelle plays Ania, the rebellious, materialistic girlfriend of a gangster played by Charles Boyer. Other important film roles include the lead in Alexander Korda's 1932 *La Dame de Chez Maxim*, in which

Florelle plays La Môme Crevette, a mischievous, sexy dancer who compli-
cates the life of a staid bourgeois doctor. Florelle also played the sympathetic
prostitute Fantine in Raymond Bernard's *Les Misérables* (1933). "Florelle
alone, in this era, could render acceptable the romanticism of the Hugolienne prostitute. Made to interpret popular heroines, she burst open the
screen with her naturalness and made her characters believable," Jacques
Siclier observes.[89] In Fritz Lang's *Liliom* (1934), Florelle plays the swagger-
ing, sexually aggressive carnival boss who tries to steal Charles Boyer from
the innocent Annabella.

She refused to make films under the German Occupation and, after the
Liberation, could not find work. Here, her life story begins to resemble that
of a realist singer. She lived in Morocco and the Ivory Coast at the end of
the 1940s, where she owned and lost a series of bistros. (Dominique Païni
compares this stage of Florelle's life to Françoise Rosay's role in Feyder's *Le
Grand Jeu*.)[90] Eventually, she returned to her hometown and died, practically forgotten, in 1974. At times, her autobiography mimics the melodramas in which she performed.

> Florelle strongly personifies, in only five years, the essence of what consti-
> tutes the fictions of the 1930s and which is summed up in the melodrama. All
> of the elements that one could easily organize into an extravagant fiction are
> brought together here [in the image of Florelle]: the joy of an overflowing life,
> the happy-go-lucky woman threatened in love, the fatal meeting with des-
> tiny . . . sickness, unhappiness, decline, exile . . . and tenderness refound.[91]

In sum, the ensemble of Florelle's film and music hall performances construct her as an emissary of the underworld, the working class, the café-
concert, and the music hall. Her star image was unusually multifaceted in a
cinema that tended to typecast its actors, at least in terms of the socioeconomic milieus they personified.

When Florelle begins her defense of Lange, she both professes her love
for him and reveals her past as an experienced woman ("He's not the first
man I've loved, but he's the one I love now"). She also announces her class
status—she is a working woman who has known poverty. Valentine is the
anchor of the courtyard in which she lives and works. She's a strong
woman—physically and psychologically, especially compared to the delicate
Estelle, who is victimized by Batala. Her defiant, "hands on hips" posture,
her verbal jousting with Batala, and her status as boss of the laundry and
confidante to her female employees all contribute to this characterization. It
is she who pursues and wins the heart of Lange, thus helping him to harness
his creativity and dreamer-quality into the Arizona Jim project. She galva-

nizes the community, organizing a party to celebrate the plans to turn the Arizona Jim *photo-romans* into a movie; and she organizes Lange's getaway after he kills Batala. She even reproaches Lange for the absence of women in his Arizona Jim serial. She represents cleanliness ("Clean white sheets are so beautiful!") and common sense in the film, but also cynicism and experience. When Lange tells her about how bandits rob the poor in Arizona, Valentine asks, "And who robs the poor here?"

The film's strong utopian element differentiates it from other, darker films of the period with working-class settings, such as *La Petite Lise, Dans les rues,* and *Coeur de Lilas.* Lange, Valentine, and the other members of the co-op are part of a "healthy" working class rather than a marginal underworld. Moreover, the film's nostalgia is more immediate and political, less for other times and other forms of community, which can be explained in part by the film's optimistic social context, the rise of the Popular Front. The character of Batala permits Renoir to criticize both capitalism and patriarchy, but Jules Berry's mannered, boulevard theater–inflected performance is so charming that it undercuts this critique. It is through his female characters that Renoir provides a glimpse of a world outside the sunny courtyard full of cooperative workers—a social order full of injustice and desperation. This is very unusual in a 1930s French film narrative. *Gueule d'amour* and *La Belle Équipe,* for example, contain biting critiques of oppressive class structures, but displace these critiques onto the figure of the *garce,* constructing women precisely as the "problem" of the film for their threats to male camaraderie. *Le Crime de Monsieur Lange,* on the other hand, emphasizes that women have been victimized doubly—through inequities related to both class and sexuality.

One of the ways in which the female characters are defined in the film is through their relationship to prostitution. The realist song, with its traditional focus on prostitutes and pimps, contributes to this characterization. The song Valentine sings to Lange, "À la belle étoile" (Under the Stars), began as a poem written by Jacques Prévert and was quite likely influenced by one of Aristide Bruant's songs, "À la Chapelle." Joseph Kosma, a Hungarian composer who had moved to Paris from Berlin in 1933, wrote the music. The two friends proposed "À la belle étoile" (sometimes called "Au jour le jour") to Renoir, who liked the song and incorporated it into the film.

Renoir loved popular music and particularly appreciated the cultural resonance of the realist singer. His 1927 *Marquitta* tells the story of a Russian prince who falls in love with—and is subsequently humiliated by—a street singer. *La Chienne* (1931) intersperses the murder of Lulu with a street performance of "La Sérénade du pavé" (Street Serenade), which was originally performed at the turn of the century by realist singer Eugénie Buffet. In *La Grande Illusion* (1937), it is Fréhel's voice we hear on the phonograph in the opening sequence performing "Frou Frou," a song popular at the turn of the century. *French Cancan* (1954), Renoir's homage to the Belle Époque music hall, contains a number of songs popular at the turn of the century, including, again, "La Sérénade du pavé," this time sung by Edith Piaf dressed up as Eugénie Buffet. Renoir himself wrote the lyrics to the realist song "La Complainte de la Butte" (Ballad of the Butte) sung by Cora Vaucaire in *French Cancan*. Lastly, in his final film, *Le Petit Théâtre de Jean Renoir* (1969), Jeanne Moreau sings "Quand l'amour meurt" (When Love Dies) a song from the café-concert era.

So, it is hardly surprising that Renoir has Valentine sing a realist song to Lange in *Le Crime de Monsieur Lange*. The song begins as a sound bridge from the train station scene to the romantic dinner scene between Valentine and Lange. Batala has just abandoned Edith to a life of prostitution. She exits the platform, weeping, on the arm of a future client, presumably, accompanied by the violin music for "À la belle étoile." A wipe returns us to the now-familiar space of the courtyard, but the location is difficult to identify at first, because it's nighttime. The camera tracks left in an exterior shot of the darkened courtyard as Florelle begins singing, but instead of cutting directly to her, the shot lingers for several seconds on an unidentified man and a woman crossing the pavement and entering the building. Are we watching Edith and her new "protector"? Or are we seeing a male client and a prostitute who is one of the "old dolls still walk[ing] the streets" of Valentine's song? It is unclear, but the shot is infused with melancholy and bears a strong resemblance to Brassaï's photographs of streetwalkers taken in the 1930s in its low-key lighting, its emphasis on the paving stones in the courtyard, and its aura of impenetrability.[92]

Finally, we track right to Valentine and Lange, who are seated at the dinner table and framed by the window. The camera tracks in and comes to rest with a static medium shot, where it will remain for the rest of Valentine's singing performance.

Boulevard de la Chapelle	Boulevard de la Chapelle
Où passe le métro aérien	Where the elevated metro passes by
Il y a des filles très belles	There are some very pretty girls
Et beaucoup de vauriens	And lots of good-for-nothings
Les clochards affamés	Starving bums
S'endorment sur les bancs	Sleep on benches
Et de vieilles poupées	And old dolls

Font encore le tapin	Still walk the streets
À soixante cinq ans.	At sixty-five years of age.
Au jour le jour	From day to day
À la nuit la nuit	From night to night
À la belle étoile	Under the stars
C'est comme ça que je vis.	That's how I live.
Où est elle l'étoile	Where is it, the [lucky] star?
Moi je n'l'ai jamais vue	Me, I've never seen it
Pourtant je me promème	Yet [still] I stroll
Dans des quartiers perdus.	In lost neighborhoods.

In the film, Valentine stops singing at this point. The remaining verses of the song continue the gesture of street-naming we see in this verse, evoking Boulevard Richard Lenoir, Boulevard des Italians, and Boulevard de Vaugirard. Each verse is a bleak vignette that evokes various social ills: factory closings, anti-Semitism, an abandoned newborn.[93] The lyrics, with their irony, cynicism, references to specific urban spaces, and awareness of social injustice, place the song squarely in the genre of the realist song. Its performance shores up the film's critique of social inequities and balances the narrative's idealism with another, darker view of society.

Valentine's song is different from the typical realist singer's performance in certain ways. The shot's high-key lighting, Florelle's quick gestures (notably her darting eyes and frequent smiles), and the fact that the performance of the song leads to her long-delayed and "healthy" seduction of Lange (as opposed to his wrong-headed earlier attempt to seduce the too-young Estelle), all lend an air of sunny optimism to the scene. Nevertheless, the song's lyrics and its placement after the train station scene allow the singing performance to accomplish the textual "work" of the more traditional realist sing performance. First, it specifically mentions prostitution ("old dolls still walk the streets at sixty-five"), a mainstay of the realist song and, in fact, an important tool for positioning the female characters in *Le Crime de Monsieur Lange*. The specter of prostitution hangs over all three female characters in the film. For Batala's mistress, Edith, the "secretary who can't type," prostitution is a certain future if she cannot maintain her status as a "kept" woman, another essential, if temporary, passage in the realist singer's autobiography. When Batala flees his creditors and abandons her at the train station, the only thing he has to give her is advice on how to pick up other men; advice she takes right away.

For Estelle, who is raped by Batala and then saved by the love of Charles, the son of the concièrge, prostitution is the "road not taken."[94] The victimization of young women is emphasized not only in her rape and unwanted pregnancy, but also through the story that Estelle tells Lange on the day they take a walk in the St.-Germain forest. When Estelle was a young girl, an old man had tried to seduce her. She resisted him, but was punished because he was a "Monsieur très bien." The story is not at all necessary in terms of character development; we already have a sense of Estelle as a tender, slightly naïve young woman. But this story of victimization and resistance adds another facet to the variety of female experiences represented sympathetically in the film.

For Valentine, prostitution is the life left behind for better things: economic stability, autonomy and the love of Lange. We know she was a prostitute for a number of reasons: her comment at the Hôtel de la Frontière that she has known other men before Lange, as well as her reluctance to reveal her past to Lange on the night of the party. Her past affair with the exploitative Batala colors her interactions with him throughout the film, and, while not proof of a past life of prostitution, further characterizes her as an "experienced" woman who has moved on to other, more egalitarian relationships.[95] The placement and lyrics of her song also point to her past as a prostitute. Her performance of "À la belle étoile" follows the scene in which Batala slips away on a train, leaving Edith to a fate of prostitution. At the moment Edith is picked up by a man on the platform, the camera pans right to the strains of "À la belle étoile," finally coming to rest on Florelle and Lange having dinner together in her apartment. Florelle's performance of "À la belle étoile," a first-person narrative, hints that she too has experienced the life of a streetwalker.

Renoir said that he "thought it would make the character of Valentine more interesting and a little mysterious to suggest in the song that she had once been a prostitute."[96] Considering that prostitutes were coded in such an obvious fashion in 1930s films, the representation of Florelle here is quite subtle. What is also unusual is the fact that she has "moved up" in the world to become the manager of a laundry—a rare fate for a prostitute in 1930s films and songs.

Yet Valentine's occupation as *blanchisseuse* is equally significant. The laundress has carried a specific erotic charge in French culture since at least the nineteenth century. She connotes sexual availability, unruliness, and physical strength from Degas's paintings through the Tradition of Quality cinema.[97] Historically, the laundress had the reputation of a street-smart, straight-talking woman prone to brawling and launching strikes.[98] In *Zouzou*, Josephine Baker plays a plucky laundress who becomes a music hall star. Arletty's character Garance in *Children of Paradise* has been a laundress before becoming a performer in the attractions on the boulevard du

Temple. Like Valentine, Garance loves an "innocent" (Baptiste) and is the frankest, most exposed character in the film.[99] A successful Tradition of Quality film, *Gervaise* (René Clément, 1955), features an extended scene of laundresses brawling with one another. In Renoir's *French Cancan*, Nini works as a laundress before becoming a cancan dancer. Renoir said of Nini: "Nothing is more seductive than a laundress walking in the street with a basket under her arm. There are no more of them today, of course, but when I was little, there were many of them, and I used to watch them."[100] Just as Degas's paintings grant laundresses "a self-sufficient dignity that belies their reputation for immoral conduct,"[101] Valentine in *Le Crime de Monsieur Lange* combines her toughness with tenderness and dignity, able to stand up to Batala and serve as a confidante to her employees.

Valentine's strength is made explicit in a synopsis of the film written during the development of the screenplay.[102] "We understand that she, like many other women, was Batala's mistress. But she is as strong as he. The adventure didn't last, and in all of the courtyard, she is the only person who dares to speak frankly to him and say what she thinks.[103] As one moves through the different drafts of the film's screenplay, one can see a conscious attempt to enrich the female characters on the part of Jacques Prévert and Jean Renoir.[104] In an early version of the script, Valentine is not a laundress; instead, she is an "ageless, lackluster woman" who edits a collection of stories called *The Petite Lisette* at the publishing company. Mlle. Marion, as she is called in this version, is in love with Lange, but Lange loves Edith, Batala's secretary and mistress. Lange's crush on the scheming Edith seems to have been conceived in visual terms as a fantasy more typical of avant-garde films of the 1920s: when Lange gets drunk in a restaurant, he sees images of Edith everywhere.[105] Later, in a nightclub, he imagines that he sees hundreds of Ediths and pursues her wildly. Marion, on the other hand, is a maternal figure. After Lange kills Batala, he "collapses at her feet, crying and clinging to her legs." Mlle. Marion "consoles Lange as one would console a child."[106] Renoir and Jean Castanier, then, apparently had a more caricatural version of femininity in mind at the beginning of the script-writing process: a spinster/mother figure juxtaposed to a pretty, coquettish young woman.

While it is true that Marion/Valentine was a key character from the beginning—it is she who encourages the print shop employees to stand up to Batala to get their pay, and she acts as Lange's defender before the impromptu "jury" of countryfolk, for example—much seems to have changed in terms of the representation of women when Jacques Prévert began working with Renoir on the script. Edith, the secretary, is fleshed out and shown to be, not only an object of contempt, but a woman with limited options, who merits our understanding. Estelle is raped by Batala the boss, and thus economic and sexual exploitation are shown to work hand in hand. Lastly, Florelle, a popular music hall performer and film actress, was cast as Valentine and transformed into a laundress.

Le Crime de Monsieur Lange thus aligns women's experience with social critique. In it, Florelle incarnates a woman characterized by both strength and vulnerability, cynicism and optimism, much like the realist singers in other 1930s French films. Her performance of the realist song, with its sense of working-class urban space, its cynicism, and its valorization of women's experience, is a key part of the film's nuanced representation of women. Furthermore, the realist song can help us read the film's famously ambiguous ending. After being acquitted by the jury of peasants, Valentine and Lange stroll along the beach into an unknown future. The music that accompanies the final scene is that of "À la belle étoile." The realist song's circularity and its pessimism thus temper the film's happy ending.

Certain elements of Florelle's star image place her in sympathetic alignment with the realist singer persona: her role as *Fantine* in the film *Les Misérables*, her aura of sexual rebellion from *Tumultes* and *Liliom*, her own roots in the café-concert, and the melodramatic portions of her autobiography. However, Florelle also evokes *La Dame de Chez Maxim*'s Belle Époque dancer/prostitute, and the glitter of the music hall world (from both her music hall career and, as we shall see in chapter 4, her role in *Faubourg Montmartre*). She is, in fact, the perfect emblem of the permeability of cinema and music hall in the first half of the 1930s in France, moving as she did with particular ease from the Folies-Bergère to the film sets of Fritz Lang, G. W. Pabst, Robert Siodmak, Raymond Bernard, Alexander Korda, and Jean Renoir. Her career is also emblematic of the international nature of early sound cinema, in that she performed in eight of the French versions of the "multiple language" films. Florelle's voice, even, is at the crossroads of the realist song and the operetta: it is often a quavering, emotional voice, like that of the realist singer, yet it is soprano, and thus quite different from the husky voices of Damia, Fréhel, Piaf, and Lys Gauty. Florelle's example, and her evocation of both realist and music hall traditions, leads us logically, in the next chapter, to an exploration of the ways in which the figure of the realist singer arises in other contexts and intersects with other performance traditions in 1930s French cinema.

In sum, the discourse on the realist singer in the interwar period retains elements of the mid-to-late-nineteenth-century accounts we investigated in chapters 1 and 2, yet the discourse changes. Like their nineteenth-century counterparts, Mac Orlan and Carco were intrigued by the realist singer's ability to convey the allure of the *pierreuse* (even as she's being replaced by the *entraîneuse*), the "street" (even as street life is changing in Paris), and the café-concert (largely a distant memory for most 1930s audiences)—in short, "Paris," at the fantasy intersection between the working class and the underworld. However, the interwar commentary generated by the flâneur has shifted in an important way: now he demonstrates an emotional investment in the realist singer that goes well beyond fascination with this feminine incarnation of the milieu to outright identification.

Likewise, we have seen that the realist singer continues to play an important role in building and sustaining her own star discourse. In most ways, this self-presentation has much in common with the nineteenth-century star's methods of self-promotion, especially in the insistence on the singer's authentic working-class origins and sensibilities. Yet Fréhel pushes this element even further than Buffet or Guilbert, focusing almost exclusively on her autobiographical intertext ("the ballad of my life"), while remaining silent about any research she might have done in the process of building her career. In Fréhel's case, "experience" carries more weight than "artistry."

Finally, as I hope my film analyses in this chapter show, the realist singer phenomenon is an expression of something well beyond the flâneur's fantasies, and beyond the authorial, self-defining gestures of the singers' themselves. She is also French interwar culture's way of preserving a radical impulse: an "investment" in the working class and in women's experience. In her ability to evoke the past, she is also a nostalgic emblem of what, in the 1930s, appeared to be the "good old days" of prewar Paris: an era unmarked by the massive human losses of World War I and untouched by the political and economic scandals of the 1930s and the economic depression that began to be felt in France early in that decade. The realist singer stands for a generalized resistance to all of these changes.

4 · The Revue Star and the Realist Singer

The Return of the Unruly Woman

Florelle's star image was unusually flexible in that it could encompass not only the positive, even "resistant" connotations of the realist singer, but the more mainstream constructions of femininity found in the image of the music hall revue star. In this chapter, we shall analyze films featuring the "queen" of the revue with the goals of assessing the ways in which 1930s French cinema represents another major category of female singer and exploring how the cinema of this era addressed one of its competitors, music hall.

As we saw in chapter 2, the fortunes of the music hall began to decline in the late 1920s and the early 1930s. One strategy adopted by the ailing music hall, we saw, was to "look back" toward the café-concert era and try to capitalize on the audience's nostalgia by showcasing singers like Damia and Fréhel. Another strategy music hall adopted was to join forces, as it were, with the cinema, its competitor. The cinema's fortunes were, in fact, linked with those of music hall long before the late 1920s. Indeed, until around 1910, music halls (as well as *cafés-concerts* and *fête-foraines*) were the primary exhibition locations for French film.[1] Beginning in 1896, the Eldorado, the Olympia, and the Casino de Paris all introduced a program of films as one of the many "numbers" in their shows.[2] Conversely, cinema programs were supplemented by live acts well into the post–World War II era. Music hall impresarios like Paul Oscar and Jacques-Charles booked their troops of chorus lines at cinemas as the pre-cinema show. Damia, Lys Gauty, and many other realist singers performed regularly in such cinemas as the Gaumont-Palace, the Rex, the Olympia, and the Alhambra.[3]

Another kind of interaction occurred between the music hall and the cinema when films told stories set in a music hall context. Music hall is celebrated in a number of films made in the 1930s, a time when it was declining, which build their narratives around the revue star and feature elaborate revue sequences as their finales. For example, in 1935, Max Ophüls directed *Divine,* an adaptation of Colette's *Music Hall Sidelights.* A backstage musical/thriller about a country girl's initiation into the seamy world of a third-rate music hall in Montmartre, *Divine* revels in the music hall's backstage chaos, its nudes, the orientalist décor of its revue, and its clandestine ring of drug dealers.[4] The most interesting interaction between music hall and cinema for our purposes, however, occurred when the music hall divas Mistinguett, Florelle, Josephine Baker, and Jane Marnac took their stage acts to the screen. Sporting fabulous feathered costumes and descending the ubiquitous staircase surrounded by a troop of devoted male chorus singers, the interwar French music hall queen exuded glamour and sophistication. While the realist singer connotes the working class and/or the underworld, the music hall queen is associated with spectacle and a hunger for power and class rise in *Zouzou* (Marc Allégret, 1934), *Paris-Béguin* (Augusto Genina, 1931), and *Le Bonheur* (Marcel L'Herbier, 1935), the films I shall address here. The realist singer and her set of values are not, however, absent from these films. On the contrary, the realist singer is still there, either literally or in a contorted, displaced form. As these films progress more resolutely toward the modern realms of the music hall and the cinema, and away from the nostalgia and underclass community of the café-concert, the singer-audience connection becomes increasingly more apparent and troubling.

FAUBOURG MONTMARTRE

Raymond Bernard's 1931 film *Faubourg Montmartre,* an adaptation of a novel written by Henri Duvernois in 1912, is a melodrama about the struggle of the Gentilhomme sisters to support themselves in the seductive, treacherous world of Montmartre. Bernard is better known for an adaptation of Roland Dorgelès's pacifist novel about World War I, *Les Croix de bois* (1931), the film he directed prior to *Faubourg Montmartre.* In 1933, he directed an even more prestigious film, *Les Misérables,* with the prominent actors Harry Baur, as Valjean; Charles Vanel, as Javert; and Florelle, as Fantine. In *Faubourg Montmartre,* Ginette (Gaby Morlay) is a naïve, yet plucky, seamstress working in a couturier's workshop, while her older sister Céline (Line Noro), works as a prostitute. Charles Vanel plays Dédé, Céline's pimp and a drug dealer. Pressured by Dédé, Céline has been urging Ginette to start working the streets too. The sisters are virtually alone in the world: their aging father is a traveling salesman, apparently unaware of the fate that awaits his vulnerable young daughters in Paris. Ginette and Céline, perched precariously on the verge of poverty, take in a provincial lodger, Frédéric, an awkward young man who reads poetry and loves the theater. Frédéric will eventually rescue the younger sister, Ginette, from the fate that befalls Céline: prostitution, drug addiction, and the asylum.

Gaby Morlay (1893–1964), a veteran of comic, melodramatic, and boulevard theater roles, plays the film's young and innocent protagonist, Ginette. Morlay was one of the most visible actresses in 1930s French cinema, but she is best remembered today for the martyr-mother figure she portrayed in the most popular film of the Occupation era, *Le Voile bleu* (Jean Stelli, 1942).[5]

Like many 1930s French films, *Faubourg Montmartre* contains stock characters from the Parisian criminal underworld—the pimp and the prostitute—and attempts to capture visually the texture of an exoticized Parisian space, in this case, Montmartre. The film's fascination with a flashy, bustling nocturnal Paris is revealed immediately. Sounds of traffic accompany an image of a street sign reading "Rue du Faubourg Montmartre." *Faubourg Montmartre* is one of the earliest French talking films, notable for its creative use of sound. Like two other films shot in 1930 that attempt a realist rendering of marginalized people—*La Petite Lise* (Grémillon, 1930) and *Paris la nuit* (Diamant-Berger, 1930)—*Faubourg Montmartre* uses music and ambient noise to sketch out, and comment upon, marginal Parisian spaces and femininity.

A high-angle long shot of the neighborhood at night reveals its busy streets and neon signs, including one that advertises "Le Palace," a music hall.[6] An aging prostitute walks along the sidewalk wearing a cheap fur coat and an animal print scarf. Another middle-aged prostitute passes, a weary expression on her face. From inside a café, a pimp surveys the women. Contemporary critics noticed the film's representation of the cityscape and praised its views of the street, the movements of the crowd, and its little bistros.[7]

Despite this, it appears that the film was not well attended. Other critics complained that its characters were of the pre–World War I moment. Bernard had failed to update the 1912 source text sufficiently, Georges Champeaux said, adding: "One only very rarely encounters fathers as blind as M. Gentilhomme, hussies as sloppy as his older daughter, Céline, and virgins as fierce as his younger daughter, Ginette."[8] Georges Charensol admired the film, but speculated that Bernard's "bold" and "moving" film was too noir for elegant audiences on the Champs-Élysées, despite its "deceptively optimistic" ending.[9] He saw a disjunction between its setting and its narrative, saying that the film's representation of the *faubourg*, with its lights, flashing signs, dance halls and sumptuous music halls, had little in common with Duvernois's 1912 portrait of the neighborhood. "No neighborhood in Paris has changed its face more in twenty years, and in such a sparkling décor, this drama of poverty and prostitution is conspicuously out of its element."[10] *Faubourg Montmartre* is, in fact, concerned precisely with the tension between "old" and "new" Paris. On the one hand, the film presents a prewar Paris where prostitutes walk the streets and popular entertainment is a woman singing a realist song in an intimate setting. On the other hand, there is the glittering surface of postwar Paris, defined by its music halls, brisk pace, and a "modern" woman—a poor but independent *midinette*, thoroughly at home in the city. This tension, uneasily resolved by the film, is played out in its juxtaposition of two different musical numbers.

Faubourg Montmartre (1931) contains two singing performances absent from both the novel and the film version directed in 1924 by Charles Burguet (which is apparently no longer extant). Raymond Bernard himself wrote the lyrics to one of the songs, "Faubourg Montmartre," performed in the film by the realist singer Odette Barencey. The first number occurs at a music hall, where Ginette, Céline, and their provincial lodger Frédéric go to watch their cousin perform. Florelle plays the music hall star Irène. The sequence begins with a high-angle shot behind the balcony seats where Ginette, Céline, and Frédéric sit. The spectators are seated according to their class; our characters are up in the cheapest seats. Down below, on stage, Florelle sings against the backdrop of a kick line of feather-clad women holding parasols. Ginette is delighted with the spectacle and chatters throughout the scene. She knows all of the dancers' names. Irène sings a cheerful tune similar to those sung by Mistinguett and Florelle herself in the music halls of Paris in the late 1920s and early 1930s. At one point in her song, Irène looks directly up at the sisters in the balcony seats and calls out "Bonjour, Céline et Ginette!" Ginette shouts back a greeting and waves, proud to know a star. But other audience members stare disapprovingly. In this instant, *Faubourg Montmartre* stages and reflects a transitional moment in popular entertainment where (some) spectators want to believe that the intimacy of the café-concert is still present in the music hall experience. But, as the other spectators' disapproval indicates, that intimacy between performer and audience is now inappropriate or illusory.

The music hall in which Irène sings is the Palace, then a real music hall in the ninth arrondissement, located at 8, rue du Faubourg-Montmartre.[11] A 1,000-seat music hall was opened there in 1921. Initially called the Eden, it did not succeed and was sublet to a number of people in the following two years, who tried producing operettas, literary theater, and revues. Finally, in January 1923, the legendary music hall directors Oscar Dufrenne and Henri Varna purchased the Eden and transformed it into one of the top Parisian music halls. They renovated it, increasing the number of seats to 1,500, redesigning the lighting and adding rose-colored furnishings, to make it one of the most beautiful music halls in the capital. They renamed it the Palace in order to associate it with the Palace in London, a music hall with which Varna and Dufrenne exchanged talent. Varna, considered an innovator, created some thirty successful revues for the Palace, typically, two per year.[12] It is this 1923–33 period of the Palace's success that is evoked in the film *Faubourg Montmartre*.

Starting around the turn of the century and intensifying after World War I, the "pact" between performer and spectator was modified by the shift from the neighborhood café-concert to the rationalized, commercial entertainment of the music hall. The café-concert spectator, accustomed to smoking, drinking, and interacting with the performers, evolved into the more sedate, prosperous music hall spectator. *Faubourg Montmartre* simultaneously mourns the real Palace music hall and the sense of community and congenial mixing of classes lost in the phasing out of the café-concert.[13] The film's characterization of the successful music hall star compounds its expression of ambivalence with regard to the music hall. The star of the revue, Irène, appears to provide a pleasurable viewing experience to her audience and to "connect" directly with her working-class public seated in the cheap seats. But her performance of warmth and gaiety are later shown to be just that: a performance. The social-climbing Irène is unsympathetic to the financial problems Ginette and Céline are experiencing, despite her own difficult past. She even seduces Frédéric, whom Ginette has started to love. It is, in fact, Irène's thoughtless seduction of the lodger that precipitates Ginette's near fall into prostitution. After the evening at the music hall and Irène's apartment, Ginette cries to Céline that, the following day, she will put on the finery her sister has provided and accompany her out.

The film's second musical performance occurs at a gathering of prostitutes. A middle-aged woman we have never seen (Odette Barencey), begins to sing a realist song written for the film. Barencey was a second-tier performer in the café-concert and then the music hall, a respected *chanteuse* at the best *concerts de quartier*. In the 1930s, like Damia and Fréhel, she was invited to perform in music halls that sought to revive the *tour de chant*. Barencey looks rather like Fréhel, in fact; she is a large woman with a weathered face. Seated at a table, smoking, and looking vaguely off into the distance, she performs a song about prostitutes who work on the rue du Faubourg-Montmartre. The scene opens just as she is finishing its first verse.[14]

Ell's n'montrent pas leur vrai visage	They don't show their true face
Caché sous le sourir' d'usage,	Hidden under the everyday smile
Celles qui, du matin au soir,	Those who, from morning to evening,
Et souvent du soir au matin,	And often from evening to morning,
Au Faubourg pass'nt pour se fair' voir.	On the Faubourg pass by in order to be seen.
Ell's s'ballad'nt le long des vitrines	They stroll alongside shop windows
Et semblent ne penser à rien	And seem to think of nothing
Qu'à montrer leur humble bobine,	Except showing their humble faces
Mais ce n'sont pas des corps sans âmes	But they are not bodies without souls
Les p'tit's femm's.	The little women.

A close-up lingers on Barencey's face as she sings.

Et y a des mômes	And there are kids
Comm' des fantômes	Like ghosts
Qui déambulent sur le trottoir,	Who pace up and down the sidewalk
Au crépuscule,	At twilight,
Cherchant chaqu' soir	Looking each evening for
Un idiot d'homme	An idiot of a man
Offrant un' somme pour s'entendr' dir' des mots d'amour.	Offering a sum to hear some Words of love.
Il faudra, pour les amuser,	They'll have to, to amuse them,
Qu'elles soient pamées	Whether they're faint,
L'coeur brisé	Broken-hearted,
Sans croir' qu' ça doit	Without believing that it
Durer toujours	Lasts forever
Car tout arriv'	Because everything happens
dans le Faubourg, un jour.	on the Faubourg, one day.

Only the prostitutes who are not hungry, the song tells us, have the luxury of rebelling against their plight. But despite these material conditions, the women hold out hope for love:

Au Faubourg, elles sont pas tout's belles;	On the Faubourg, they aren't all beautiful;
Y en a des pâl's qui sont rebelles.	There are some pallid ones who are rebels.
C'est p't' êtr' qu'ell'es ont moins d'appétit	Perhaps it's because they have less appetite
Car c'est au fil' pour la vertu,	Because the virtuous girl
D'avoir un estomac petit.	

Mais la rue est inexorable,	Has a small stomach.
Et le destin est très têtu.	But the street is inexorable
	And destiny is stubborn.
Et y a des mômes	And there are kids
Comm' des fantômes	Like ghosts
Qui déambulent sur le trottoir,	Who pace up and down the sidewalk
Au crépuscule,	At twilight,
Et dont l'espoir	And whose hope
Est si tenace	Is so tenacious
Que rien ne lasse leur croyance	That nothing exhausts their belief
En un bel amour.	In a great love.
De Montmartre, ces humbles fleurs,	From Montmartre, these humble flowers,
Sortent du ruisseau tout en pleurs.	Come out of the gutter all in tears.
Ell's s'ront heureus's	They'll be happy
Quand c' s' ra leur tour	When it's their turn
Car tout arriv' dans le Faubourg, un jour.	Because everything happens on the Faubourg, one day.

The sequence is structured by a series of close-ups that constitute a departure from the visual style of much of the film. The camera lingers on each woman's tired, longing face, as she stares at the singer, mesmerized. The room is dim and smoky, unlike the brightly lit music hall where Irène performs. Shots of eerie-looking dolls are interspersed with the tight shots of the women's faces. The setting appears to be a cheap, furnished room where the prostitutes and their pimp have gathered before beginning their evening's work. Typical of realist songs, "Faubourg Montmartre" evokes the daily lives of prostitutes, humanizing them, and capturing the monotony and heartbreak of their lives. The sequence communicates a sense of female community in an otherwise bleak existence.

The performance also initiates a powerful opposition to the revue sequence, in terms of the representation of the internal audience. While the realist singer and the community of prostitutes cannot offer Ginette the giddy spectatorial pleasure she experiences at the music hall or the financial safety net of the bourgeois family, they furnish the solace of female solidarity in a difficult existence. In the music hall sequence, we saw that Ginette transgresses by attempting to breach the gap between performer and audience when she shouts "Bonjour." Eschewing the kind of reaction her outburst at the music hall elicits, the prostitutes respond out loud to the song. Between two verses of Barencey's song, one prostitute exclaims, "Ah! You know men. . . ." Likewise, in contrast to the hierarchical seating at the Palace, the prostitutes are seated loosely in a circle, each in intimate proximity to the performer. In further contrast to the relatively static, "tableau" perspective of Florelle and the chorus line at the music hall, the camera here moves in and out of the group of women, offering us close-ups and medium shots of the singer and her audience from a variety of angles. While Irène's performance connotes artificial, mass-produced gaiety, Barencey's moving performance reflects the texture of the difficult, yet compelling lives of these prostitutes and their tenuous sense of community. The film thus contrasts two very different urban spaces and two different types of entertainment: the modern music hall, with its kick lines and glamorous star, and the furnished room, with its "authentic" prostitutes and the realist song.

Faubourg Montmartre, like the films discussed in chapter 3, also lays out distinctly different scenarios relating to the trajectory of women living on the margins of society. Just as Florelle represents the "upper class" of the world of entertainment, Barencey is the "working class" of that same universe. The larger narrative trajectory of Ginette and Céline further mimics this polarization of women's material condition, again using "place" to comment on class structure and the female condition. Neither sister remains on the rue du Faubourg-Montmartre for long. The film's resolution of the problem of two poor, unmarried sisters living in Paris is to "save" Ginette by marrying her off to Frédéric and moving her to the country, while disposing of Céline, who becomes a cocaine addict, in an asylum. Ginette, then, after hovering precariously between the levels of *midinette* and prostitute, gets pulled miraculously into the provincial bourgeoisie. This politically conservative resolution to the film's narrative is tempered, however, by the film's representation of the city.

While on one level the film folds Ginette into the provincial setting, it also acknowledges that she cannot forget the city. Despite its apparent valorization of provincial life, care is taken to represent pleasures available to women in the city. Early on, Ginette giggles and eats chocolate with her friend on a busy boulevard. She clowns around at work with friends and behaves irreverently toward a wealthy customer. Leaving the couturier's workshop at the end of her working day, she is jostled by the crowd, eyed by an older man, and followed. But she is no victim of the hustle and bustle; rather, she contributes to it. She buys a snack from a street vendor and argues about the price, participating in the ebb and flow of city life. She is a spunky young woman, vulnerable to prostitution, but fully at home in the urban environment.

Although Ginette moves away from rue du Faubourg-Montmartre, this Parisian space remains with her. The signifying power of the words "Faubourg Montmartre" is made clear near the end of the film, when

Ginette has moved to the provinces, initially seeking refuge with Frédéric and his mother. Dédé tracks her down and tries to take her back to the city. When she refuses to return to Paris with him, he gossips to the villagers. All he needs to say in order to discredit Ginette is that she is from Faubourg Montmartre. Scandalized, the villagers burn effigies of Ginette and Frédéric. The provincial setting will eventually serve as a haven for Ginette, but at this moment, it is a place of intolerance and ignorance.

The film ends with a representation of Paris that emphasizes its seductiveness more than its infamy. The final sequence takes place in a candy store belonging to Ginette's aunt in Paris. Ginette calls her aunt from the country, finally accepted in her provincial life, but missing Paris, nonetheless. She telephones specifically because she wants to hear the noises of Paris. The aunt obliges and holds the telephone out to the traffic-filled rue du Faubourg-Montmartre. It is here that the film ends, with the valorization of the city's aural texture and seductiveness. Despite the film's moralistic solution to the sisters' dilemma, it communicates above all the magnetism of the urban space and the ideal of female community not found in bourgeois marriage.

The remaining films under consideration in this chapter—*Zouzou, Paris-Béguin,* and *Le Bonheur*—all feature the music hall queen as protagonist. They activate fantasies and anxieties similar to those we saw in *Rigolboche,* but they generate other meanings, as well, around the female star character. *Zouzou, Paris-Béguin,* and *Le Bonheur* bring together the powerful female star with the virile "man of the people." The films juxtapose the worlds of the working class (or, in the case of *Paris-Béguin,* the underworld) with that of the glittering music hall, addressing, in the process, gender and class difference.

An examination of these films is also instructive in that it reveals the extent to which the aura of the realist singer permeates 1930s French cinema, even when there is no realist singer in the film. None of these films contains a Fréhel or a Damia, or even an actress playing the role of the realist singer. True, Jane Marnac sings a realist song in *Paris-Béguin,* but she was known as a revue star and did not even carry the *parigote* connotations we identified in Mistinguett's star image. Gaby Morlay, who plays a music hall star in *Le Bonheur,* was much better known for her roles in Henry Bernstein's boulevard theater dramas. Nevertheless, these films draw on the realist universe, albeit in a manner quite different from that of the films examined in chapter 3. *Zouzou, Paris-Béguin,* and *Le Bonheur* place the aura of the realist singer in their male characters. Jean Gabin (in *Zouzou* and *Paris-Béguin*) and Charles Boyer (in *Le Bonheur*) play characters imbued with the authenticity previously attributed to female singers such as Fréhel and Barencey. Here, the men are emissaries of the working class or the underworld, while the women move up the socioeconomic hierarchy. As we shall see, this elevation in the status of the *chanteuse* is carried out with considerable ambivalence.

ZOUZOU

Zouzou (Marc Allégret, 1934) stars Josephine Baker, the African American dancer who made her début in 1925 at the Théâtre des Champs-Élysées in the Revue nègre. At first glance, it may seem curious to include Baker in a study of the French realist singer and the revue star in 1930s French film. After all, Baker's appeal in the 1920s and 1930s responded to a very different fantasy circulating in French culture that conflated "blackness," "femininity," "animalistic sexuality," and "primitivism." The qualities she evoked according to the mythology of this fantasy seem very different from those of both the revue star (class mobility, glamour) and the realist singer (the tragic lives lived out in the marginal landscapes of Paris). However, much like the French female stars of the café-concert and the music hall, Baker utilized the intertext of her own life to construct an appealing star image that dovetailed with French fantasies of social transcendence and exotic "otherness." First, she incarnated the poor girl from the slums of St. Louis who astounded Paris at the Revue nègre. Next, in the late 1920s, she metamorphosed from the girl in the banana skirt to the *grande dame du music-hall*. Elegant, French-speaking, and in possession of a trained singing voice, she became the glamorous *parisienne* heading up revues at the Folies-Bergère and the Casino de Paris.

Both of Baker's sound films, *Zouzou* and *Princesse Tam-Tam* (Gréville, 1935), were written for her and recycled the "rags to riches" and "primitive to *parisienne*" narratives at the center of her star image. The realist singer, as we have seen, renders the marginal spaces of Paris exotic: the fortifications, the *faubourgs*, the rough dance hall, and the old café-concert. Baker utilizes the same mechanism—but trades instead on the exoticism of America, jazz, the jungles of Africa, and the South Seas—and supplements this image with the patina of Parisian music hall glamour.

Zouzou opens in Toulon during the childhoods of Zouzou (Baker) and her adoptive brother Jean (Jean Gabin). The children perform as circus freaks with their kindly adoptive father, Papa Mélé (Pierre Larquey). Mélé displays the children as twins, claiming they are a "miracle of nature" from an island in the Polynesian archipelago. Their parents, he explains to the fascinated fairground audience—a Chinese mother and a "redskin" father—turned the children away because their colors did not match those of their parents. Racial difference is the stuff of spectacle, as is sexual difference: our first glimpse of Zouzou is through the eyes of a group of boys who are peeping at her in her dressing room tent as she applies white powder to her face.

The children grow up: Jean becomes a sailor in the French Navy, while Zouzou and Mélé move to Montmartre and Zouzou finds work as a laundress. *Zouzou*, like *Faubourg Montmartre*, contrasts two different kinds of singing performance, which we may broadly differentiate as "realist" and "spectacular." The realist performances draw on the intimacy and the working-class character of the café-concert and the bal musette, while the spectacular performances take place in the modern music hall. Both Baker and Gabin, in fact, perform in the realist style early in the film in settings other than the music hall. Zouzou sings in the laundry; Jean dances and sings at the bal musette. Another performer represents the "false" values of the modern music hall: Miss Barbara (Ila Merry), the capricious blond star whose heart is with her Brazilian lover, not the overweight patron underwriting her show. The "tragedy" of the film is that, in the end, Zouzou is relegated to the artificial, joyless universe of the music hall, leaving Jean in the arms of another laundress and in the warm, "authentic" realist world.

Zouzou's first singing performance occurs at the laundry where she works and consists of an improvised parody of the singing style of Miss Barbara. She sings "C'est lui" (It's Him, or He's the One) to her fellow laundresses:[15]

Vingt fois par jour, par douzaines	Twenty times a day, by the dozens
Des Messieurs très amoureux	Very smitten gentlemen
Me props'nt un' vie de reine	Offer me a queen's life
Pour que je m'donne à eux.	So that I'll give myself to them.
Y en a qu'un qu'a su me plaire.	There's only one who knows how to
Il est moche et n'a pas l'sou.	please me.
Ses histoir's ne sont pas claires,	He's ugly and doesn't have a penny.
Je l'sais bien mais j'm'en fous;	His stories aren't always clear,
Pour moi y a qu'un homm' dans	I know this very well, but I don't give
Paris,	a damn;
C'est lui!	For me there's only one man in Paris
	It's he!

Like Fréhel's performances in *Coeur de Lilas* and that of Odette Barencey in *Faubourg Montmartre*, "C'est lui" is presented as Zouzou's own fabrication, performed for the members of her community. Zouzou sings the song at the urging of her fellow laundresses, who gather around her in a circle. Centered in the frame, Zouzou sings directly to her friends, accompanied by another laundress with a harmonica. Zouzou sings joyously, screams, tosses laundry into the air, rolls her eyes, contorts her face, and generally hams it up with great verve.

This performance sequence features a rather unusual relay of the gaze between the characters, as well as between the performers and the implied film audience. Although she is centered in the frame, Zouzou never once looks into the camera, as if to imply that this spectacle is for the laundresses only, and not for the film's spectators. Just as unusual for the classical cinema is the "reciprocal gaze" between Zouzou and her fellow laundresses: a gaze between the female performer and her female spectators, as it were. The sequence lacks point-of-view shots that might grant us a closer, voyeuristic look at Zouzou. In a cinema that usually grants the power of the gaze to male characters and to the (implied) male spectators, *Zouzou* seems to privilege, if only briefly, a noncontrolling gaze at the female performer.

The scene cuts directly, in mid-song, to the performance of the "real" music hall star, Miss Barbara, rehearsing the same song at the music hall. In contrast to Zouzou's audience of laughing laundresses, who participate in the performance, Miss Barbara's auditors are the music hall's director and her fawning protector. She sings in a flat voice utterly lacking in conviction. She is depressed because her true love, a Brazilian man who "takes her like a jaguar," is leaving Paris.

The film's next realist performance occurs in a bal musette, where Zouzou, Claire (Yvette Lebon), her friend from the laundry, and Jean go to dance. While dancing with Claire, Jean accompanies the accordion band in a jaunty waltz called "Viens Fifine."[16]

Ah! Viens Fifine:	Ah! Come along Fifine;
De la rue des Halles à la rue d' la Huchette	From the rue des Halles to the rue d' la Huchette
On connait Fifine, la rein' des bals musette.	We knew Fifine, the queen of the dance hall.

Other dancers join Jean in the chorus, and, like Zouzou's performance in the laundry, his number is integrated into the narrative. He sings, casually and spontaneously, to Claire and to Zouzou in the bal musette, a mythical space of working-class community. Jean's singing performance does not isolate him from his community visually—he moves about the floor among other dancing couples, singing "naturally." Here, as in his other singing performances in 1930s films, Gabin's conduct consolidates his membership in the community of the proletariat.[17]

Zouzou's second performance begins with the aura of friendly female complicity we saw in the laundry scene, but becomes something different. While delivering laundry to the music hall, Zouzou cavorts with chorus girls in a dressing room. They dress Zouzou in a sparkly, scanty costume. Zouzou runs to show it to Jean, now an electrician working at the music hall. Jean directs Zouzou to the stage while the curtain is closed and shines a floodlight on her, ostensibly to test the lighting. He instructs her where to stand, directing her to "stay put." She begins to dance, casting shadows in the shape of animals on the wall. Unbeknownst to Zouzou, Jean raises the curtain, exposing her to the music hall directors sitting in the empty theater. In contrast to Zouzou's improvised performance in the laundry, it is Jean who "directs" the spectacle of Zouzou. This spectacle is made up, in part, by a huge black shadow—an extreme, potentially dehumanizing, abstraction of a black woman. Her dance, in which she imitates the head-bobbing movements of a chicken, walks on all fours, and does the Charleston, reproduces the combination of sensuality, animality, jazz, and primitivism that Baker had symbolized for French audiences since her debut in the Revue nègre.

Zouzou offers a literal enactment of the mechanism explored fruitfully by feminist film theory: the production of female spectacle orchestrated by a man for the desiring gaze of (presumed) male spectators. In *Zouzou*, however, this moment both participates in the fetishization of the female body and reveals the aggression inherent in this system. We watch, along with Jean and the producers, while Zouzou dances. But when she realizes her antics are being observed, she flees in horror, and suddenly we too are complicit. Crucially, the sequence represents the music hall stage as an alienating space outside the woman's control, in which she is subject to manipulation and scrutiny. In contrast to her song in the laundry, Zouzou's performance is, quite literally, authored by, and presented to, men.

Zouzou's next performance occurs on the music hall stage once again, but this time, she performs as a star. When Jean is falsely accused of murder and needs money for his defense, Zouzou agrees to perform at the music hall in order to raise funds. Ironically, Zouzou replaces Miss Barbara, the woman she had previously mocked and who has now abandoned the stage to follow her Latin lover. Perched in a huge birdcage wearing a feathered costume, Zouzou sings "Haïti."[18]

Once again, we have a representation of racial difference as a mark of the "primitive," and the exotic. The feathered costume, the gilded cage, and the reference to a love call point to both Zouzou's construction as an untamed creature and a confining metaphor for a certain image of spectacular women. As in this sequence, Baker came to represent any number of "exotic" cultures, playing, for example, an Arab Tunisian woman in *Princesse Tam Tam*, who inexplicably breaks into the Charleston at one point in the film.

Zouzou's exchange of the camaraderie of the laundry and the bal musette for imprisonment in the music hall is completed in the final sequences. Between numbers during the opening night of her revue, Zouzou manages to identify the real murderer and secure Jean's release. Back at the music hall, she sings "C'est lui" again, this time dressed in a satin evening gown. The performance lacks both the element of parody and the sustained interaction with the appreciative female audience from the laundry.

The shift in performance context of a song from a more "private" performance to a public domain carries with it unfortunate consequences for the female protagonist. Zouzou's success in the music hall coincides with the loss of the man she loves. Jean does not recognize Zouzou's sacrifice and chooses her friend Claire instead. Zouzou may have experienced a class rise—she has exchanged her simple cotton dresses for satin gowns and fur-trimmed suits—but has lost the only thing she wants: Jean. The film closes with an image of Zouzou singing "Haïti" for the hundredth time in her gilded prison.[19] The music hall itself functions here as a sort of cage: an oppressive milieu for both Miss Barbara and Zouzou. Notwithstanding the rather extraordinary revue sequences in *Zouzou*, the film mounts a kind of critique of this artificial world, valorizing the working-class camaraderie and modest urban spaces of the dance hall and the laundry.

Baker's performances in *Zouzou* evince not only the intertext of the realist representation of the proletariat essential to realist singer texts but also that of the different stages of Baker's life as it was disseminated in her autobiographies and publicity. At the beginning of *Zouzou*, she is the poor little black girl defined exclusively by the spectacle of her race (i.e., the freak of nature). Her acrobatic shadow dance at the music hall, directed by Jean, corresponds to her Revue nègre phase, with its emphasis on exoticism and racial otherness. Finally, her star appearance in the music hall revue evokes the "real" 1930s Baker: the elegant *meneuse de revue* who has conquered Paris.

Zouzou may have lost her man, but she has gained something that was a crucial aspect of every music hall revue star's persona: citizenship of Paris. The film's treatment of Parisian urban space is similar, in some ways, to that of other 1930s French realist films. The gritty fortifications and the enchanting Les Halles in *Coeur de Lilas*, the courtyard in *Le Crime de Monsieur Lange*, and the prostitutes and the honking cars on the rue du Faubourg-Montmartre in *Faubourg Montmartre* have their counterparts in Zouzou. Scenes of everyday life in Montmartre are represented with detailed texture and considerable affection. Zouzou shops at street markets in friendly day-time Montmartre, while Jean's inadvertent involvement in murder takes place in a noir-ish nocturnal Montmartre familiar from poetic realist films. However, once Zouzou becomes a music hall star, she leaves Montmartre and enters a paste-diamond Paris. In the opening-night revue sequence, an elegant Zouzou sings against the backdrop of a heavily stylized Paris, represented by the huge obelisk at the place de la Concorde and the distorted bridges of the Seine. Clearly, the Paris Zouzou has won is not Paris *populaire*. This "Paris" offers the chanteuse only the admiring glances of male chorus singers, denying her an authentic love affair with a "real" man. This trade-off, which we shall explore more fully, characterizes all the films featuring the music hall queen.

PARIS-BÉGUIN

Paris-Béguin (Augusto Genina, 1931) anticipates poetic realism in its use of moody exteriors, low-key lighting, and the shadowy universe of prostitutes and criminals. But the film is just as indebted to the backstage musical, chronicling the rehearsals and opening night of a music hall revue, in which the real life music hall star Marnac performs both a realist song and a revue number. One of the paradoxes of *Zouzou* is that its female protagonist experiences a vertiginous class rise, and achieves social ascendancy in the glittering Paris of the music hall world, at the expense of personal happiness and the presence of a "real" man in her life. *Paris-Béguin*, likewise, features a rich, powerful star denied the man she loves. The plot concerns a star named Jane Diamond (Jane Marnac) who cannot perform her songs with sincerity until she experiences the virility of the *réaliste* universe through her attraction to a dangerous gangster, Bob, played by Gabin. On opening night of the show, however, Jane loses Bob. In the first of Gabin's many photogenic deaths in 1930s cinema, a rival gangster guns him down in front of the music hall. Like *Zouzou*, *Paris-Béguin* plays out a fantasy around the encounter between the rich, female star and the virile "man of the people."[20]

The film opens in Jane's sumptuous apartment before she has met Bob. The opening scene, notable for its camera movement and construction of a fragmented space, establishes Jane as an imperious star leading a decadent life. The camera travels slowly through her luxurious, cluttered bedroom to the strains of a jazzy tune on the radio. High-heeled shoes, a fur coat, cigarettes, a slumbering lapdog, and an empty champagne bottle are strewn about. A close-up reveals a woman's leg as she puts on stockings. A tight close-up fragments Jane's face as she applies mascara. She speaks rudely to her protector on the telephone, then leaves for the music hall, where she must rehearse.

At the Folies de Paris, a fictitious music hall, the rehearsal of the revue "Paris-Béguin" is under way. Jane observes a rehearsal of a dance, judging it "idiotic." The rehearsal of her own number, the "Moroccan Tableau," is fraught with problems. The narrative concerns the rape of a woman by a North African gang leader and her eventual love affair with him. Jane speaks the first lines of the scene in an old-fashioned declamatory style, with one arm raised, gesturing toward the sky. She then interrupts the rehearsal, claiming that the story feels false because a woman would never fall in love with an intruder and allow him to spend the night with her. She demands of the author that he change the scenario. She is at the top of the power hierarchy, ruling over servants, a lover, the director and the author of the revue, and her fellow actors. Crucially, all the men shown thus far are emasculated: her wealthy, but ridiculous protector, the overwrought director and his incompetent assistants, the elderly, foppish author, and especially Jane's co-star, clearly coded as homosexual. When he learns that his role in the revue may be diminished, he stomps off furiously, his male lover in tow. In response, Jane stamps her foot and demands "a man, a man, a man!"

In contrast to Mistinguett's star vehicle, *Rigolboche*, which wholeheartedly celebrates the ascent of the music hall queen, *Paris-Béguin* mourns the emasculation of the modern music hall, commenting critically on its imperious female star, its artificiality, and its homosexual male star, who here undergoes a specifically "oriental" feminization, in that his role within the Moroccan revue is that of the Arab male character. As if in answer to Jane's demand for a "real" man (i.e., straight, white, and French), the following sequence introduces Bob (Jean Gabin), a hardened yet seductive gangster. A modern apache, he wears eyeliner, a fedora, a pinstriped suit, and two-toned patent leather shoes. Bob's milieu is carefully established: the scene begins with a shot of the elevated metro line, an icon of Paris *populaire*, as a train pulls into the Barbès-Rochechouart station in the eighteenth arrondissement. According to the film's promotional material, this scene was meant to resemble the intersection of the boulevard de la Chapelle and the rue de la Charbonnière, known for prostitution.[21] The publicity proudly notes that "real regulars from the boulevard" were used as extras in the location shooting, indicating a "professional consciousness and care for the truth pushed to the extreme limit ... that does honor to French production."[22]

Bob enters a bistro to plan a jewel heist with a fellow gangster, Dédé (Jean Max). He encounters Gaby (Rachel Berendt), a prostitute and his former lover.[23] "Je suis chipée pour toi," she says using underworld argot to express her desire for him. But Bob spurns her and brags of other conquests. Later, as a reinforcement of this popular atmosphere, one of Mistinguett's realist songs plays on the bistro phonograph, nursing Gaby through her depression over the loss of Bob.

Paris-Béguin continues its alternation between Bob's noir universe and the star's opulent surroundings. After drinking champagne and flirting at an elegant restaurant, Jane returns home. While in her bath, she hears a sound and finds Gabin in her room. They size one another up in a series of shot/reverse shots. Bob reveals his revolver. A smile spreads across his face: he stares at her exposed leg. The phallic gaze and fetishistic camera work prefigured in the opening sequence could not be more explicit here. Jane stares back mutely, fascinated and horrified. When she breaks away and calls for help, Bob kisses her brutally and leads her to bed off-screen, ignoring her cries of protest. The following morning, Bob slips away, leaving her jewels. Jane awakens and smiles contentedly, caressing the bed Bob has just left.

The effect of this sexual encounter, coded initially as a rape, is a radical shift in Jane's personality and performance style. In a repetition of the opening sequence, the transition from boudoir to theater could not possibly be in greater contrast. At the dress rehearsal for the revue, she is affectionate toward the music hall personnel. The ballet she found idiotic is now "charming"; she deems unnecessary the reduction in her stage lover's role. Her encounter with Bob results in a complete loss of her mastery, figured here as amiability, if not utter complacency. Furthermore, she restages the rape in the music hall narrative, orchestrating her powerlessness in a highly ambivalent, if suggestive gesture that does nothing to restore her primacy in this space. She requests that the Arab threaten her with a revolver instead of a saber and that he kiss her roughly when she tries to call for help. In short, she transforms the exotic context of her North African showpiece to that of the Montmartre underworld. Once her stage lover has been killed by the guard, she sings a realist song called "C'est pour toi que j'ai le béguin" (I Have a Crush on You) over his dead body.[24]

C'est pour toi que j'ai l' béguin,	It's for you that I have a crush,
Mon chéri tu l' sais bien,	My darling you know it well,
J' t'ai dans la peau,	I've got you under my skin
J' suis plus moi-même,	I'm no longer myself,
Laisse toi donc enlacer,	Let me take you in my arms
Laisse moi t'embrasser.	Let me kiss you.

The audience of music hall performers and stagehands, particularly the female spectators, is hypnotized by Jane's performance. Four separate reaction shots reveal women mesmerized by Jane's antics; one strokes her feather boa absentmindedly, while another mechanically eats a chocolate bar.

The song recounts a *béguin* (crush) that begins promisingly, but ends violently, with the woman shooting her lover dead as he tries to leave her. It does not exactly illustrate what we have just seen on the stage, but rather predicts the outcome of the relationship between Bob and his former lover, Gaby. The link between Jane's emotions and her "authentic" expression of them made possible by her encounter with underworld masculinity is underscored in the sequence that takes place the following night during the opening performance of the revue.

Just before Jane's performance, Bob is shot dead in front of the music hall. The visually striking scene is filmed in low-key lighting, with an emphasis on the formal beauty of an iron fence nearby that casts shadows in the shapes of bars along the wall. The scene climaxes with Bob dying gracefully in Jane's arms beneath a huge, abstract poster of the music hall star resembling the art deco posters created for Mistinguett by Gesmar in the 1920s. A fade connects a shot of Jane cradling Bob in her arms to that of Jane cradling her stage lover during her performance a bit later in the music hall. She sings "I Have a Crush on You" for the second time, crying "genuine" tears. This time it is the well-to-do spectators who are transfixed by this expression of authentic emotion. We saw earlier how Jane's performance, infused through Bob with the virility and authenticity of the underworld, affected her fellow female music hall performers. Now this experience also filters to the bourgeois spectators of the modern music hall. Jane has taken the realist song from the seedy hotel room and the laundry to the music hall stage, recapturing, for a moment, the intimacy, the emotion, and the authenticity felt to be missing from the music hall experience.

Like *Faubourg Montmartre*, *Paris-Béguin* wants to give us both the frisson of the underworld and the sophistication of the music hall. Despite Jane's devastation, the show must go on, and here *Paris-Béguin* finally fulfills its other function: the celebration of the *music-hall à grand revue*. Jane pulls herself together and performs the final number, which features a troop of male chorus singers in top hats and tails, as well as women in evening gowns and feathers. Forming a glittering, colorful kaleidoscope, the dancers ascend and descend the huge staircase dominating the stage. Reversing the film's earlier ridicule of the music hall's artificiality and incompetence, this sequence celebrates its spectacular quality. Jane appears at the top of the staircase wearing an enormous feather headdress and sparkly black tights. She descends regally and sings the other song written for the film, "Paris-Béguin," in her quavering operetta soprano. In contrast to her performance of the realist song that elicited such intense involvement on the part of the internal spectators, this sequence eschews "reaction" shots of the audience, privileging instead a view of the performance consisting of frontally shot long takes.

In the logic of the film, then, it takes a sexual encounter with a "real" man, an emissary of the underworld defined in direct opposition to the aristocratic cuckold and the effeminate men of the glittering music hall world, to tap Jane's sexual potential. This process can be read as both a valorization of the exoticism and authenticity of the marginal people and spaces of Paris and a textual mechanism for containing the "woman on top." Jane's encounter with Bob can be read not only as a utopian sexual awakening, but also as a foreclosure of her position of control. If their "lovemaking" was a quasi-rape, the conquest is short-lived, according to the terms set by the man, for the morning after their encounter, Bob flirts with Jane's assistant, hinting that she will soon usurp a different male subjectivity: that of the cuckold, a figure once possessed of authority, but subsequently undermined.

LE BONHEUR

Le Bonheur (Marcel L'Herbier, 1934), offers a critique of the overarching ego and social power of a female music hall star. The film is an adaptation of boulevard playwright Henry Bernstein's melodrama *Le Bonheur*, created at the Théâtre du Gymnase in 1932 with Yvonne Printemps. In both the play and the film, Charles Boyer played a man of modest means who, disgusted by the cult of celebrity, shoots a star. He is convicted of the crime and spends time in prison. Upon release, the former anarchist and the star (played by Gaby Morlay in the film) fall in love. In Bernstein's play, the star is a theater actress. L'Herbier's film, which enjoyed critical and popular success, transforms Bernstein's theater star into a film star, thereby not only mounting a critique of the star system but characterizing the cinema as a hypnotizing, emasculating medium.

Philippe Lutcher (Boyer) is a caricaturist for *L'Anti-Sociale,* an "anarchist, revolutionary" newspaper. He is assigned to sketch the arrival at the train station of the film star Clara Stuart, just back from Hollywood. That night, Philippe attends Clara's singing performance, given before the screening of her latest film. Wearing a feathered costume connoting excessive luxury, the prima donna sings a waltz about the fragility and happiness of love to enthralled, mute spectators.[25] The number is edited in a highly fragmented fashion, revealing images of Clara from a number of different angles. Clara's mesmerizing power is further emphasized in close-ups of

Philippe and Clara, which create the illusion that she is singing directly to him. Philippe is shown to experience, despite himself, the hypnotizing power of the star's performance.

The active spectator is thus transformed into the compliant spectator when the female singer appears. In depicting this, L'Herbier's film taps into a long tradition of ambivalence about the female singing star—a tradition we have traced back to the mid nineteenth century in Veuillot's condemnation and fascination with Thérésa. However, the opposition to the power held by the chanteuse has shifted somewhat. Veuillot was afraid that Thérésa would incite unrest, that her working-class "aggression" would spill out into the streets or contaminate the bourgeois strata, and bourgeois women in particular. Here, we have a critique of the female star's ability to paralyze the male spectator and render him apolitical. This critique conforms to the views expressed by Pierre Bost's *Le Cirque et le music-hall,* which celebrates the lowly circus acrobat while excoriating the new female music hall star (Mistinguett, in particular). *Le Bonheur* updates Bost's lament, criticizing both the power of the diva in live performance and the cinematic apparatus (its star system, its publicity apparatus, its hypnotic power over its spectators, and its highly rationalized spectacle of technology and dehumanized performers).

In the sequence following Clara's performance, Philippe attempts to murder her. His motive, he explains at his trial, was the desire to commit an anti-social act by killing a powerful person. He reasoned that in today's world, the contemporary figure whose murder would garner maximum publicity was not the traditional holder of power, the politician, for example, but the new idol: the film star. However, once in the theater, he finds himself transfixed by Clara, transformed from anarchist to compliant spectator. This potentially subversive theme in *Le Bonheur*—the protest against the paralyzing neutralization of the anarchist—is neutralized itself, as we shall see, by the end of the film.

Just as Philippe has been unexpectedly touched by Clara, Clara is now strangely attracted to Philippe. She testifies at his trial, begging the judge to show mercy. Philippe spends a few years in prison, then is united with Clara on release. Their passion flourishes until Clara decides to make a film chronicling Philippe's attempt on her life and their subsequent love. Philippe protests that the story is his. Responding that it is her story too, she proceeds to make the film in secret.

He leaves her, but not explicitly for her appropriation of their private love story for a narrative destined for the mass audience, as one would expect. Oddly, he explains that he is abandoning Clara because he realizes that her ex-husband, a minor character played by Jaque Catelain, still loves and needs her. He leaves Clara not with bitterness, but with tenderness and self-sacrifice, asking only that she direct her special "look" at him while singing in her films, a look he will recognize, he tells her. The final image is a close-up of Philippe gazing lovingly at Clara up on the screen, presumably imagining that she is singing directly to him. The representation of Clara singing in a film at the end of *Le Bonheur* replicates her earlier mesmerizing effect, depicted in the live performance shown at the beginning of the film. Whether in the music hall or the cinema, *Le Bonheur* implies, female performance possesses an overwhelming and destabilizing power, rendering spectators mute, incapable, apolitical.

Like *Paris-Béguin*, *Le Bonheur* celebrates the male protagonist with ties to *le peuple* at the expense of other, feminized male characters, and especially at the expense of the female protagonist possessed of wealth and power. Although Philippe is not, properly speaking, a proletarian figure— he's a trained lawyer and painter turned anarchist—he is nonetheless aligned with the working class through his humble surroundings and in his oppositional stance to the power structure of his society, incarnated in the dominant cinema idol. Clara's manager (Michel Simon) and husband (Jaque Catelain) are "inadequate" men: Simon's character is ridiculed for his homosexuality, and Catelain plays an idle, impoverished aristocrat. Just as in *Paris-Béguin*, in *Le Bonheur* a female star is flanked by a homosexual and a compliant aristocrat in order to highlight the virility of the proletarian-identified male. Likewise, Philippe is posited as an "authentic" man, sensitive to his surroundings, whereas Clara is egotistical and artificial.

Le Bonheur's construction of gender is unusual not only on the thematic level but also in terms of its visual style. During the sequence in which Clara performs live, the film's representation of her as object of desire is fairly conventional: her body is fragmented, and lighting and costumes abet a process of fetishization. But Philippe is framed in a fashion usually reserved for female characters in the classical film. In this, and many other sequences, his face is filmed in lengthy, filtered close-ups as he watches Clara, enthralled. Moreover, the close-ups that align their gazes are highly ambiguous. Philippe's gaze is not the masculine look that "freezes" the body of a woman, reducing her to an erotic image. It is a gaze connoting subjugation and disorientation. Clara's gaze, directed at Philippe through the editing, reduces him, as well as the other spectators, to paralysis. He is revealed to be "too close" to the image, reflecting the more traditional construct of the woman's "excessive" proximity to the image, taken up by Mary Ann Doane in her defining study of the woman's film.[26]

Although it would be rash to infer that its "feminization" of a masculine character in this manner functions to overturn the gender hierarchy that traditionally accords men primacy, we can, nonetheless, identify in *Le Bonheur* an important disruption in the codes of gender coding. A norm has been disturbed on the level of the visual organization of the gaze and in terms of cinematography, and this coincides with the film's unusual portrayal of a socially powerful female protagonist. The scenario of alienation represented in *Le Bonheur* operates further in opposition to what Dudley Andrew identifies as the more prevalent tendency in French cinema at this time:

> Through the direct address of stars, the cinema evoked the memory of simpler forms of pleasure, of a lost community surrounding street singers, of revelers at spontaneous outdoor stage shows, of good times in the army, and so forth. As France's economic and international situation grew more disturbing; as its increasingly urban populace became more alienated, the cinema conveyed the security of a former identity, the persistence of an endless *belle époque*.[27]

The effect of Gaby Morlay's Clara could hardly be more different from the impact of Odette Barencey's presence in *Faubourg Montmartre* or Fréhel's nostalgic presence in *Pépé le Moko, L'Entraîneuse,* and *Coeur de Lilas*. Rather than transport her spectators back in time to an imaginary space of community and melancholy, Clara isolates them in a cold, mechanized relationship with her image. *Le Bonheur's* internal spectators, far from interacting with the singer, as the laundresses did in *Zouzou*, are hypnotized and mute.

In sum, in 1930s French film, the character of the music hall queen constitutes a rich site of anxieties and desires centered around gender and class issues. As we have seen in the four films discussed above, the music hall queen is used as a vehicle through which the music hall as institution is simultaneously celebrated and criticized. These films reveal her impossible will to "have it all." In *Zouzou, Paris-Béguin,* and *Le Bonheur,* the star wants both the glamour and social power (denied to the lowly realist singer figure in 1930s films) *and* the intimacy, authenticity, and underworld allure of the realist singer's universe.[28]

Ultimately, the trajectory of realist values (working-class camaraderie, authenticity, and so on) mapped in these four films is not haphazard. In the first, *Faubourg Montmartre,* this impulse resides in a historical realist singer (Odette Barencey). Next, in *Zouzou,* the realist tradition is embodied by a male-female duo (Baker and Gabin). In the third film, *Paris-Béguin,* it is invoked by the figure of a woman (Marnac) liberated by the intervention of a man, when a virile, underclass gangster transmits his "realist" values to a frigid, unaffecting artist, thawing her innate expressive self, which she then takes to the music hall stage. Finally, *Le Bonheur* locates its realist values squarely in the character of a man, who cannot, in the end, successfully transfer them to the woman. This trajectory not only leads further and further away from the thrilling, communal dynamism of the underworld toward the dehumanized, spellbinding attractions of the music hall and the cinema, it also displaces the woman. The idealized images of prostitutes and laundresses generating female performance for a female community in *Faubourg Montmartre* and *Zouzou* give way to the construction of male spectatorship evident in the classic fetishization and objectification of the spectacular image of women *(Zouzou* and *Paris-Béguin)*, and, finally, to the disenfranchisement of both the internal male spectator and the female star *(Le Bonheur)*.

The mechanized version of the female star, as we shall see in the next chapter, inscribes male spectatorship in an uneasy vis-à-vis with the image of the female performer, already evident in the system of gazes between the protagonists of *Le Bonheur,* not only foregrounding the anxiety that transgressive female spectacle produces in men but generating an ominous tension around how that anxiety is resolved.

Edith Piaf, Polydor
Catalogue, February 1936,
"A Singer Who Lives Her Song."
Author's collection.

Lucienne Boyer,
Columbia Catalogue,
August–September 1935.
Author's collection.

Lys Gauty, sheet music for "Le Bonheur est entré dans mon coeur" from the film *La Goualeuse.* Author's collection.

"Chansons de Films" listing in mid-1930s record company catalogue. Author's collection.

"La Nouvelle Chanson de Thérésa" caricature by André Gill, *La Lune*, September 9, 1866. © Roger-Viollet.

Folies-Bergère (date unknown). © Roger-Viollet.

Yvette Guilbert, 1890s.
© Roger-Viollet.

Mistinguett, queen of the music hall, final number of revue
"Féerie de Paris," Casino de Paris, December 1937. © Roger-Viollet.

Mistinguett and Max
Dearly in "La Danse
du pavé," a version
of the apache dance.
© Roger-Viollet.

Rigolboche
(Christian Jaque, 1936),
poster for film, with
Mistinguett. Courtesy
Bibliothèque nationale
de France.

"Valse chavirée: Étude réaliste,"
performed by Fréhel, 1910,
sheet music. © Éditions Fortin.

Fréhel, late 1930s. Courtesy
Bibliothèque nationale de France.

Pépé le Moko (Julien Duvivier, 1936), Lucas Gridoux and Fréhel.
Courtesy Bibliothèque du film.

Coeur de Lilas
(Anatole Litvak, 1931),
sheet music for "Dans la
rue," performed by
Fréhel in the film.
Courtesy Bibliothèque
nationale de France.

Coeur de Lilas (Anatole Litvak, 1931), Fréhel and Jean Gabin.
Courtesy Bibliothèque du film.

L'Entraîneuse (Albert Valentin, 1938), Fréhel. Courtesy Bibliothèque du film.

La Revue des revues, film directed by Alex Nalpas and Joé Francis, 1927.
Courtesy Bibliothèque nationale de France.

Mistinguett at the A.B.C. music hall, 1937. © Roger-Viollet.

Faubourg Montmartre (Raymond Bernard, 1931), with Line Noro and Gaby Morlay. Courtesy Bibliothèque du film.

Zouzou (Marc Allégret, 1934), Josephine Baker sings to the laundresses.
Courtesy Bibliothèque du film.

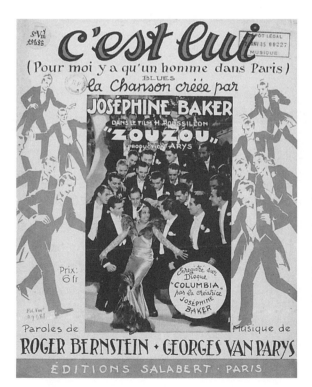

Zouzou
(Marc Allégret, 1934),
sheet music for
"C'est lui," performed
by Josephine Baker
in the film. Courtesy
Bibliothèque
nationale de France.

Paris-Béguin (Augusto Genina, 1931), with Fernandel, Gaby Morlay, and Jean Gabin. Courtesy Bibliothèque du film.

Paris-Béguin (Augusto Genina, 1931), poster featuring Gaby Morlay. Courtesy Bibliothèque nationale de France.

Le Bonheur (Marcel L'Herbier, 1934), Charles Boyer, mesmerized by the *chanteuse*. Courtesy Bibliothèque du film.

Damia, 1930s.
Courtesy Bibliothèque
nationale de France.

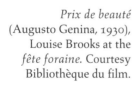

La Tête d'un homme (Julien Duvivier, 1932), Damia. Courtesy Bibliothèque du film.

Prix de beauté
(Augusto Genina, 1930),
Louise Brooks at the
fête foraine. Courtesy
Bibliothèque du film.

Prix de beauté (Augusto Genina, 1930), Louise Brooks as "Miss France." Courtesy Bibliothèque du film.

Prix de beauté (Augusto Genina, 1930), Louise Brooks in the final scene. Courtesy Bibliothèque du film.

Edith Piaf on stage
near the end of her life.
Author's collection.

La Garçonne (Jean de Limur, 1936), Edith Piaf as lesbian *chanteuse*.
Courtesy Bibliothèque nationale de France.

5 · Violent Spectatorship

Mechanical Reproduction, the Female Voice, and the Imaginary of Intimacy

In *L'Atalante* (Jean Vigo, 1934), a film now legendary for its aesthetic innovation and its realistic, yet magical images of working-class life, there are two scenes in which the recorded and broadcast human voice functions as a key causal element in the narrative. Juliette, a young bride who sails the canals in a barge with her husband, is irresistibly drawn to Paris when she hears a radio announcer reporting on the latest fashions. Soon thereafter, on an impulse, she steals away from her husband's barge to explore the city. He sails off, abandoning her, and is subsequently miserable with longing and regret. The two are eventually reunited through the magical intervention of his shipmate Père Jules and a popular record. Juliette now works at a Pathé Chansons Palace (Song Palace), where people listen to records on an early form of the jukebox while wearing headphones. The song palace is emblematic of the kind of media experience one could have in modern 1930s Paris.[1] It was a public space but did not offer live performance such as that found in the music hall or in the *guingette*, seen in an earlier sequence in *L'Atalante*. The Chansons Palace offers music, although music mediated by technology. Initially, the scene underscores the loneliness of modern urban life, and indicates how technology serves to undermine community. Here, music is offered in a public space, yet the earphones isolate people from one another. Juliette, clearly miserable and lonely, puts on "Chanson des Mariniers" (Song of the Bargemen), a song that she and her husband had sung together on the barge in happier times. The song is broadcast onto the street by a loudspeaker and, improbably, heard by Père Jules, who just happens to be strolling by. The song draws him into the Chansons Palace, where he finds Juliette. They return to the barge, where she is reunited with her husband and all is forgiven. *L'Atalante*'s optimistic vision of the intersection of modern technology, recorded music, and femininity is quite rare; 1930s French films were more likely to posit a troubling relationship between the technologies of mechanical reproduction and the female voice, a relationship that is the topic of this chapter.

The poet Léon-Paul Fargue complained in 1938 that the language used by Aristide Bruant had disappeared.[2] Due to the radio and the record, he laments, the nineteenth arrondissement is starting to resemble every other arrondissement in Paris: "The tripe butchers . . . the extras at the [Théâtre des] Bouffes du Nord [on the boulevard de la Chapelle], those who work on the canals, the wine merchants of the quai de l'Oise and the mechanics of the place de Joinville are for comfort and do not disdain to listen to *Faust* or to Beethoven's *Ninth* when their dumpy, greasy loudspeakers vomit out good music."[3]

"Street musicians are disappearing," *Paris-Soir* complained in January 1930; "people have no time to listen, the traffic makes it awkward to hear. Gramophones first, then radios cut into the street musicians' audience."[4]

Is Anouk Adelmann correct in arguing that modern public address systems, with their microphones and tinny, disembodied echoes, had invented a new mode of listening, just as the photograph and the cinema offered new modes of seeing?[5] This suggests, as we began to see in the case of *Le Bonheur*, not only a new relationship between performer and audience, but also a change in the response to that new, electronic voice. On the one hand, there is an imagined intimacy of address: Charles Boyer's character in *Le Bonheur* not only believes that the woman is singing exclusively, directly to him, he is encouraged by her to believe this. One casualty of this intimacy, however, is loss of the community, of a shared listening, that was a key element of the nostalgia and appeal of the café-concert and the realist aesthetic. Despite the imaginary of intimacy, of individual address, new technologies of recorded or cinematic entertainment undeniably placed a greater distance between the performer and her audience, whether through the intermediary of projected shadows or amplified signals. Adelmann characterizes this new regime of listening as one in which audience members no longer sing along with the performer. The audience are now "impotent, with only their vocal chords to compete with the magnetic echo."[6]

Without carrying the Freudian implications of this characterization to absurd lengths, the question arises, nonetheless, of how this effect of distance or powerlessness is articulated in the case of female performance, and to what extent it is projected on the woman herself. In *Le Bonheur*, Philippe is overcome by the impulse to lash out at a powerful person after he sees Clara perform. The anxiety provoked by independent and sexually aggressive *réaliste* performers and by the threat of an unconstrained sense of community among unruly women is amplified as the modes of their production become associated with the threat of new technology, emblemized first by the music hall and subsequently by the talkies. Certain 1930s films foreground female performance, associating it with female mobility, whether social or technological, and with male powerlessness and anxiety. The imaginary of intimacy becomes an imaginary of distance, isolation, and impotence; an unstable psychic state from which, more often than not, a violent impulse must erupt. The figure of Damia in *La Tête d'un homme* (Julien Duvivier, 1932), *Sola* (Henri Diamant-Berger, 1931), and Louise Brooks's performance in *Prix de beauté* (Augusto Genina, 1930) suggest a far more disturbing response to the incarnation of the realist singer than we have seen thus far, one that is linked specifically to modern technologies of reproduction: the phonograph and the sound cinema.

LA TÊTE D'UN HOMME

Julien Duvivier was attuned to the power of the realist singer as a potent symbol of the past. But long before he made *Pépé le Moko*, Duvivier cast another realist singer in a 1932 film about a criminal figure and impossible desire. *La Tête d'un homme*, an unjustly neglected early sound film adapted from the novel by Georges Simenon, tells the story of a murder, the ensuing bribery and psychological manipulation of the man who commissioned it, and the sexual obsession experienced by the killer for a woman who remains inaccessible to him. The killer, an impoverished and embittered Czechoslovakian medical student named Radek (Valéry Inkijinoff), murders a wealthy elderly woman in her home, then bribes the man who hired him to commit the murder, the old woman's playboy nephew Willy Ferrière (Gaston Jacquet). Radek is obsessed with Ferrière's girlfriend, Edna (Gina Manès). Commissaire Maigret of the *police judiciaire* (Harry Baur) investigates the crime.

La Tête d'un homme anticipates poetic realism in terms of its narrative and visual style. The plot chronicles a murder, a police investigation, a male protagonist's obsession with a woman and his subsequent downfall, as in *La Bête humaine* and *Le Jour se lève*. The film's visual style is edgy and varied, containing smoky, shadowy interiors, mobile framing, and contemplative, lengthy close-ups of characters' faces. The interiors mix art deco décor reminiscent of late 1920s French cinema with the cafés and furnished rooms of the realist song and 1930s poetic realism. The sound track, dense and multilayered for an early sound film, has much in common with the sound in Grémillon's *La Petite Lise* and Renoir's *La Chienne*, other innovative early sound films. Here too diegetic music is used not only to establish verisimilitude but to punctuate moments of emotional and psychological intensity. Like so many poetic realist films, *La Tête d'un homme* features a realist singer.

Next door to Radek, the murderer, lives a mysterious woman who sings, unseen by Radek (or by the film's spectators), in a plaintive, broken voice. The singing neighbor is played by the realist singer Damia (Marie-Louise Damien, 1892–1978), Fréhel's direct contemporary. Simenon's novel contains no such character; Duvivier, like so many other 1930s film directors, inserted the character of the realist singer and even wrote the lyrics of her song. Here, Damia helps to establish *La Tête d'un homme*'s urban texture and to bring into relief the bleak existences lived out in cheap, furnished rooms. Moreover, she haunts Radek throughout the film, exacerbating his obsession with Edna. Damia's name appears at end of the credit sequence, after the names of the more prominent film actors Harry Baur, Gina Manès, and Valéry Inkijinoff. Her character remains nameless; she is called, simply, *la femme lasse*, the weary woman. As is so often the case with the realist singer's film appearances, Damia's symbolic importance in the narrative far outweighs her actual screen time. Her visual presence is, moreover, far exceeded in importance by her aural presence in the film.

Damia sings a fragment of a song written in the realist style in *La Tête d'un homme* that reaches us in several different ways and with increasing intensity. We first hear her singing voice during the credit sequence, which gives way to the aggressive sounds of car engines and honking in nocturnal Montparnasse, sounds that also served to establish the urban context of Faubourg Montmartre. Next, there is a close-up of a street singer performing in front of the café. She is played by a real 1930s chanteuse named Simone Missia, and serves to foreshadow Damia's importance in *La Tête d'un homme*.[7] The film's narrative of crime and obsession is overlaid with the Montparnasse setting, still associated in the early 1930s with Man Ray and Kiki, café life, and libertine sexuality. This setting, in its evocation of a modern bohemia, thus constitutes an updating of the apache culture of the exterior boulevards.[8] The realist song, while still considered appropriate for the evocation of this updated milieu, takes on a different function, as we shall see.

We hear Damia's voice for the second time in Radek's apartment after the murder has occurred and Commissaire Maigret has come to investigate. Radek stares intently into the camera in a static medium shot, listening to the voice of his neighbor. He does not even know what she looks like, he tells

Maigret, and does not want to know her. "I know her through listening to her. . . . I put a face onto this voice. The face of someone. "

The notion that Radek's neighbor possesses a voice with hypnotic power would have seemed perfectly understandable to the viewers of the film, who were also undoubtedly fans of Damia. Damia began singing in music halls in 1911. Like Yvette Guilbert and Eugénie Buffet before her, Damia performed both literary songs written by poets (Jules Jouy's "La Veuve" [The Widow] and Verlaine's "D'une prison" [From a Prison], for example) and the "worst romances of the beuglant."[9] Damia was also known for her performances of authentic sailor songs. Her biggest hit was "Les Goëlands" (The Seagulls), a song about the death of sailors at sea.

Damia was praised for her sculptural body, her muscular, expressive arms, and her powerful voice. Her star image relied somewhat less heavily on her private life as an "intertext" than those of the other realist singers did.[10] What we do know about her, we owe to critics and enthusiasts of the period, rather than to industry-generated star biographies. According to the music hall historian Pierre Philippe, everyone from conservative war veterans to homosexuals revered her.[11] In histories of music hall, she is always credited with bringing the principles of mise-en-scène to the tour de chant, applying the lessons she learned about lighting while touring with Loïe Fuller during World War I. Her use of high-contrast lighting in her music hall performances, combined with her trademark sleeveless black velvet dress, produced a stark, dramatic staging.

Like all of the realist singers, Damia brought to her films specific connotations relating to the Parisian *peuple* and to specific Parisian spaces. One writer (perhaps Gustave Fréjaville, a distinguished critic of the newspaper *Paris-Midi* and one of Damia's most fervent admirers) associates her with the desolate space of the military fortifications just beyond the *barrières* of Paris: "She is the Eve whose sin gave birth to our punishment, she is the sentimental, lovesick seamstress, she is the girl from the city ramparts whose male terrifies her, she is the murderess, haunted by remorse, she is the hustler, she is Nana with spirit. She is all of that because she believes herself all of that, because she believes in all of that."[12] Another contemporary critic, Georges Saint-Bonnet, places her in the mythology around the Parisian *faubourgs:* "Damia expresses, with this sort of tragic morbidness so often exploited since Carco, all the poetry of the troubled, shady, uncertain, often unhealthy, but always profoundly human existences that swarm in the *faubourgs.*"[13] For the historian Louis Chevalier, Damia symbolized Montmartre. In his sprawling history of that *quartier*, Chevalier writes that his memory of seeing Damia perform "seems to sum up and resuscitate, to capture the *fête* of these years [the mid 1930s]."[14] He recounts that Damia "occupied an immense place" in his life from 1934 on. Chevalier and his friends, fellow students from the prestigious École normale supérieur, formed an informal fan club devoted to Damia. Calling themselves *les Damiaques*, they played her records, watched her perform at the Européen music hall, and even followed her after performances down the boulevard Clichy to a bar where she customarily had a drink with a friend.[15]

Damia's singing voice was considered imperfect, but extremely charismatic:

> Damia starts to sing. The diction is strongly marked, the articulation almost brutal. The voice is deep, almost hollow; I won't hide that she sings through her nose at times and surprises the ear with sudden defects, followed by abrupt starts that owe nothing to the methods of any classical training. But soon she warms up, raises her voice, sweeps her arms outward, exalts in piercing shrieks, chokes sobs like gravel carried downstream by the current. . . . She also knows how to make herself infantile and languorous, to soften herself in murmurs, to melt into sighs. A voice no doubt difficult to classify, whose rich and deep cello tones ally themselves with the lament of the oboe or the call of the French horn. When Damia lives her songs, the very flaws of this voice add to the pathos of her oratory and gestures. One could not imagine a more perfect harmony.[16]

The avant-garde composer Darius Milhaud described Damia in similar terms as "a *tragedienne* who doesn't let a word go until she's expressed it thoroughly, she bites the phrases she sings, she makes the sounds that she pulls from her throat weep, a type of dramatic baritone ready to tighten around our throats like a sob."[17] Other critics indicate a rough, hard quality to Damia's voice. Words like "brutal" and "hoarse" come up repeatedly. The body—either Damia's or that of her listener—is constantly emphasized. Henri Béraud wrote of

> her famous voice, made of a sob and of a revolt—this voice that has nothing of the professional singer about it, nor even the voice of the *diseuse*, this true voice of flesh, made through and through of the breath of woman, a voice that delivers the very tone of a being, and that groans or cries, knowing only how to stretch itself to the limits of our anguish, to break without fail at the moment when our resistance exhausts itself.[18]

This "voice of flesh" had, in turn, a direct and profound effect on the bodies of Damia's listeners. "[E]lle touche l'auditeur tout droit, à la poitrine ou au ventre [She hits the listener head on, in the chest or gut]."[19]

Damia was born on the rue Jeanne d'Arc in the working-class thirteenth arrondissement of Paris.[20] Raised in Lorraine in a family of eight children by a strict police sergeant, she ran away from home at the age of fifteen after a brush with reform school. She went to Paris, worked as a model in Montmartre, and found bit parts at the Théâtre du Châtelet. In 1910, at the age of seventeen, she danced the *valse chaloupée* with Max Dearly in London. She began to sing on the advice of Roberty, Fréhel's impresario husband, and debuted at the Pépinière in 1911.[21] Next, still only nineteen years old, she performed at the prestigious Alhambra. She went on to perform in all of the major music halls in the following years, including the Ambassadeurs, Casino de Paris, Bobino, Olympia, Palace, Européen, Empire, and Folies-Bergère. During World War I, she sang at the front.

After the war, Damia toured with Loïe Fuller, performing patriotic songs. Fuller taught her to incorporate a sophisticated use of lighting and spotlights into her performance. Damia altered the traditional mise-en-scène of the tour de chant in another way by substituting a simple black curtain for the traditional painted backdrop, which typically represented the Temple de l'Amour at the Trianon or the fountains of Versailles.

The popular press usually described Damia as a realist singer and spoke of her in connection with Fréhel and Yvonne George, but some critics insisted that she transcended the category. Fréjaville claimed, "Damia n'est plus une chanteuse réaliste: c'est une grande tragédienne [Damia is no longer a realist singer, she's a great tragedienne]."[22] Like Buffet, Guilbert, and Mistinguett, then, Damia was both of the *peuple* and an artiste in her own category. She knew how to elevate the tawdry *fait divers* (short news item) to a virtuoso feat.[23] The perception that Damia transcended the category of realist singer allowed critics to embrace her even as they rejected the realist song as a genre.

Contradictions abound both in the critical discourse surrounding Damia and in the persona she mobilized. She is masculine and feminine; classical and modern. First, her physical power is emphasized: "the powerful head," "this first impression of tranquil force." But these "masculine" terms are quickly balanced by discussion of her charming, feminine smile. Her virile grace reminds one of the "beautiful figures of the Italian Renaissance," and her eyes are those of an "androgynous Bacchus," yet her smile is "adorably modern."

The emphasis on Damia's physicality runs through much of the discourse on the realist singer. The dance critic André Levinson's compared Damia to "a fairground boxer in repose."[24] Louis Chevalier also linked the realist singers with boxers, perceiving in Fréhel's liaison with a boxing promoter in the mid 1920s a synthesis of the two grand passions of the people of Montmartre: boxing and the realist song.[25] Both the boxer and the realist singer, he noted, meted out violence: "Two kinds of violence fairly similar to each other: the blow from the mouth [*coup de gueule*] and the blow of the fist to the stomach [*coup de poing à l'estomac*], not to mention the powerful arms of the realist singers, the arms of Damia, and the biceps of Fréhel, which everyone was allowed to touch."[26] This notion not only excavates the undercurrent of violence that circulates in certain cinematic representations of the realist singer but also suggests an ambivalence on the part of the audience, which seeks out two forms of popular entertainment, one violent on the surface, the other analogous in terms of its latent revolt. What lies beneath the realist singer's codified performance is, we are to believe, far more threatening.

Damia connotes the psychological as well as the physical: "Damia does not describe, she lives. Her commentary is all psychological and interior. She translates the movements of her soul into stylized gestures and synthetic poses."[27] Her "interiority" makes her the perfect sound track to Radek's obsession in *La Tête d'un homme*. Her haunting voice and repeated performances of the same song function both as a partial explanation for Radek's madness and an evocation of his experience of that madness.

As the film progresses, Radek becomes increasingly obsessed with Ferrière's lover, Edna. We first encounter Edna in a Montparnasse café where Ferrière secretly makes contact with Radek to arrange the murder. There are two distinctive shots of Edna in this scene. First, she scans the café in a lengthy point-of-view shot, attempting to figure out what Ferrière is planning. Next, there is a close-up of her face, smiling knowingly. She looks around actively, aggressively, in order to interpret what is happening and store it away for future advantage. Later in the film, she is dubbed "une femme exigeante" (a demanding woman), and we are eventually led to understand that Ferrière ordered his aunt's murder because he needs money to maintain the materialistic Edna in style. When Radek attempts to bribe him after the murder, the indecisive and weak Ferrière freezes. Edna, nonplussed, takes over the negotiations with Radek. Ferrière, increasingly ineffectual, commits suicide when his arrest is imminent. Significantly, the textual force of this emasculating feminine figure is shared by two women in *La Tête d'un homme*: Edna and Damia.

Damia's third performance occurs at the film's climax. Radek has finally managed to coerce the object of his obsession, Edna, into his room. This, he says, is the moment he has dreamed of every night watching Edna at the Eden, a Montparnasse nightclub. He rips off her coat and begins to assault her. Damia's off-screen singing voice then penetrates Radek's room. Until this scene, Damia has served as an aural displacement for an unspecific, idealized woman, a repository for Radek's despair and rage over a woman he cannot have. Now, he makes explicit the fact that all this time, Edna has been the visual analogue of Damia's voice. "J'ai mis ton image sur la voix de cette femme qui vit là et tout le temps, j'ai rêvé que tu chantais pour moi. Pour moi. Pauvre Radek [I superimposed your image on the voice of that woman who lives there and always dreamed that you were singing for me. For me. Poor Radek]." In connecting Damia's voice with Edna's face, Radek engages in a metaphorical operation akin to dubbing. In a quasi-directorial role, Radek creates his dream woman, fusing the voice of one with the body of the other, as it were. This "merging" of the two characters is underscored by their resemblance to each other. Though Damia was brunette and Manès blond, both had strong, broad features and sculptural figures.[28] One way Damia functions, then, is as the aural component of Radek's obsession, "Edna displaced."

Once again, as in *Le Bonheur*, we have a male auditor who imagines for himself an intimate narrative with respect to an idealized singer. Again, that fantasy, and the repeated isolation that the mechanized, disembodied voice imposes on him, incites the male figure to violence. Radek forces Edna into Damia's room next door, as if hoping to unite his fantasy female voice and body at last. Curiously, when we are finally granted a glimpse of the mysterious Damia, we discover how little the fantasy corresponds with reality—a reality that refers back to more classical representations of the realist singer. Through a haze of cigarette smoke, Radek and the film's spectators see Damia for the first and only time. She is centered in the frame in a medium shot, sitting on a bed with her back against the wall in a dim room crowded with drunken, down-and-out revelers. She looks depressed and seems distanced from the revelry around her. Radek, Edna, and the other people in the room crowd the edges of the frame, leaving a small performance space for Damia. Accompanied by a phonograph that is on the bed next to her, Damia sings a portion of the song that has been haunting Radek throughout the film:

Toute est brume et tout est gris	All is mist and all is gray
Sans tendresse.	Without tenderness.
J'ai . . . mon destin	I have . . . my fate
. . . et la nuit m'envahit . . .	. . . and the night invades me . . .

As she repeats the final words of the song, "et la nuit m'envahit/tout est brume, tout est gris," a close-up reveals Damia framed by photographs of

men. We can assume that they are former lovers—lovers who have aban
doned her, conquests of an earlier time, when she might have exerted the
same physical magnetism that her detached voice is still capable of producing. It is the classic trope of the realist singer, immortalized by Fréhel in
Pépé le Moko.

Both the phonograph and the photographs in this scene reinforce the
sense of nostalgia and the feeling of loss: loss of looks, loss of lovers. As in
Pépé le Moko, both the record and the photograph (of a younger Fréhel)
preserve the idealized version of the singer. Both technologies are thus
shown to be capable of generating modern anxiety, when divorced from the
humanity of their earlier context: the café-concert, the community of a
marginal working-class that, despite social obstacles, looked after its own.

The phonograph and the photographs merely extend the film's obsession
with presence and absence, the copy and the original, and loss. Damia's body
remains motionless throughout the sequence, as if paralyzed by the weight
of her cares. She closes her eyes, then stares into the distance, her brow
creased with despair. The disembodied singer finally attains a bodily presence, only not in the body the voice-fantasy evoked. As static as this mise-
en-scène of Damia may appear, the power of the detached voice points to a
woman with far greater mobility, the ambitious Edna. This moment revealing Damia's "presence," so long awaited in the film, is ultimately unfulfill-
ing, both for Radek and the spectator, as reality and fantasy confront one
another violently. Upon seeing and hearing Damia, Radek is driven to
greater madness; he attempts to rape Edna, then stabs a detective to death.
When the audience finally see Damia, with a heightened sense of anticipation produced by the film's narrative and extratextual connotations, they
are, doubtless, disappointed. The film's "internal" audience of rowdy drunks
crowd the frame, competing with Damia for centrality within it. Their
cries—and those of the neighbors, irritated by all the noise—drown out her
voice at first. The underlying message seems to be that the mechanized production of the voice, that is, modern entertainment, leads inevitably to dis-
proportionate expectations, if not outright, possibly violent, fantasy, and
that ultimately the content or human form behind this production is disil-
lusioning, if not entirely corrupt.

Damia's furnished room is a performance space of sorts, but one far
removed in tone from the music hall or even the warmth of the café-concert
stage. Much as in the scene in *Faubourg Montmartre* in which Odette
Barencey sings to the prostitutes seated around her, or the scene in *Dans les
rues* (Pierre Chenal, 1933) in which the realist singer Charlotte Dauvia sings
to a doomed young couple, Damia provides the film with a kind of private,

interiorized performance that constitutes a chorus about the bleak fate of the film's marginalized inhabitants.

The role of the urban milieu in Radek's demise is evident. Pursued by Maigret and his men, Radek stabs Maigret's assistant and then runs blindly into the street, where he is hit by a car. The aggressivity of another aural component of the film's world, that of the hectic city traffic, brings about his death. We hear Damia's song yet again as Radek dies under the car, muttering, "C'est moi . . . moi qui a tout combinée, tout executé. Moi, moi. Radek. C'est un beau crime, eh Commissaire? [It was I, I who planned everything, executed everything. Me, me. Radek. It was a beautiful crime, wasn't it, Commissaire?]" Radek insists that he is the executor of everything, but by the perverse effect of their identification through voice, Damia and Edna are shown to be the motors of the narrative, in the sense that they elicit his obsession. "If the performer of this melody had not been Damia, one might have said that she added nothing to the value of the film, but this sorrowful voice is all that is needed for the simple verses to become, on the contrary, a powerful dramatic element," one critic said of Damia's performance.[29]

For a time, it is as if the film cannot really "decide" what motive to assign to Radek's murder of the old woman or his manipulation of Ferrière and Edna. Class jealousy and hubris are Radek's ostensible motives, but it is ultimately Radek's obsession with a haughty, materialistic woman that serves as the primary force driving both him and the narrative. Damia's voice functions, I would argue, as the aural equivalent of Edna's inaccessibility. *La Tête d'un homme*'s placement of the realist singer in an alienating urban space creates, not a nostalgic vision of a working-class or criminal community, but a sinister world of cacophonous traffic, menacing foreigners, and demanding, knowing, inaccessible women. The realist singer's connotations, then, have shifted from community, nostalgia, and female solidarity to inaccessibility and obsession. Instead of establishing a connection between her audience and herself, the realist singer now evokes the idea of separation and distance: the separation of a performance from its generic context, the separation of the voice from the body, and the distance between the male auditor's fantasies and reality. The danger in the social mobility of women, it would appear, is the possibility that men will not find them safely contained within the bodies their male fantasies project.

SOLA

In Henri Diamant-Berger's *Sola*, the disembodied female voice of the realist singer once again has the power to undermine a man's sanity. Conceived for Damia, *Sola* chronicles the fall from glory experienced by a music hall singer and her demise at the hands of an obsessed fan. The film begins in a recording studio, where Sola, at the height of her fame, records a song called "Tu ne sais pas aimer" (You Don't Know How to Love).[30] The song, about a failed love affair, is addressed by a woman to her lover, whom she chastises for lacking the capacity for love. The film's opening scene emphasizes the modernity of the recording industry: the studio is decorated in sleek art deco style, and the sound technician and recording equipment are shown. The scene even contains a quasi-documentary in which the process of mass-producing records is explained. Technology is presumed to be a source of fascination for the spectator, but it will metamorphose into a threat for both the realist singer and one of her listeners.

Sola embarks on what is supposed to be a six-month world tour with her companion. However, while on the ship, her lover dies. Having left her jewels and money in her lover's safe, to which she is denied access after his death, Sola finds herself penniless and alone in Singapore. She sings at a run-down café-concert called the Café de Paris, trying to earn enough money to return to Paris. Drawing heavily upon the image of the abandoned, vagabond realist singer (particularly the image Fréhel nurtured), the film chronicles emotional loss, a decline in fortune, and exile.

Meanwhile, a Frenchman named Jeff embarks on a two-year stay at a plantation in Malaysia. He looks forward to enjoying his collection of French records, but his Hindu servant clumsily drops the box containing them, leaving only Sola's "Tu ne sais pas aimer" unbroken. He listens to her record repeatedly as he becomes increasingly isolated, homesick, and ill. As in *Pépé le Moko* and *Amok*, the female voice is associated with the heartbreak of exile and with a lost Paris, but here, as in *La Tête d'un homme*, there is the additional connotation of male madness and anxiety.[31] When two years have passed, Jeff heads back to Paris, but he first stops in Singapore to see Sola. His Hindu servant is uneasy with the presence of the phonograph on board the ship and claims that they are all doomed. "It's as if a woman is closed up in the box . . . the soul and the voice are separated. Throw the box in the sea before it's too late." The film gives explicit voice, through the figure of the "primitive," to the spiritual malaise technology engenders.

When Jeff arrives at his room at the Café de Paris, he brings out Sola's record and explains to a friend that it was his "only company" while in Singapore and, paradoxically, that Sola is "a real woman." He imagines that she is "beautiful" and "pure." His friend tries to explain that Sola is no longer beautiful and pure, but to no avail. They go to the bar, where they see

Sola sing "La Fille aux matelots" (The Sailors' Girl). Sola gives a raucous, vulgar performance, showing her legs to all the men in the bar. She is behaving this way, in fact, in an altruistic attempt to discourage the affection of an amorous younger man with whom one of Sola's friends is in love. Jeff calls Sola over and asks her to sing the song on his record, "Tu ne sais pas aimer." She is drunk (or pretends to be, perhaps) but begins to sing anyway. Shots of various spectators gazing at Sola reveal fascination, even a kind of hypnosis among the audience. However, Sola interrupts her singing abruptly and lets out a horrible laugh, before continuing to sing unsteadily while sitting in the lap of an old man. This was a marked departure from the classicism and tragic dignity Damia usually evoked in her singing performances, described earlier.

Jeff is horrified as Sola then dances with a sailor, laughs coarsely, and orders more drinks. When he tries to speak with her at the bar, she laughs and sings mockingly to him. Outraged, he pounces on Sola, screaming, "You will no longer soil your voice. . . . This voice that I love" and then abruptly strangles her to death. A crowd gathers, whereupon he flees to his room and plays Sola's record once more. When the police come to arrest him, he shoots himself off-screen, while Sola's voice on the phonograph continues to sing. The mechanically reproduced female voice preserves not only the idealized youth of the *chanteuse réaliste*, as we saw in *Pépé le Moko*, it survives her entirely.

Tragically, Jeff makes the mistake of believing that Sola's persona in the song "Tu ne sais pas aimer" is the real Sola. The shock of the contrast between the Sola of his imagination and the actual Sola performing, apparently drunk and flirtatious, completes his breakdown. Like Fréhel in *Coeur de Lilas*, Damia offers a vision of a woman's sexual autonomy, yet as in the case of Fréhel, it does not extend past the performance space. While Sola has the power to take on the identity of a drunken reveler to suit her purposes, she does not have the power or mobility in the narrative to escape her own destiny of loss, loneliness, and exile. Unlike Fréhel in *Pépé le Moko* and *Coeur de Lilas*, however, the narratives of Damia's films construct distance, by means of the technologically produced distance of the recorded voice, between what her fans (within the films) think she is and what she "really" is. In *La Tête d'un homme*, as we saw, Radek imagines what his singing neighbor is really like but avoids meeting her, which allows her singing to function all the more effectively as the sound track to his private agony. When he finally encounters Damia in the flesh, he, like Jeff in *Sola*, goes mad.

The critical reception of *Sola* was mixed. Contemporary critics recog-

nized the notion of a recording exerting a hallucinatory effect as a particu
larly modern scenario:

> The idea is that a gramophone disc can, in certain cases, take on its own exis-
> tence; that the mechanical voice acts on a man to the point of exerting over
> him the influence of a real presence, one artificially constructed by his imag-
> ination. In the past, in novels, we saw extravagant madmen walk the four cor-
> ners of the earth in search of the model for a statue or a portrait. Today, it is a
> sheet of black wax that serves to develop the illusion.[32]

However, the film's visual style, characterized by frontal, static shots against
flat, often black backgrounds, was criticized. Émile Vuillermoz condemned
the slow pace of all contemporary films, citing *Sola* as an example, yet he
admired the basic plot idea.[33] The influential fascist critic François Vinneuil,
for his part, was merciless:

> Of the cinematography, the actors, the mise-en-scène, it is impossible to say
> anything. Its incompetence is not even worth mentioning. There remains
> Damia. Dilettantes of the music hall whose taste we do not contest have cre-
> ated around her a fairly ingenious little mythology: humanity and tragedy in
> insignificant songs. It can be done. Personally, we don't like it very much. We
> argue only that Damia possesses enough tricks in her bag not to be worse
> than any other star in the studio, but she doesn't know how to adapt her stage
> routine to film. Go see instead the spontaneous reactions of Marlene Dietrich
> in front of the camera. There is someone who is lively and cinematic.[34]

Other critics, in fact, appear just as invested as the film's characters in
Damia's performance mythology: Philippe Soupault found that "Damia has
nothing of the actress about her. . . . Yet, cleverly, they have her sing often,
and there we discover once again the strange power of the *real* Damia"
(emphasis added).[35]

Sola contains a mixture of the old and the new: a melodramatic narrative,
the performance of Damia, a music hall star whose career began before
World War I, and the performance of songs whose style had been popular
for decades and would soon be overshadowed by newer currents, such as the
jazz-inflected melodies, clever wordplay, and sunny optimism of Charles
Trenet. But *Sola* also presents a fascination with the technology of contemporary sound recording, and a female character whose powerful, hypnotic
voice triggers male obsession. The realist singer—and all that she represents—is figured as so powerful that her effect extends well beyond the live
performance. Indeed, the message of both of these films suggests that the
threat she represents is contained by the live performance space, only posing
a threat when technology separates the voice from the body. Fetishization of

the voice, then, is dangerous when there is no visual field within which the gaze may frame the body.

PRIX DE BEAUTÉ

The most vivid representation of the connection between male anxiety and the recorded singing voice of the modern woman can be found in Augusto Genina's *Prix de beauté*. René Clair was initially slated to direct the film, but he stepped down after a dispute with the producers well into the project's development. Genina, a respected Italian director best known for his films featuring the diva Carmen Boni, replaced Clair. The production conditions of *Prix de beauté* were unusual. First planned as a silent film, then reconceived as a talkie, it was, nevertheless, shot silently and postsynchronized, allowing Genina an unusual freedom in camera movement.[36] The film was both critically and commercially successful; its mixture of dialogue, noise, and song was especially admired. "The score, composed judiciously, supports the images quite well. The lines are concise, reduced to their essentials, generally expressive enough not to give the impression of 'filling.' In any case, very little appears superfluous or insufficient."[37]

Louise Brooks, appearing in her only French film, plays Lucienne, a secretary who wins a beauty contest. Brooks exuded modernity in the late 1920s and early 1930s. She was American, she wore her hair in the quintessentially modern hairstyle, the bob,[38] and she had just embodied Weimar Germany's modern woman in G. W. Pabst's *Pandora's Box* (1929) and *Diary of a Lost Girl* (1929). Brooks's character in *Prix de beauté* provides a sharp contrast to Fréhel and Damia, with her bobbed hair, cloche hats, love of women's fashion magazines, and secretary's job. This chanteuse is an ambitious member of the modern workforce, not a denizen of the underworld. Although the milieu in *Prix de beauté* is quite different from that represented in *Coeur de Lilas, Faubourg Montmartre*, and *La Tête d'un homme*, the female singer nevertheless still functions as a symbol of the malaise around gender relations and the transformation of Parisian working-class culture. If Damia's film appearances in *Sola* and *La Tête d'un homme* constitute the beginning of a shift in the representation of the realist singer from nourishing voice of nostalgia to alienation, exile, and madness, Louise Brooks's character in *Prix de beauté* goes even further in evoking the anxiety associated with the modern, post–World War I woman.

Lucienne sings a song that plays a crucial role in *Prix de beauté* in marking the modern woman's transgression and in commenting upon the shift away from community-based, neighborhood entertainment to that of mass culture. She performs the song, entitled "Je n'ai qu'un amour, c'est toi" (I Have Only One Love, It's You), [39] in the first and last sequences of the film. The first performance occurs in the opening sequence at a crowded public beach, where Lucienne, her boyfriend André (Georges Charlia), and André's friend are spending their day off. Wearing a bathing suit, Lucienne cavorts and does calisthenics on the beach, oblivious to the attention she attracts. André scolds her for making a spectacle of herself. Lucienne then sings to André in an attempt to neutralize his jealousy:

Ne sois pas jaloux, tais-toi	Don't be jealous, hush
Je n'ai qu'un amour, c'est toi.	I have only one love, it's you.
Il faut te raisonner	You must be reasonable
Tu dois me pardonner	You must forgive me
Quand un autre me dit que	When another tells me that I
je suis belle.	am beautiful.

Here, the song is a reassuring, personal, private message from Lucienne to André.

In its portrayal of the *petit peuple* of Paris, *Prix de beauté* shares an emphasis on realism with the films addressed in chapter 3. The film's settings—a crowded public beach, a *fête foraine* (fairground), a bistro, and the typography workroom and secretary pool of a daily newspaper—all possess a remarkable documentary texture, aided by the frequent use of location shooting, nonprofessional actors, and ambient noise. Here, however, specific neighborhoods are not identified; rather, a generic, modern, urban "working class" is presented. Outside the newspaper office, high-angle shots reveal crowds moving down a large, busy boulevard. The passers-by pause, listening to a voice on a loudspeaker urging women collectively to enter the beauty contest. Inside the newspaper building, tracking shots linger on the rows and rows of identical typewriters and linotype machinery, as if to emphasize the anonymity and uniformity of contemporary culture.

When *Prix de beauté* zeroes in on individual, idiosyncratic faces, it is not with the aim of valorizing marginalized people, as in *Coeur de Lilas* or *Faubourg Montmartre*. Instead, the stifling crowds at the Neuilly Fair disgust our protagonist. For example, a black man is shown in a tight close-up eating a hot dog. Lucienne looks on in distaste as the man eats hungrily, with his mouth wide open, laughing uproariously. Next, she is repulsed by the sight of a man kissing a woman brutally. The crudeness in behavior at the fair seems to infect André, who, in turn, kisses Lucienne roughly after winning a strength contest.

Another incident at the fair disturbs Lucienne profoundly. When André and Lucienne have their photograph taken, Lucienne seems numb and unable to respond to the photographer's efforts to pose the couple and make them smile. In *Pépé le Moko* and *La Tête d'un homme*, we saw that the photograph of the realist singer points to an anxiety about loss—loss of youth, loss of lovers. In *Prix de beauté*, the very act of being photographed renders Lucienne mute and paralyzed. Here, the film seems to point to an anxiety about loss of individuality. The crowded fair rendered Lucienne anonymous earlier; now the photographer attempts to pose the couple using the same stiff pose he uses for all of his photographs of couples. It is at this moment, precisely, that Lucienne seems to become acutely aware of her need to escape this standardized existence.

This milieu—and this confining relationship—is something to escape. The people at the fair represent a crowd instead of a community. What Lucienne desires is social mobility and the pleasures of consumption that accompany it. These desires are represented as specifically feminine in *Prix de beauté*. Lucienne gazes longingly at the pages of a fashion magazine, a pleasure her boyfriend disdains. She parades up and down for André in the luxurious dresses and furs she receives upon winning the beauty contest. Numerous shots of Lucienne gazing appreciatively at her image in a mirror emphasize her narcissistic pleasure in her new appearance. This is a new kind of woman, *Prix de beauté* asserts, who wants more than a traditional working-class or petit bourgeois marriage and the ordinary pleasures of an urban fair.

Lucienne's ticket out of this world is the beauty contest. This scenario draws on an existing stereotype in French culture in the early 1930s. In a tongue-in-cheek book about the cinema milieu written in 1929, René Jeanne, a film critic for the popular daily *Le Petit Journal*, describes all the types of people who tend to become afflicted with the desire to become cinema stars, a desire he calls "la cinématomanie." On his list of those who are the most typical victims of *cinématomanie* are "les dactylographes ambitieuses au point de ne pas se contenter de devenir la maîtresse ni même la femme légitime de leur patron [secretaries who are ambitious to the point where they're no longer content with becoming the mistress or even the legitimate wife of their boss]."[40]

Lucienne is chosen "Miss France" the following day on the basis of her photograph. After being outfitted with evening gowns and furs, she is whisked into a first-class train compartment and sent to San Sebastián, Spain, for the Miss Europe contest. At an outdoor amphitheater, the contestants parade up and down the catwalk in bathing suits and high heels. Lucienne wins the contest based on the audience's approval, measured by an applause meter. That night, she is fêted at an elegant party by a movie producer/prince and a maharaja. André, who has followed her to the contest, gives her an ultimatum: "Come back with me tonight to Paris or we're finished." At the last second, Lucienne joins him in the third-class section of the train, conspicuously out of place in her fur coat.

Now married and living with André in a modest apartment in Paris, Lucienne spends her days reading her fan mail and keeping house. She's bored and miserable, cut off from her previous life as a secretary and her brief life of luxury as Miss Europe. When the film producer offers her a contract for a worldwide publicity campaign and, even more important, in terms of *cinématomanie*, for screen tests, she leaves André.

The second performance of Lucienne's song occurs in the film's extraordinary final sequence, in which Lucienne's first rushes are screened. Lucienne and her producer/boyfriend view the image, pleased with the promising footage. The film within the film is of Lucienne singing, once again, "Je n'ai qu'un amour, c'est toi." The song's function and context have changed from private to public address, just as Lucienne herself is no longer the possession of a single man, but the property of the (masculine) public through the miracle of mechanical reproduction. In *Zouzou*, we saw that the shift in performance context from "private" to "public" coincided with grave consequences for the female protagonist. Zouzou's rise to stardom coincides with her loss of the man she loves. In *Prix de beauté*, Lucienne's ascent into the arena of public performance (the cinema) results in far greater tragedy.

André has learned of the projection and sneaks into the dark screening room, where Lucienne and the producer/prince watch the film. André looks at Lucienne's image on the screen for a moment, then looks at her, holding hands with the producer, and shoots her. The film continues to run and the reflection of Lucienne's image flickers across her lifeless face, creating an abstract play of light and shadow, a stunning homage to Brooks's beauty. An eerie disjunction between her body (now dead) and her voice is created. Lucienne "the woman" has been sacrificed to her film image.[41] As in the opening sequence, the performance of the song is associated with male rage, but this time, the machines of modern media are also indicted, in the sense that Lucienne has been "consumed" by the cinema.

The cinema is implicated in her death in several ways. It is an indirect cause of her death in that its star-making function facilitates Lucienne's autonomy and thus fuels André's rage. On a less literal level, the cinematic apparatus "consumes" Lucienne by turning her face into a screen onto which the film projects her own image. In one respect, the scene is reminiscent of Gabin's aesthetically pleasing death near the end of *Paris-Béguin*.

Both Lucienne and Bob die as a result of an apparatus (both social and technological) of modern popular entertainment. Music hall (represented by the poster of the revue star visually and by the liaison with Jane more generally) causes Bob's demise, while the cinematic apparatus is implicated in Lucienne's death.

In many ways, *Prix de beauté* inscribes itself in the new urban milieu of the late 1920s and early 1930s: a machine-filled, media-saturated space. The film conveys a fascination with the spaces and technology of the new urban proletariat, both in its work and its leisure spaces. In contrast to the lengthy close-ups of the *zoniers'* faces in *Coeur de Lilas, Prix de beauté* offers many lengthy, documentarylike shots devoted to the printing machines at the newspaper where André and Lucienne work, as well as to the film projector during the final sequence. Moreover, there is a fascination in *Prix de beauté* with public address systems: Lucienne finds out about the Miss France contest via a loudspeaker, while other pedestrians mill around her on a busy boulevard; the Miss Europe contest is emceed over a loudspeaker. Lastly, Lucienne devours women magazines, which were a new phenomenon in France at the time of the film's release.

The film expresses ambivalence about the new woman of post–World War I France, but also about other cultural shifts. Just as Lucienne's song shifts from private performance to mass-produced commodity, the older forms of leisure represented in the film, such as fairground attractions and the neighborhood bistro, give way to mass-circulation magazines, international beauty contests, and the cinema. An important component of this new urban space was, of course, the increased visibility and mobility of women, which is reflected in *Prix de beauté*. Lucienne works as a "modern" secretary (for a mass-circulation daily newspaper, no less), is ambitious, and acts against her more traditional boyfriend's wishes. Just as Fréhel's mobility in *Coeur de Lilas* is limited, and just as Damia pays the price for her hypnotic powers in *Sola*, the trajectory of Brooks's character in *Prix de beauté* is unforgivingly contained on the level of plot.

In the René Clair papers at the Bibliothèque de l'Arsenal in Paris, there are several different versions of the scenario of *Prix de beauté*.[42] They provide an interesting range of the narrative possibilities imaginable at this time in a film about an ambitious young woman. The film's creators had difficulty deciding on the ending of the film. The scenarios are similar until the moment in which Lucienne wins the Miss Europe contest, but thereafter, they vary considerably. In one version, Lucienne becomes the mistress of the newspaper editor to whom she owes her election as beauty queen. Alas, she has no acting talent whatsoever and loses her studio contract. She is no longer welcome in her parents' humble home. She wants her boy-friend back, but a series of unfortunate circumstances prevent this. Years pass, and Lucienne has many different lovers (i.e., she becomes a fallen woman). While walking in the Bois de Boulogne one day, she sees her for-mer boyfriend, now happy, with his wife and young daughter. Broken-hearted, she turns away.

In a second version, again Lucienne has no acting talent and loses her studio contract. She cannot return to her working-class family or to her boyfriend. She regrets everything, is hit by a car, and dies.

In a third version, she becomes the mistress of the assistant film director after winning the beauty contest. She still has no talent, however, and loses the studio contract. She becomes a fallen woman but gets back together with her working-class boyfriend, whom she has never stopped loving.

In a fourth version, she again has no acting talent and loses her contract. She is about to embark on a trip with the assistant director as his mistress, but she decides against doing so at the last minute because "she wanted to work; to have a career—not to travel as the kept woman of a rich man!" In the end, however, she reunites with her working-class boyfriend. In this version, a different woman initially wins the beauty contest, but her hus-band forbids her to accept the title because "he wants a good, honest, wor-thy wife for a true family life." Presumably, a similar fate awaits Lucienne.

In the fifth version, which is closest to the final form of Genina's *Prix de beauté*, she becomes the mistress of the director's assistant. She possesses talent and is well on her way to stardom. She wants to get back together with her former boyfriend, but she feels unworthy of him. The former boyfriend discovers the affair and kills her in the film studio, while her first film continues to run in the nearby projection room.

Thus, in two of the five versions, Lucienne is denied an acting career because she is revealed to lack acting and singing talent, but she manages to get her old boyfriend back at the end. In two other versions, Lucienne loses her career *and* her boyfriend, and is passed from one man to another. In one of these versions, she loses her life as well in a car accident. In the only ver-sion of the screenplay in which she possesses talent *and* the possibility of a career, her boyfriend murders her. A successful career and satisfying love life are absolutely incompatible for our female protagonist, then, not only in *Prix de beauté*, but in all of the films about female stardom, including those analyzed in chapter 4: *Paris-Béguin*, *Le Bonheur*, and *Zouzou*. Significantly, with talent and mobility, through the intervention of the media and new technology, the female star becomes a fantasy available to all, yet the dis-tance imposed by that technology means that she, the person behind the star image and the fantasy, is, in fact, available to no one, not even herself.

Although my project has been to consider the possibility of female subjectivity and mobility when the figure of the realist singer is taken up by the French cinema, these narratives of male anxiety produced by the female voice suggest a broader field of application for the sexual mechanism of visual and aural fetishization, whether for both feminist and psychoanalytic approaches to film criticism. As a cinema that privileges male communities, subjectivity, and anxiety, 1930s French cinema is not that different from 1930s Hollywood cinema, except perhaps in its tendency to give freer reign to less normative male fantasies (e.g., the older man–younger woman couplings analyzed by Ginette Vincendeau, or narratives that center more candidly on prostitutes, etc.). But as a cinema that is widely perceived to offer even less interesting, more constraining representations of women in the interwar period than its dominant, mainstream Hollywood counterpart, the possibility in the French cinema of transgressive, powerful representations of women is particularly intriguing, even more so if it suggests a resistance, through the voice, to a traditionally constraining practice of visual fetishization. Narratives in which the threat of a powerful woman is resoundingly checked by violence, then, underscore this potential resistance. The record played repeatedly in colonial exile, the voice coming through the wall, have the power to take Jeff (in *Sola*) and Radek (in *La Tête d'un homme*) to a place of melancholy, loss, and madness. Little wonder, then, that they provoke murderous passions, particularly when placed in the context of the realist singer.

Conclusion

French cinema of the 1930s draws upon a figure dating back to the mid-nineteenth century, in whom a tradition of song meets a very particular construction of femininity: the realist singer. She embodies multiple qualities, some of which appear to contradict one another. She stands for strength and vulnerability, earthy sexuality and melancholy; she is defined by the singularity of her body and the intensity of her emotions; she evokes nostalgia for the past and anxiety with regard to the future; she performs a version of her personal history overlaid with other literary, musical, and cinematic codes. The realist singer functions as a representative of radical cultural impulses: she is a mark of authenticity in the representation of the sordid and violent underworld; she is a symbol of transgressive female sexuality and solidarity, she is a glue that binds an underclass together. Yet at the same time, she is the repository of anxiety over new cultural roles for women and over new forms of entertainment that are increasingly dependent upon the technologies of recording. Above all, she inscribes herself, and is inscribed by others, in the Parisian landscape, a cultural space that is resolutely urban and working class. Buffet, Guilbert, Fréhel, and Damia sing of and embody the marginal spaces of Paris, such as the fortifications and the neighborhoods of northern and eastern Paris, as well as the more general space of the "street," with its connotations of poverty, prostitution, despair, but also seduction.

The *meneuses de revue* Mistinguett and Baker, we found, absorb certain aspects of the realist singer persona. They too align themselves with urban space, but they situate themselves in the urban topography in a more inclusive fashion: they claim the entire city of Paris for themselves. Actually, Mistinguett's and Baker's alignment with place extends even beyond the city limits of Paris: Mistinguett represented France itself to the foreigners who came to the Casino de Paris and the Folies-Bergère and to audiences of her tours of Europe and South and North America. Baker adopted Paris as "her country" in her signature song, "J'ai deux amours (Mon pays et Paris)" and evoked, as well, a wide range of "exotic" places, from America to the jungles and deserts of Africa to the tropical spaces of the Caribbean. As the music hall progressively rids itself of acts perceived as too "local" in their appeal as part of its transformation into an international, automated form of entertainment, the music hall queen too incarnates nothing so specific as the military fortifications or Montmartre or the *faubourgs* of Paris, but rather "Paris"—and France—itself. Regardless of the exact locations or the geographical scale represented by the realist singer, she is an "author" of the city of Paris and must be seen as a corrective to the generally held idea that modern Paris was uniquely the province of the nineteenth-century flâneur and the interwar men of letters.

Analysis of the realist singer in 1930s French cinema has shown that this figure—in both her purest form (as a performer designated as a "realist singer") and her "queen of the music hall" incarnation—accomplishes a surprising number of textual and cultural functions. For the fullest readings of the films that feature the realist singer, one must understand the lengthy tradition behind her—from Thérésa to Yvette Guilbert and Eugénie Buffet; from the tour de chant in the café-concert to the revue in the music hall. In chapter 3, we saw how she both represents and narrates *Paris populaire*. She narrates its prostitutes and its poverty in *Pépé le Moko, L'Entraîneuse,* and *Coeur de Lilas;* Fréhel's performance of "La Môme Caoutchouc" in *Coeur de Lilas* reveals that the bawdiness of Thérésa and the early café-concert, and the right to narrate transgressive female sexuality, are by no means absent from 1930s cinema.

In chapter 4, we find the realist singer, this time incarnated by the music hall queen, or, more properly, the men around her, embodying another shift in the meaning of the female singer, popular commercial entertainment, and Paris. *Paris-Béguin* and *Le Bonheur* offer an uneasy mixture of gritty Paris and glitzy Paris, oscillating between these two visions of urban space and imbuing the male characters, this time, with the positive realist qualities. Likewise, Paris is still present in *Zouzou* (and *Rigolboche*, discussed in chapter 2), but its realist spaces (Montmartre and Dakar) compete with a glossy Paris emanating from the music hall, which bears little resemblance to the working-class urban spaces seen in *Coeur de Lilas* and *Faubourg Montmartre* or to the imaginary Paris dreamed from exile in *Pépé le Moko* and *Sola*.

In chapter 5, we saw that the realist singer still carries with her associations with specific spaces, but those spaces have shifted. In *La Tête d'un homme*, Montparnasse has replaced Montmartre, the *faubourgs*, and the fortifications; Damia represents a distant Paris for the exile depicted in *Sola*. *Prix de beauté* replaces the characters who roam the periphery of Paris, the *pierreuse* and the apache, with those who work on the *grands boulevards* of central Paris, the secretary and typesetter. The underworld and artisanal working class give way to a bustling modern work environment. Connections between inhabitants of this Paris are forged, not in the popular bistro or the Foire de Neuilly, but through a mediascape consisting of daily newspapers, women's magazines, voices projected over loudspeakers, and international beauty contests. This movement away from the traditional urban spaces inhabited by the realist singer corresponds to a connection between the "feminine" and obsession and deception; she is now a screen onto which the male characters project their fantasies and anxieties, yet the media that project her, whether recorded sound or cinema, deny anyone the possibility of realizing their fantasies: the male characters are powerless in their dreams of possessing that which they fetishize; the women themselves are prevented from fulfilling their ambitions.

And what had become of the realist singer by the late 1930s? Two things, I would suggest, as a conclusion: (1) her cultural legacy persisted beyond the 1930s through the persona and performances of Edith Piaf; and (2) her textual functions in the cinema were, in part, absorbed by Jean Gabin. In a sense, the 1930s saw the apotheosis of the realist singer in French culture and cinema. Damia and Fréhel were still as popular as ever. Their live performances were supplemented by cinema roles and by phonograph recordings, increasing the size of their audiences. The fin-de-siècle realist song had been updated and renewed by the 1930s through the contributions of new lyricists and composers such as Raymond Asso ("Mon légionnaire," and "Elle fréquentait la rue Pigalle"), Michel Vaucaire ("Sans lendemain"), and Maurice Vandair ("Tel qu'il est" and "Ou sont tous mes amants?"). The populist literature written by Carco, Dabit, Mac Orlan and others throughout the teens, twenties, and thirties only reinforced the fascination for stories of the criminal world. Another reason for the realist song's continued strength was the emergence of Edith Piaf, "the greatest, the most popular, the most admired of the French chanteuses."[1]

EDITH PIAF

Piaf, who was born Edith Giovanna Gassion (1915–63), made her début in a cabaret in 1935 and performed, recorded, and toured until her death at the age of forty-seven. In contrast to the other realist singers, her renown extends well beyond the contexts of the realist song and French popular entertainment. Like Judy Garland and Marilyn Monroe, Piaf belongs to the select gallery of female stars revered for their perceived personal suffering and courage, as well as for their acting and singing talent, and she has an enormous cult following to this day.[2] Because of her continued popularity and her international profile, it is tempting to think of Piaf as a case apart from Damia and Fréhel. However, Piaf's star persona and performance style were not, in fact, unique.

The legend of Piaf's humble beginnings is an important part of her star persona, just as it was for the other realist singers. Born in working-class Belleville (literally on the street, according to some accounts) to itinerant street performers, she was soon abandoned by her alcoholic mother, and she was raised by her grandmother, who ran a brothel in Normandy.[3] By the age of twelve, she was on the road with her father, a street acrobat. At fifteen, she supported herself by singing in the streets. She gave birth to a baby girl at the age of seventeen and then lost her to meningitis two years later. For a number of years, she lived in Pigalle in the criminal milieu, singing in the streets and paying the neighborhood pimps for "protection." Her first break came in 1935, at the age of twenty, when a cabaret owner, Louis Leplée, heard her sing in the street and offered her a singing engagement. Leplée was murdered not long afterward, an event that both enhanced Piaf's notoriety and slowed the progress of her career somewhat. Her romantic and professional liaison with the songwriter Raymond Asso finally launched her career: in 1937, she débuted at the A.B.C., a prestigious music hall, performing Asso's "Mon légionnaire" and "Le Fanion de la Légion." Years of successful tours in Europe and the United States followed, as well as scores of hit recordings, including "L'Hyme à l'amour," "Non, je ne regrette rien," and "La Vie en rose." Alternating with this rags-to-riches story is the chronicle of Piaf's personal misfortunes: the untimely death of a lover, the boxer Marcel Cerdan, years of drug and alcohol addiction, tumultuous and well-publicized romances with singers and songwriters (Yves Montand, Georges Moustaki, Jacques Pills, etc.), and illnesses that sent her into comas on three separate occasions and caused her to collapse on stage before she died, penniless.

Some have argued that Piaf constituted a radically new phenomenon. According to the music hall historian Lucienne Cantaloube-Ferrieu, the "quality of her performance," the "marvelous instrument of her voice," and her ability to "shake up the audience" constituted a real "upheaval," despite the apparent familiarity of her repertoire and persona.[4] Maurice Chevalier called her a "unique case" and a "little phenomenon with guts of steel."[5] In fact, the critical and fan discourse surrounding Piaf is quite similar to that which had attended her predecessors Fréhel and Damia.

Critics and biographers emphasize her "authenticity," her skill at self-promotion, her "carnal" quality, her cycles of success and misfortune, and her evocation of the poor people and places of Paris. For Maurice Laporte, writing in 1944, she was more authentic than the other realist singers:

> The street, the pain of the girl who clung to a passer-by one night, the humble and beaten love of a woman worker for a tough guy, ten singers for whom we have invented the qualification "realist" have sung of these before her. But despite their black dresses and their red scarves, it was "from outside" that they recounted their songs. It was in literary terms that they expressed their unadorned loves. . . . [But Piaf is illuminated] . . . from inside by that authentic ardor, [and] we perceive that the banal words were so infallibly chosen, with such a sense of symbol![6]

Léon-Paul Fargue wrote in 1946: "She sings because song is part of her, because drama is part of her, because her throat is full of tragedy."[7] Cantaloube-Ferrieu observes: "What immediately imposed itself was the burning authenticity that the living, real being lent abruptly to the character. The girl who, one night in February 1936, in the closed and protected world of a luxurious cabaret, sang 'Les Momes de la cloche,' then 'L'Etranger,' coming so obviously from the street."[8] The realist singer, here again, owes at least part of her talent and success to the fact that she has lived what she sings. Not only has she lived her material, she knows how to shape her autobiography into something that can serve her embryonic star persona. According to her childhood friend and biographer Simone Berteaut:

> To develop Edith's personality [Raymond Asso] made her talk for hours on end. She would tell him stories and she loved to chat. She always knew what to say to hold a man's interest. Instinctively she told him what he wanted to hear, and she was never wrong. Raymond was entitled to the same treatment as the others, only for him she gave it a poetic twist. She was the poor little girl from the back streets, a little lost, but so appealing. She took care over the details: her family, the men she had had; the miserable evenings she had spent alone; everything that had happened. True or false, Raymond did not care. She helped him to fashion and fill in the details of her "personality."[9]

Commentators focus also on her body, either to emphasize its frailty and Piaf's unattractiveness or its relationship to the quality of her voice. "Here is a voice that comes from the gut," Jean Cocteau wrote.[10] "[S]he had a way of pronouncing certain words that gave them an extraordinary carnal dimension," the singer Claude Nougaro commented in 1963.[11] Once again, the realist singer is associated with marginalized people and places: "Piaf loaned . . . her voice to the poor girls of the people, the kid from Aubervilliers, the exhausted worker or the dishwasher of the café."[12] Piaf constitutes, not a radical break with previous models of the realist singer, but instead a particularly distilled form of her ancestors: Thérésa, Eugénie Buffet, Yvette Guilbert, Damia, and Fréhel. She may have been more popular, more "pathetic," more powerful in performance than her predecessors, and more international in her appeal, but she is properly placed squarely in the tradition of the realist singer because of her realist repertoire, her performance style infused with autobiographical authenticity, her connections with the Montmartre underworld, her drug abuse, her precarious health, her huge voice emanating from a peculiar, waiflike body, and, above all, her ability to forge an intense emotional connection with her devoted audience.

If the realist singer reached her purest and most extreme form in the persona of Edith Piaf, the argument could also be made that the 1930s saw a gradual displacement of the realist singer onto other figures, at least in the cinema. The film appearances of the realist singer are clustered in the first half of the decade. As the decade wears on, her appearances become less frequent. It is striking, for example, that despite Piaf's overwhelming popularity in the late 1930s and throughout the 1940s and 1950s, her film performances were few and far between.[13] She had a small but interesting role in *La Garçonne* (Jean de Limur, 1936), an adaptation of the 1922 novel by Victor Margueritte, featuring Marie Bell as a young woman who walks away from a wealthy, unfaithful fiancé and into a world of opium dens and lesbian cabarets. Piaf plays a singer who flirts openly with Bell's character and sings a song, "Quand même, fais-moi valser" (All the Same, Waltz with Me).[14] The film also features Arletty and the singer Suzy Solidor as lesbians, which may explain in part why it was censored. In 1941, Piaf played a role written for her in *Montmartre sur Seine* (Georges Lacombe, 1941). Here, she is a flower seller in Montmartre who becomes a successful cabaret singer but fails to attract the man she loves. The film was panned by most critics for its weak script, formulaic images of Montmartre, and casting of Piaf as a romantic female protagonist, but it is of interest to us in its continued insistence on the realist singer's ultimate exclusion from viable romantic relationships. In *Étoile sans lumière* (Star without Light) (Marcel Blistène, 1945), Piaf plays a naïve maid persuaded to loan her powerful singing voice to a beautiful star (Mila Parely) of the silent cinema whose career is in jeopardy at the coming of sound. When Piaf's character, Madeleine, decides to build her own career as a singer, the film star commits suicide. Wracked with guilt, Madeleine faints on stage during her music hall debut. In contrast to the upbeat Hollywood version of this story (*Singin' in the Rain*), *Étoile sans lumière* ends with Piaf walking down a deserted Paris street at night, dejected and alone. One explanation for the paucity of Piaf's film roles (ten in all) is that her early career coincided with the Occupation, an era that constituted an enormous rupture in French film history in terms of both industry organization and narrative preoccupations. The dark, moody films of poetic realism that so easily accommodated the realist singer gave way to films with higher production values, more literary scripts, and more uniform performance styles. "The masterpieces of Occupation cinema tended to emphasize a more uniform, distanced, and homogeneous playing style based on that of the artistically advanced Parisian stage (as opposed to boulevard theatre and music hall)," Alan Williams observes.[15] The popular café-concert and music hall tunes that fill 1930s French cinema give way somewhat to lush, symphonic scores.[16]

We must query the fate of the realist singer in French cinema even before the Occupation era, however, as we search for an explanation for her waning importance as the 1930s progressed. Poetic realism, which shares the realist singer's sensibility, characters, and emphasis on place, emerged in the early to mid 1930s. It is worth considering for a moment that the components of the realist singer image—emotion, loss, authenticity, sexuality, the link to the socially dispossessed and the marginal spaces of Paris, and femininity, certainly—were transferred in their most concentrated form in the 1930s cinema to poetic realism's male star, Jean Gabin, who so often performed his own songs, sometimes right alongside the realist singer in her 1930s film appearances. As we saw in chapter 4, the spectacle of the *chanteuse* was already giving way to the spectacle of the male spectator, the fetishized to the fetishizer.

JEAN GABIN

Fréhel and Jean Gabin share the stage for a moment during the performance of "La Môme Caoutchouc" in *Coeur de Lilas* (1931), in which, for the first time, Gabin plays a seductive, virile *mauvais garçon*. His character is linked initially to the prostitute Lilas but is not actually the film's protagonist. Fréhel is a used-up prostitute, whose "Dans la rue" expresses both the melancholy and the defiance of the inhabitants of the neighborhood. On the dance floor at the bal musette, she deftly takes over where Gabin leaves off in the performance of "La Môme Caoutchouc," transforming the song into a bold expression of female sexuality. By the time the two performers next appeared together in *Pépé le Moko* (1936), Gabin's persona, so familiar to us from poetic realism, was fully established. He was, at this point, a star, with *La Bandera* (Duvivier, 1935), *La Belle Équipe* (Duvivier, 1936), and *Les Bas-fonds* (Renoir, 1936) behind him.

Gabin sings again in Pépé le Moko in celebration of his fledgling romance with the glamorous Parisian Gaby (Mireille Balin), before an audience of women going about their daily tasks in the Casbah of Algiers. Fréhel and Gabin come together for the last time when Fréhel sings her mournful "Où est-il donc?" (Where is it, then?) to Pépé in an attempt to help him *changer d'époque* (go back in time). It would seem that Fréhel, more than any other woman performer in France at this time, was perfectly positioned to be the "female voice" of poetic realism. But in fact, Fréhel and the other realist singers remained on the margins of poetic realism when it flowered in the latter half of the decade.

Poetic realism is generally understood to refer to those pessimistic urban dramas made during the latter half of the 1930s in France featuring a proletarian or criminal hero destined for a violent death. The films tend to be set in working-class Paris or, less frequently, some "exotic" colonial outpost. Gabin occupies center stage in these films and in poetic realism in general. Following *Pépé le Moko,* he would continue his 1930s string of phenomenally successful work in *La Grande Illusion* (Renoir, 1937), *Gueule d'amour* (Grémillon, 1937), *Quai des brumes* (Carné, 1938), *La Bête humaine* (Renoir, 1938), *Le Jour se lève* (Carné, 1939), and *Remorques* (Grémillon, 1939).

Gabin embodied the typical working-class hero imbued with authenticity, a sense of tragic destiny, and Popular Front values, as Ginette Vincendeau has forcefully established.[17] As is the case with the realist singers, Gabin's myth is constructed around oppositions: hero/ordinary man; strength/vulnerability; virile male friendships/romantic relationships with women, and so on. Like the realist singer, Gabin is understood as a "natural" from the beginning of his career. He was generally not seen to be acting in films like *La Bête humaine, Le Jour se lève,* and *Quai des brumes;* he was just "being himself." Vincendeau reveals the process by which this impression of naturalness was constructed through her analysis of acting practices and Gabin's autobiographical texts.

In addition to similarities in their shared connotations (Paris *populaire,* authenticity, etc.), there are other parallels between the realist singer and Gabin: a minimalist performance style, certain characteristics of their mise-en-scène, and the conflation of their lives with their roles. Gabin utilized a new, more sober acting style that departed radically from other types of 1930s film acting derived from boulevard or classical theater. This style, characterized by Vincendeau as the reduction of body gestures and an emphasis on facial expressions, was enhanced by poetic realism's reliance on the close-up and low-key lighting. The pared-down, subtle movements interrupted by dramatic, violent outbursts quite closely resemble the descriptions of the live performances of the interwar realist singer. Damia, in particular, with her relative immobility, her "boxer in repose" stance, followed by her sudden, dramatic movements with her powerful arms, shares Gabin's performance aesthetic. Piaf, likewise, kept her use of gesture and facial expression to a minimum.[18] Moreover, just as poetic realist films rely heavily upon the close-up and noir lighting, it was Damia who began to use dramatic, high-contrast lighting in her singing performances. This lighting style, coupled with the black dress that "erased" her body and her pale skin, emphasized her face, creating a kind of "close-up."[19] Piaf's mise-en-scène often reduced her body to a white face and white hands.

Just as the realist singer carefully built up a convincingly authentic persona through interviews and memoirs, Gabin was careful to modulate his image early on in his film career. Six articles in *Pour vous* in 1935 under the title "Quand je revois ma vie" (When I Look Back on My Life) shape his life into a story in which every past event became significant a posteriori.[20] The elements of the Gabin film persona—earthiness, a tendency to violence when provoked, the importance of male friendship, and so on—are all found in Gabin's life story. This process by which the star's autobiography enters into subsidiary forms and then feeds back into films, astutely analyzed by Vincendeau, is exactly that by which the star discourses of Thérésa, Guilbert, Buffet, and Fréhel were formulated.

Vincendeau has argued that, in a cinema that overwhelmingly favors male groups and male friendships over female characters, Gabin incarnates both the masculine and the feminine.[21] Is it possible that the "feminine" side of Gabin is, more accurately, the legacy of the realist singer? In order to respond to this question, of course, a more sustained analysis of Gabin's poetic realist roles is necessary. If the realist singer first evoked a certain loss of community, only to be displaced by male anxiety and impotency in an increasingly technological world over which men are no longer master, or even the directors of their own fantasies, it seems that the male emblem of this community, Gabin, was equally destined to be displaced, this time by the community's failure to shoulder, much less survive, the demise of the Popular Front, the rise of fascism, and the advent of a far more sinister technology in the war to come.

For her part in providing a key to understanding the overarching themes and concerns of French cinema of the 1930s, the realist singer is a crucial character in the French cultural landscape. Above and beyond the context of the cinema, the realist singer played a fundamental role in the construction of the modern French star system and the fantasies it engendered, helping to mold the café-concert and the music hall into environments that retained a place for the expression of women's autonomy and sexuality. Finally, she added a female voice to the crowded gallery of male authors of the city of Paris.

The realist singer, and all that she connotes—audacity, resilience, the working class, the pleasures of female community—resonated most strongly in the 1930s, but her relevance as a symbol of female rebellion can be felt even decades later. As late as 1962, at the height of the New Wave cultural and aesthetic upheaval, the realist singer reappears. In Agnès Varda's *Cléo de 5 à 7 (Cléo from 5 to 7)*, a petulant and fearful pop singer rebels against her composer, thus setting in motion her transformation from pampered doll to thoughtful and independent woman. Alone in her dressing room, Cléo discards her white, feathered peignoir in favor of a little black dress identical to those worn in the 1930s by Damia and Fréhel. A photograph of Edith Piaf hangs on the wall.

Select Filmography

The Realist Singer in 1930s French Film

1930

Chiqué (Pière Colombier)
Paris la nuit (Henri Diamant-Berger)
Prix de beauté (Augusto Genina)
Tu m'oublieras (Henri Diamant-Berger)

1931

Coeur de lilas (Anatole Litvak)
Faubourg Montmartre (Raymond Bernard)
Paris-Béguin (Augusto Genina)
Sola (Henri Diamant-Berger)
Tumultes (Robert Siodmak)
Un Soir de rafle (Carmine Gallone)

1932

La Tête d'un homme (Julien Duvivier)

1933

Dans les rues (Victor Trivas)
La Maternelle (Marie Epstein and Jean Benoit-Lévy)
La Rue sans nom (Pierre Chenal)

1934

Amok (Fédor Ozep)
Zouzou (Marc Allégret)

1935

Le Bonheur (Marcel L'Herbier)
Le Crime de Monsieur Lange (Jean Renoir)
Princesse Tam-Tam (Edmond T. Gréville)

1936

La Garçonne (Jean de Limur)
Pépé le Moko (Julien Duvivier)
Rigolboche (Christian-Jaque)
Le Roman d'un tricheur (Sacha Guitry)

1937

Le Puritain (Jeff Musso)

1938

La Maison du Maltais (Pierre Chenal)
L'Entraîneuse (Albert Valentin)
Une Java (Claude Orval)
Prisons de femmes (Roger Richebé)
La Rue sans joie (André Hugon)
La Goualeuse (Fernand Rivers)

Notes

1. Michèle Lagny, Marie-Claire Ropars, and Pierre Sorlin, *Générique des années 30* (Paris: Presses universitaires de Vincennes, 1986), 179–83.

2. Ibid. Colette Darfeuil and Marguerite Moreno also each appeared in more than thirty films in the 1930s, but they drop out of the top tier of the chart when we take into account the relatively high number of small roles they played. In other words, women were certainly visible in 1930s French cinema, but they were far less likely to play the lead role. However, actresses are represented in the second tier—those who played more than twenty lead roles—and include Gaby Morlay, Josselyne Gaël, Danielle Darrieux, Annabella, Suzy Prim, Elvira Popesco, Renée Saint-Cyr, Marie Bell and Edwige Feuillère. Those actors in the second tier include André Luguet, Jean Gabin, Jean Murat, and Pierre-Richard Wilm.

3. In "French Cinema in the 1930s: Social Text and Context of a Popular Entertainment Medium" (diss, University of East Anglia, 1985), 179, Ginette Vincendeau also points to the relative paucity of prominent women actors in 1930s French film: "We only need first to look at film credits. Taking as an example the top movies in the 1936 and 1937 survey, and comparing the number of leading actors and actresses of equal stature, we find on the male side, Raimu, Pierre Fresnay, Victor Francen, Charles Boyer, Jean Gabin, Louis Jouvet, Fernandel, Guitry, Charles Vanel, Michel Simon and Harry Baur; while actresses are represented only by Gaby Morlay, Danielle Darrieux, Annabella, Arletty, Edwige Feuillère and Marie Bell."

4. For an analysis of Arletty and gender, see Keith Reader, "'Mon cul est intersexuel?': Arletty's Performance of Gender," in *Gender and French Cinema*, ed. Alex Hughes and James S. Williams (New York: Berg, 2001), 63–76.

5. "Complainte" (1932), lyrics, Julien Duvivier; music, J. Dallin. "[L]a nuit m'envahit/toute est brume et tout est gris." Translations are my own unless otherwise indicated.

6. "Faubourg Montmartre" (1931), lyrics, Raymond Bernard, music, André

Roubaud. "Ell's s'hallad'nt le long des vitrines/Et semblent ne penser à rien/ Qu'à montrer leur humble bobine/Mais ce n'sont pas des corps sans âmes/Les p'tit's femm's."

7. "La Môme Caoutchouc" (1931), lyrics, Serge Veber; music, Maurice Yvain. "Je peux bien vous dire entre nous/Et bien la môme caoutchouc, c'est ma pomme/Et oui, c'est comme ça qu'on me nomme."

8. "Je t'aime d'amour" (1930), lyrics, Henri Diamant-Berger and Jean Lenoir; music, Jean Lenoir.

9. "L'Amour des hommes" (1938), lyrics, André Hugon and Géo Koger; music, Vincent Scotto.

10. "Le Grand Frisé" (1931), lyrics, Léo Daniderff; music, Emile Ronn.

11. "Mon homme" (1920), lyrics, Albert Willemetz and Jacques-Charles; music, Maurice Yvain.

12. Jean-Pierre Jeancolas, *15 ans d'années trente: Le Cinéma des Français, 1929–1944* (Paris: Stock, 1983), 93.

13. Ibid. In this "filmed song," Gilles and Julien perform "Nini," a "gently parodic realist song."

14. Guisy Basile and Chantal Gavouyère, *La Chanson française dans le cinéma des années trente: Discographie* (Paris: Bibliothèque nationale, 1996).

15. According to Raymond Chirat's *Catalogue des films français de long métrage: Films sonores de fiction, 1929–1939*, 2d ed. (Brussels: Cinémathèque royale de Belgique, 1981), there were approximately 1,300 feature-length French films made in the 1930s. Films designed as vehicles for singers and adaptations of operettas generally contain even more songs. *Naples au baiser de feu* (Genina, 1937), a Tino Rossi vehicle, contains six songs. The Paramount-produced *Un Soir de réveillon* (1933) contains sixteen songs. But even films that are neither adaptations of operettas nor set in an entertainment milieu frequently contain several songs. *Tumultes* (Siodmak, 1931), for example, which features Charles Boyer as a petty criminal and Florelle as his unfaithful girlfriend, contains three songs. The discography also lists the recordings made of songs outside the context of the films, information that usefully indicates the resonance of a particular song. Many films now completely forgotten, or at least disdained by film historians, contain songs that went on to be recorded by scores of singers. For instance, *Sola*, an all-but-forgotten film directed in 1931 by Henri Diamant-Berger, contains five songs, one of which, "Tu ne sais pas aimer," was recorded by ten different performers for ten different record companies. *Capitaine Craddock* (Vaucorbeil/Schwartz, 1931) contains a song called "Gars de la marine," which was recorded by nineteen different singers. Conversely, the discography reveals that the songs in films that are today highly regarded often experienced a surprisingly minimal afterlife. Not a single person recorded "À la belle étoile" after it was sung by Florelle in Renoir's *Le Crime de Monsieur Lange*.

16. Jean-Pierre Jeancolas notes in *15 ans d'années trente*, 93, that the average working-class household did not possess a radio until after 1935, and only the middle class could afford phonographs until late in the decade.

17. Anouk Adelmann, *Chansons à vendre* (Paris: Cujas, 1967), 193.

18. With the exception of Piaf's performance in the film *La Garçonne* (De Limur, 1936), her film work took place in the 1940s and the 1950s and is thus beyond the scope of this book. Her film career merits extensive study.

19. Ginette Vincendeau, "The *Mise-en-Scène* of Suffering: French *Chanteuses réalistes*," *New Formations* 3 (1987): 113. Lucienne Cantaloube-Ferrieu, *Chanson et poésie des années 30 aux années 60* (Paris: A. G. Nizet, 1981), 29, also establishes the roots of the realist song in naturalism: "Ces chanteuses qui ont nom Fréhel, Germaine Lix, Irène de Turcy, Damia, poursuivent l'oeuvre d'Eugénie Buffet. À travers elles, il est vrai, c'est encore souvent Fantine qui, par-delà Rose-blanche, nous revient. Mais les existences en marge qu'elles incarnent, pour être nées dans *Les Misérables*, n'en ont pas moins été modelées, désormais, par É. Zola et les Goncourt, avant d'être finalement transmises à la chanson réaliste par l'intermédiaire de Bruant dont le 'naturalisme nouveau' est toujours influent."

20. Vanessa R. Schwartz, *Spectacular Realities: Early Mass Culture in Fin-de-Siècle Paris* (Berkeley: University of California Press, 1998).

21. On this topic, see Molly Nesbit, *Atget's Seven Albums* (New Haven, Conn.: Yale University Press, 1992), and Marja Warehime, *Brassaï: Images of Culture and the Surrealist Observer* (Baton Rouge: Louisiana University Press, 1996). See also the numerous photographic books on Paris that emerged in the 1930s: André Warnaud, *Visages de Paris* (Paris: Firmin-Didot, 1930); Brassaï, *Le Paris secret des années 30* (Paris: Gallimard, 1976), trans. Richard Miller as *The Secret Paris of the Thirties* (New York: Pantheon Books, 1976); Brassaï, *Paris de nuit* (Paris: Arts et Métiers graphiques, 1933); André Kertész, *Paris vu par André Kertész*, text by Pierre Mac Orlan (Paris: Plon, 1934); and Francis Carco and René Jacques, *Envoûtement de Paris* (Paris: Grasset, 1938).

22. For examples of literary populism, see Francis Carco, *Jésus-la-Caille* (1932; reprint, Paris: Albin Michel, 1985), Pierre Mac Orlan, *Quai des brumes* (Paris: Gallimard, 1927), and Eugène Dabit, *L'Hôtel du Nord* (1921; reprint, Paris: Denoël, 1977). For examples of nonfiction populist literature on Paris, see Pierre Mac Orlan, *Images secrètes de Paris* (Paris: René Kieffer, 1930); id., *La Lanterne sourde* (1953; reprint, Paris: Gallimard, 1982); and Eugène Dabit, *Ville lumière* (Paris: Dilettante, 1990). See Dudley Andrew's useful chapter on the literary populism and its relation to poetic realism in *Mists of Regret: Culture and Sensibility in Classic French Film*, (Princeton, N.J.: Princeton University Press, 1995).

23. On the ideological ramifications of Bruant's performance of poverty, see Dietmar Rieger, "'J'cass'rai la gueule aux proprios': Aristide Bruant et la chanson 'naturaliste' fin-de-siècle," in *La Chanson française et son histoire*, ed. id. (Tübingen: Gunter Narr, 1988).

24. Laura Mulvey, "Visual Pleasure and Narrative Cinema," *Screen* 16, no. 3 (1975); reprinted in E. Ann Kaplan, *Feminism and Film* (Oxford: Oxford University Press, 2000), 40. "A woman performs within the narrative; the gaze of the spectator and that of the male characters in the film are neatly combined

without breaking narrative verisimilitude. For a moment the sexual impact of the performing woman takes the film into a no man's land outside its own time and space."

25. For a selection of essays charting new directions in the relationship between psychoanalysis and the cinema, see *Endless Night: Cinema and Psychoanalysis, Parallel Histories* (Berkeley: University of California Press, 1999).

26. See the following useful accounts of this shift from early feminist criticism to models that engage more directly with history and culture: Janet Bergstrom and Mary Ann Doane, "The Female Spectator: Contexts and Directions," *Camera Obscura* 20–21 (1989): 5–27; Patrice Petro, "Feminism and Film History," *Camera Obscura* 22 (1990): 9–28; and esp. Judith Mayne, *Cinema and Spectatorship* (New York: Routledge, 1993).

27. Mayne, *Cinema and Spectatorship*, 63.

28. Lea Jacobs, *Wages of Sin: Censorship and the Fallen Woman Film, 1928–1942* (Madison: University of Wisconsin Press, 1991).

29. Judith Mayne, *Directed by Dorothy Arzner* (Bloomington: Indiana University Press, 1994).

30. Miriam Hansen, *Babel and Babylon: Spectatorship in American Silent Cinema* (Cambridge, Mass.: Harvard University Press, 1991).

31. Monica Dall'Asta, *Un Cinéma musclé: Le Surhomme dans le cinéma muet italien (1913–1926)* (Paris: Éditions Yellow Now, 1992). Dall'Asta examines the "strong man" film of the silent Italian cinema, addressing its "excessive" male body, its generic form, and its links to Italian fascism.

32. Mayne, *Cinema and Spectatorship*, 64–68.

33. Ibid., 64.

34. Mary Ann Doane, *The Desire to Desire: The Woman's Film of the 1940s* (Bloomington: Indiana University Press, 1987).

35. Rhona J. Berenstein, *Attack of the Leading Ladies: Gender, Sexuality, and Spectatorship in Classic Horror Cinema* (New York: Columbia University Press, 1996).

36. Mayne, *Cinema and Spectatorship*, 64.

37. For particularly useful studies of stardom, see Edgar Morin, *Les Stars* (Paris: Seuil, 1972); Richard Dyer, *Stars* (London: British Film Institute, 1990), Richard deCordova, *Picture Personalities: The Emergence of the Star System in America* (Urbana: University of Illinois Press, 1990), Judith Mayne, *Cinema and Spectatorship* (New York: Routledge, 1993), Pamela Robertson, *Guilty Pleasures: Feminist Camp from Mae West to Madonna,* (Durham, N.C.: Duke University Press, 1996), Ramona Curry, *Too Much of a Good Thing: Mae West as Cultural Icon* (Minneapolis: University of Minnesota Press, 1996), and Linda Mizejewski, *Ziegfeld Girl: Image and Icon in Culture and Cinema* (Durham, N.C.: Duke University Press, 1999).

38. Colin Crisp, *The Classic French Cinema, 1930–1960* (Bloomington: Indiana University Press, 1997).

39. Sandy Flitterman-Lewis, *To Desire Differently: Feminism and the French Cinema* (Urbana: University of Illinois Press, 1990).

40. Geneviève Sellier, *Jean Grémillon: Le Cinéma est à vous* (Paris: Méridiens Klincksieck, 1989).

41. Ginette Vincendeau, "Daddy's Girls: Oedipal Narratives in 1930s French Films," *Iris* 8 (1988): 70–81.

42. Ginette Vincendeau, "Melodramatic Realism: On Some French Women's Films in the 1930s," *Screen* 3 (1989): 51–65, looks at four melodramas structured around female characters: *Jenny* (Carné, 1936), *Hélène* (Epstein and Benoit-Lévy, 1936), *L'Entraîneuse* (Valentin, 1938), and *Angèle* (Pagnol, 1934). France never produced a cycle or genre such as the Hollywood "woman's film" in the 1930s and 1940s.

43. Claude Gauteur and Ginette Vincendeau, *Jean Gabin: Anatomie d'un mythe* (Paris: Nathan Université, 1993); Edward Baron Turk, *Child of Paradise: Marcel Carné and the Golden Age of French Cinema* (Cambridge, Mass.: Harvard University Press, 1989); and Noël Burch and Geneviève Sellier, *La Drôle de guerre des sexes du cinéma français, 1930–1956* (Paris: Nathan, 1996).

44. See esp. Ginette Vincendeau, "Community, Nostalgia and the Spectacle of Masculinity," *Screen* 26, no. 6 (1985): 18–38, and "French Cinema in the 1930s."

45. Caryl Flinn, *Strains of Utopia: Gender, Nostalgia, and Hollywood Film Music,* (Princeton, N.J.: Princeton University Press, 1992), 117.

46. Ibid., 151–52.

47. Susan McClary, *Feminine Endings: Music, Gender, and Sexuality* (Minneapolis: University of Minnesota Press, 1991), 153.

48. In this regard, I was inspired by Linda Mizejewski's interdisciplinary, feminist history of the "Ziegfeld Girl," *Ziegfeld Girl: Image and Icon in Culture and Cinema* (Durham, N.C.: Duke University Press, 1999).

49. The key texts on *flânerie* include the prose and poetry of Charles Baudelaire and Walter Benjamin's *The Arcades Project,* trans. Howard Eiland and Kevin McLaughlin (Cambridge, Mass.: Harvard University Press, Belknap Press, 1999). For useful critical analyses see Susan Buck-Morss, *The Dialectics of Seeing: Walter Benjamin and the Arcades Project* (Cambridge, Mass.: MIT Press, 1989), and *The Flâneur,* ed. Keith Tester (New York: Routledge, 1994).

50. Priscilla Parkhurt Ferguson, "The *Flâneur* on and off the Streets of Paris," in *The Flâneur,* ed. Keith Tester (New York: Routledge, 1994), 22.

51. Keith Tester, "Introduction," in *The Flâneur,* ed. id. (New York: Routledge, 1994), 2. Here Tester is writing specifically about Baudelaire's conception of the flâneur as poet.

52. For arguments against the existence of the flâneuse, see Susan Buck-Morss, "The Flaneur, the Sandwichman and the Whore," *New German Critique* 39 (Fall 1986): 99–140; Janet Wolff, *Feminine Sentences: Essays on Women and Culture* (Berkeley: University of California Press, 1990); and Janet Wolff, "The Artist and the *Flâneur:* Rodin, Rilke and Gwen John in Paris," in *The Flâneur,* ed. Keith Tester (New York: Routledge, 1994), 111–37.

53. Wolff, *Feminine Sentences,* 47.

54. Buck-Morss, "The Flaneur, the Sandwichman and the Whore," 112.

55. Deborah L. Parsons, *Streetwalking the Metropolis: Women, the City, and Modernity* (Oxford: Oxford University Press, 2000), 4. For other works that raise the possibility of the flâneuse, see Elizabeth Wilson, *The Sphinx in the City: Urban Life, the Control of Disorder, and Women* (Berkeley: University of California Press, 1991). For examinations of the relationship between the female writer and the city, see Alex Hughes, "The City and the Female Autograph," *Parisian Fields*, ed. Michael Sheringham (London: Reaktion Books, 1996), 115–32, and Susan Merrill Squier, *Women Writers and the City* (Knoxville: University of Tennessee Press, 1984).

56. Anne Friedberg, *Window Shopping: Cinema and the Postmodern* (Berkeley: University of California Press, 1993).

57. Parsons, *Streetwalking the Metropolis*.

58. Vincendeau, "*Mise-en-Scène*," 107–28.

59. "Elle fréquentait la rue Pigalle" (1939), lyrics, Raymond Asso; music, L. Maitrier.

60. "Entre Saint-Ouën et Clignancourt" (1937), lyrics, André Mauprey; music André Sablon.

61. "À Paris dans chaque faubourg" (1932), lyrics, René Clair; music, Maurice Jaubert.

62. Adrian Rifkin, *Street Noises: Parisian Pleasure, 1900–40* (Manchester: Manchester University Press, 1993), 73: "Baker's famous theme song, 'I have two loves, my country and Paris,' was the proclamation of her adoptive Frenchness, a move so crucial to her image that it gave her a man's rights to address the city as a lover. But for the ensemble of women singers, they never, so to speak, embrace it as a whole. If Chevalier has the right to sing Paris as if it were a woman, the woman singers are never more than one of its types of woman, even if, like Mistinguett, they might masquerade the whole gamut in a single show, and even though, once famous, they might get to choose their leading men as colleagues or as lovers."

63. Ibid., 73.

64. Vincendeau, "*Mise-en-scène*," 114. The realist singer in turn serves to authenticate seedy settings in films. For example, in *Paris la nuit* (Henri Diamant-Berger, 1930) and *Chiqué* (Pière Colombier, 1931), wealthy people visit the dance halls on the exterior boulevards of Paris in search of a frisson of danger. In these films, the realist singer connotes authenticity in these marginal urban spaces; she serves to assure the interlopers that they are in the real underworld.

CHAPTER 1. *CAF'-CONC'*: THE RISE OF THE UNRULY WOMAN

1. Louis Veuillot, *Les Odeurs de Paris* (Paris, 1866), 141, quoted in T. J. Clark, *The Painting of Modern Life: Paris in the Art of Manet and His Followers* (1984; rev. ed., Princeton, N.J.: Princeton University Press, 1999), 209 (Clark's translation): "ELLE allait paraître, un tonnerre d'applaudissements l'annonça. Je ne la trouvai point si hideuse que l'on m'avait dit. C'est une fille assez grande, assez

découplée, sans nul charme que sa gloire, que en est un, il est vrai, de premier ordre. Elle a, je crois, quelques cheveux; sa bouche semble faire le tour de la tête, pour lèvres, des bourrelets, comme un nègre; des dents de requin. . . . Elle sait chanter. Quant à son chant, il est indescriptible, comme ce qu'elle chante. Il faut être Parisien pour en saisir l'attrait, Français raffiné pour en savourer la profonde et parfaite ineptie. Cela n'est d'aucune langue, d'aucun art, d'aucune vérité."

2. Ibid., 140. Clark's translation, 209.

3. Ibid., 141: "La musique a le même caractère que les paroles; un caractère de charge corrompue et canaille, et d'ailleurs morne comme la face narquoise du voyou. Le voyou, le Parisien naturel, ne pleure pas, il pleurniche; il ne rit pas, il ricane; il ne plaisante pas, il blague; il ne danse pas, il chahute; il n'est pas amoureux, il est libertin. L'art consiste à ramasser ces ingrédients dans une chanson, et les auteurs y arrivent neuf fois sur dix, la chanteuse aidant."

4. *Dictionnaire historique de la langue française* (Paris: Le Robert, 1992), s.v. *voyou*.

5. Fernand Léger, "Bal," in *Functions of Painting*, trans. Alexandra Anderson (New York: Viking, 1965), 74–77.

6. Veuillot, *Odeurs de Paris*, 138: "La présence de ces femmes 'comme il faut' donnait à l'auditoire un cachet tout particulier de débraillement: le débraillement social!"

7. My account of the prehistory and early history of the café-concert is particularly indebted to Concetta Condemi, *Les Cafés-Concerts: Histoire d'un divertissement (1849–1914)* (Paris: Quai Voltaire Histoire, 1992), and François Caradec and Alain Weill, *Le Café-Concert* (Paris: Atelier Hachette/Massin, 1980). For straightforward factual information, such as the addresses and years of existence of particular cafés-concerts and music halls, see André Sallée and Philippe Chauveau, *Music-Hall et café-concert* (Paris: Bordas, 1985).

8. Condemi, *Cafés-Concerts*, 19.

9. Ibid., 21.

10. Ibid. It is precisely this latter category of popular theater that Marcel Carné celebrates in *Les Enfants du paradis* (1945), an homage to pantomime, melodrama, and fairground attractions set during the 1830s on the boulevard du Temple.

11. For an account of the ways in which these laws were, nevertheless, abused, and for information on the more political *goguette*, see Jacques Rancière, "Good Times, or, Pleasure at the Barriers," in *Voices of the People: The Social Life of "La Sociale" at the End of the Second Empire*, trans. John Moore, ed. Adrian Rifkin and Roger Thomas (New York: Routledge & Kegan Paul, 1988) 45–94.

12. Condemi, *Cafés-Concerts*, 27.

13. Clark, *Painting of Modern Life*, 211.

14. Caradec and Weill, *Café-Concert*, 36.

15. Sallée and Chauveau, *Music-Hall et café-concert*, 12.

16. Ibid., 186, quoting Maurice Chevalier, *Ma route et mes chansons*: "Le

public se composait, en majorité, de vieux rentiers paillards qui venaient avec des jeunes femmes qu'ils entretenaient. Ce public de presque vieillards vicieux et de poules intéressées formait le noyau journalier de l'établissement. Le reste de la salle se complétait d'une audience de passage, le concert étant placé sur le boulevard de Strasbourg, boulevard excessivement vivant et mouvementé. Beaucoup de commis-voyageurs attendant l'heure d'un train pour la gare de l'Est. Mauvais public, indifférent aux efforts des artistes, d'ailleurs recrutés dans la plus lamentable qualité de la profession par des agents lyriques de même envergure. Il arrivait très souvent que des tours de chant entiers se produisaient sans un seul applaudissement, tellement tous ces vieux 'michés' étaient intéressés par leurs histoires personnelles et leurs chassés-croisés. Toute la maison, depuis la direction jusqu'aux garçons de café, avait d'ailleurs l'empreinte de cette atmosphère, et si un artiste avait, par extraordinaire, eu suffisamment de talent pour être applaudi bruyamment, je crois qu'il aurait alors été résilié comme dérangeant la douce quiétude de ce mélange de café-concert et de maison close."

17. Jean-Claude Klein, *La Chanson à l'affiche: Histoire de la chanson française du café-concert à nos jours* (Paris: Du May, 1991), 23.

18. Sallée and Chauveau, *Music-Hall et café-concert,*139, quoting Chevalier.

19. Ibid., 139, quoting Chevalier: "Un gros type, pilier de tous les cafés du faubourg, faisant office de monologuiste et qui avait aussi la faveur des ouvriers. Il zozotait, était toujours entre deux vins . . . et blaguait en argot, n'ayant la plupart du temps pas travaillé ses chansons. Lui et le patron Verner jouaient toujours en fin de spectacle une pièce en un acte dont ils n'avaient appris que le commencement et la fin."

20. Condemi, *Cafés-Concerts,* 60.

21. Ibid., 60.

22. Sallée and Chauveau, *Music-Hall et café-concert,* 13.

23. Ibid., 13.

24. Condemi, *Cafés-Concerts,* 84.

25. Jean-Claude Klein, *Chanson à l'affiche: Histoire de la chanson française du café-concert à nos jours* (Paris: Du May, 1991), 29, provides a useful chart of the various performance genres .

26. See Rae Beth Gordon's wide-ranging and original analysis of the "epileptic" mode of performance in *Why the French Love Jerry Lewis: From Cabaret to Early Cinema,* (Stanford, Calif.: Stanford University Press, 2001).

27. Klein, *Chanson à l'affiche,* 31.

28. Sallée and Chauveau, *Music-Hall et café-concert,* 177.

29. Caradec and Weill, *Café-Concert,* 33.

30. Clark, *Painting of Modern Life,* 244, quoting Guy de Maupassant, *Bel-ami,* ed. G. Delaisement (Paris, 1959), 16: "[D]errière nous, le plus drôle de mélange qui soit dans Paris. . . . Il y a de tout, de toutes les professions et de toutes les castes, mais la crapule domine. Voici des employés, employés de banque, de magasin, de ministère, des reporters, des souteneurs, des officiers en bourgeois, des gommeux en habit, qui viennent de dîner au cabaret et qui sor-

tent de l'Opéra avant d'entrer aux Italiens, et puis encore tout un monde d'hommes suspects qui défient l'analyse."

31. Edmond and Jules de Goncourt, quoted in Caradec and Weill, *Café-Concert,* 42: "Au fond, un théâtre avec une rampe; là-dessus, j'ai vu un comique en habit noir. Il a chanté des choses sans suite, coupées de gloussements, de cris de basse-cour en chaleur, d'une gesticulation épileptique . . . . La salle était ent-housiasmée, délirante. . . . Je ne sais, mais il me semble que nous approchons d'une révolution."

32. Condemi, *Cafés-Concerts,* 88.

33. Marcel Carné celebrates precisely those devoted fans seated in *le paradis* in *Les Enfants du paradis* (1945).

34. *La Vagabonde,* trans. Charlotte Remfry Kidd (1910; New York: Bantam, 1994), 50–51.

35. Yvette Guilbert and Harold Simpson, *Yvette Guilbert: Struggles and Victories* (London: Mills & Boon, 1910), 106.

36. Mistinguett, *Toute ma vie* (Paris: René Julliard, 1954), 1: 47: "Ba-ta-clan, l'Eldorado, le Casino Montmarpasse et le Casino Saint-Martin, étaient les caf' conc' les plus populaires. Aux places bon marché, on voyait en foule des femmes en cheveux et des casquettes à carreaux. On ne se gênait pas pour dire leur fait aux artistes et quand leur tête ne plaisait pas, on les bombardait de noyaux de cerises et de pelures d'oranges. Le public n'avait pas l'applaudissement facile et il en voulait pour son argent. Mais lorsqu'il vous adoptait, il reprenait votre chanson aux refrains. C'était comme une promesse de mariage."

37. Laurent Tailhade, *Quelques fantômes de jadis,* quoted in Caradec and Weill, *Café-Concert,* 51–52: "Quand elle parut, avec son masque de louve, sa taille maigre et déhanchée, avec ses bras trop courts, ses belles mains qu'elle ne ganta plus depuis un certain soir où l'Empereur en avait fait l'éloge, avec sa voix qui mordait, riche en inflexions, Thérésa prit immédiatement sur la foule une autorité qui n'appartient qu'aux rois de scène, aux artistes souverains."

38. T. J. Clark, "The Bar at the Folies-Bergère," in *Popular Culture in France: The Wolf and the Lamb,* ed. Jacques Beauroy, Marc Bertrand, and Edward T. Gargan (Saratoga, Calif.: Anma Libri, 1977), 241.

39. Ibid., 247.

40. Ibid.

41. In addition to the work of T. J. Clark, I have relied upon the following for general background information on Thérésa: Sallée and Chauveau, *Music-Hall et café-concert*; Chantal Brunschwig, Louis-Jean Calvet, and Jean-Claude Klein, *Cent ans de chanson française* (Paris: Seuil, 1981); Caradec and Weill, *Café-Concert*; Klein, *Chanson à l'affiche*; and Thérésa, *Mémoires de Thérésa,* 2d ed. (Paris: E. Dentu, 1865).

42. Klein, *Chanson à l'affiche,* 17.

43. Ibid., 18.

44. Thérésa, *Mémoires,* 314: "Le succès d'une de mes chansons nouvelles me préoccupe tout autant, sinon plus, que le succès d'une grosse opération finan-cière n'inquiète les frères Péreire."

45. Klein, *Chanson à l'affiche,* 17.

46. Colin Crisp, *The Classic French Cinema* (Bloomington: Indiana University Press, 1997), 218.

47. Brunschwig, Calvet, and Klein, *Cent ans de chanson française,* 364.

48. Ibid.

49. Thérésa, *Mémoires,* 233–34: "J'attache un grand prix aux applaudissements du public en général, mais j'avoue que j'ai un faible pour la partie malheureuse de la population. Est-ce parce que je suis fille du peuple et que j'ai été malheureuse comme eux? Non! Mais il me semble que ceux-là méritent tout notre intérêt. De loin en loin ils arrachent une soirée libre à leur vie de fatigue et de travail. Il faut les amuser à tout prix, car ils n'ont pas les moyens de revenir le lendemain."

50. Ibid., 2.

51. Ibid., 9–10.

52. Ibid., 300.

53. Ibid., 230.

54. Ibid., 14: "Il me semblait tout simple qu'on chantât comme on mangeait, pour obéir à la voix de la nature."

55. Ibid., 15: "J'avais le sentiment de l'indépendance comme toutes les filles de ma condition qui ont grandi en plein air; mon père m'avait appris à lire et à écrire; je n'avais jamais fréquenté une école, personne ne m'avait jamais imposé sa volonté; mon caractère s'était développé librement avec les instincts de ma nature un peu sauvage."

56. Ibid., 153: "[J]'ai eu mon idylle, ma pastorale pleine de poésie et de douleur. . . . L'amour n'est-il pas, lui aussi, une religion dont les femmes sont incessamment les apôtres? J'ai aimé. J'ai aimé avec frénésie, avec délire."

57. Eugénie Buffet, *Ma vie, mes amours, mes aventures* (Paris: Eugène Figuière, 1930), 12.

58. Ibid., 13: "[L]e charme de la musique, la magie du chant, l'ardeur des bravos, le rappel fait aux artistes, me transportaient, me rendaient folle. . . . Mon rêve prenait une forme; mon âme avait une vie; j'étais plus une enfant inconsciente et désorientée; j'étais une artiste déjà, par l'ampleur de mon enthousiasme et la puissance de mon désir. Ma décision était prise, inébranlable. J'aurais renversé désormais de mon coeur tous les vieux préjugés sentimentaux, pour que triomphât ma volonté suprême: faire du théâtre."

59. Ibid., 25: "Toutes les femmes qui, comme moi, ont souffert et lutté, toutes celles qui portent en elles le fier idéal du courage et la haine des promiscuités injurieuses de l'homme, comprendront les angoisses torturantes que j'éprouvai à la pensée que, pour échapper à un sort de misère et à une défaite artistique finale, il me faudrait peut-être connaître une destinée plus honteuse encore, me ravaler au rang des pauvresses obligées de subir de dégradants baisers, en échange des quelques louis qui les font vivre!"

60. Ibid., 19: "Etait-ce ma faute si une volonté supérieure à la mienne, me poussait vers le théâtre, vers la chanson, vers l'art?"

61. Ibid., 27–28: "Il était un peu semblable à ses explorateurs qui, revenus de

leurs voyages à travers les steppes et les pampas, promènent avec orgueil et ostentation des collections d'insectes bizarres, et traînent avec eux de jolies tigresses à peine apprivoisées qui font peur à tout le monde."

62. Ibid., 28: "Tout me plaisait en lui: ses chansons, pleins de souffrance et de révolte, sa diction simple et pathétique, sa voix mordante. Ce fut une révélation. J'allais l'entendre souvent et, un soir, je l'abordai et lui dis: 'Si l'on mettait en scène ces malheureuses telles que vous les dépeignez, qu'en diriez-vous?'"

63. Caradec and Weill, *Café-Concert*, 95.

64. Vincendeau, *"Mise-en-Scène,"* 113.

65. *Dictionnaire historique de la langue francaise*, s.v. *pierreuse*.

66. Alain Corbin, *Women for Hire: Prostitution and Sexuality in France after 1850*, trans. Alan Sheridan (Cambridge, Mass.: Harvard University Press, 1990), 148.

67. Bernard Marchand, *Paris, histoire d'une ville XIXe–XXe siècle* (Paris: Seuil, 1993) 209–10.

68. Klein, *Chanson à l'affiche*, 70–71.

69. Ibid., 71.

70. "L'Hirondelle du faubourg" (1912), lyrics, Ernest Dumont; music, Louis Benech.

71. Buffet, *Ma vie*, 56–57: "Je ne dormais plus, je ne mangeais plus, je ne vivais que dans l'ambiance de mes chansons. Je les vivais elles-mêmes, comme un écrivain qui fait un roman et qui s'enfonce dans le milieu où évoluent ses personnages. La nuit, je suivais les radeuses des boulevards extérieurs, par tous les temps. Tapie dans l'ombre des ruelles, j'épiais leurs appels aux passants, les filais de loin, en rasant les murs, écoutais leurs propos dans l'encorgnre des portes d'hôtel borgne; parfois même, maquillée et vêtue comme elles, je me glissais parmi les tables des bouges et je me mêlais à leur conversation."

72. Ibid., 60: "[C]e n'était plus une individualité que je montrais, mais l'image d'un type générique, et c'est par là qu'on voulut bien reconnaître que s'affirmait ma personnalité! La livrée de l'amour errant que je portais, la défroque usée de la Prostitution que je revêtais chaque soir, c'était l'image même de la misère sociale de la femme."

73. Rieger, "'J'cass'rai la gueule aux proprios,'" 215.

74. Buffet, *Ma vie*, 69: "Georges Daniel, reporter du *Journal*. . . . désirait faire un reportage sur les chanteurs ambulantes, les chanteurs des rues, mail il voulait, avant tout, que les décors et les personnages fussent pittoresques, et, pour tout dire, son intention intime était de [truquer] son reportage afin d'en corser l'originalité. Il ne souhaitait rien moins, pour la réalisation de ce project, que d'opérer avec de véritables artistes. . . . la supercherie journalistique de Daniel m'avait séduite, plus que séduite; subjugée. Chanter ainsi pour le peuple, dans le peuple, avec lui, c'était une partie de mon rêve réalisé."

75. Ibid., 69: "Le peuple aime les chansons. Il les a toujours aimées. Il les aimait surtout de mon temps, avec une ferveur naïve et passionnée. Il fallait voir, les soirs d'été, à la lueur de quelque lampe à pétrole, ces groupes d'ouvriers et d'ouvrières écouter, sur les boulevards populaires les refrains d'amour, les cou-

plets sentimentaux ou patriotiques qui faisaient monter aux yeux bien des larmes et passer dans les fibres d'ardents frissons! Quel spectacle simple et réconfortant! Quel touchant tableau!"

76. Cécile Giteau, "Yvette Guilbert et la Bibliothèque nationale," in *Yvette Guilbert: Diseuse fin de siècle* (Paris: Bibliothèque nationale, 1994), 67.

77. Noëlle Giret, "Le Cinéma selon Madame Yvette Guilbert," in *Yvette Guilbert: Diseuse fin de siècle* (Paris: Bibliothèque nationale, 1994), 41–47.

78. Ibid., 41.

79. Ibid., 43.

80. Guilbert and Simpson, *Struggles and Victories,* 56.

81. Rifkin, *Street Noises,* 60.

82. Ibid.

83. Ibid., 61.

CHAPTER 2. MUSIC HALL MISS

1. Klein, *Chanson à l'affiche,* 40–41.

2. Ibid., 41.

3. Sallée and Chauveau, *Music-Hall et café-concert,* 154.

4. Louis-Jean Calvet, *Chanson et société* (Paris: Payot, 1981) 70.

5. Charles Rearick, *The French in Love and War: Popular Culture in the Era of the World Wars* (New Haven, Conn.: Yale University Press, 1997) 83.

6. Ibid., 95.

7. Ibid., 95.

8. The music hall critic Gustave Fréjaville emphasizes the distinction between extravagant, *féerie*-inspired revue and the older *revue littéraire,* sometimes called the *revue satirique.* The *revue littéraire* developed in the *cabarets de chansonniers* and were meant to appeal mainly to the mind. The new *revue à spectacle* was understood to appeal primarily to the eye. Fréjaville, *Au music-hall* (Paris: Monde nouveau, 1922), 27.

9. Jean-Claude Klein, "Borrowing, Syncretism, Hybridisation: The Parisian Revue of the 1920s," *Popular Music* 5 (1985): 177.

10. Ibid., 177–78.

11. Ibid., 180.

12. Ibid., 181.

13. Ibid., 180, quoting Louis Roubaud, *Music-hall* (Paris, 1929).

14. Klein, "Borrowing," 180.

15. Pierre Bost, *Le Cirque et le music-hall* (Paris: René Hilsum, 1931), 25.

16. Ibid., 26–28: "La recette, la voici. On prend deux vedettes de bonne grosseur, ou une seule, si elle est d'une grosseur exceptionnelle (de celles-ci, on n'en compte guère que quatre ou cinq à la surface des terres habitées); une paire de danseurs virtuoses, un comique (indispensable); deux comédiens honorables; une danseuse nue, un grand truc de mise en scène; une danseuse (ou comédienne) 'originale'; un orchestre étranger et enfin (indispensable) une troupe de *girls* bien entraînées, qui sont d'ailleurs, en général, le meilleur de tous

ces ingrédients. Si possible (de plus en plus recommandé) une troupe de *boys*. On alterne les scènes de danses, les évocations historiques, le sketch comique, le sketch dramatique (facultatif); on met autour de tout cela une nombreuse figuration, de la lumière, un brin de fausse poésie, quelques grammes de tragique épais (facultatif), un peu de polissonnerie, une chanson anglaise, une ou deux plaisanteries d'actualité, genre Montmartre (qui ratent à coup sûr), et l'on sert. Deux actes, quarante tableaux, cinq cents artistes, trois mille costumes, demandez le programme, esquimaux, chocolats glacés, pochettes surprises, vestiaire, promenoir. . . . Fauteuil d'orchestre quatre-vingts francs, salle comble pendant six mois."

17. Louis Léon-Martin, *Le Music-Hall et ses figures* (Paris: Éditions de France, 1928), 22.

18. Legrand-Chabrier, "Le Music-Hall," in *Les Spectacles à travers les âges* (Paris: Cygne, 1931), 278–79.

19. Fréjaville, *Au music-hall*, 28: "Les revues à spectacle ont pris pendant la guerre un développement remarquable. Du tumulte et de la lumière, des couleurs aveuglantes, une profusion d'effets décoratifs, peu ou point de texte: voilà où nous en étions en 1919. Une foule se ruait aux lumières, ivre d'incertitude, avide de bruit, de mouvement et de couleur. Une seule pensée hantait les cerveaux, pensée poignante, atroce, qu'il s'agissait de mettre en fuite pour une heure ou deux. Tous les stupéfiants semblaient bons pour cet office. On se saoûlait de jazz-band, de cuisses levées, de gros rires, de grosse sottise, de grossiers symboles, d'étendards brandis on cadence par des femmes demi-nues, de lourdes plaisanteries, de panaches et de paillons. De la rue baigné de ténèbres, où planaient des souffles de mort, on passait avec délices à cet enfer éblouissant."

20. Ibid., 95: "les coeurs battent d'un rythme unique et répondent à chaque intention du chanteur."

21. Ibid.: "la chanson, dans sa variété infinie, tour à tour tendre, enthousiaste, malicieuse, héroïque, frondeuse, ironique, libertine ou même gauloise."

22. Léon-Martin, *Music-Hall et ses figures*, 61: "L'orchestre, qui jouait en sourdine, attaque de tous ses archets et de tous ses cuivres; au bout des bras les cannes se lèvent, et les projecteurs, se concentrant en haut de l'escalier, vont chercher une femme vêtue de tulle et de perles et que couronne une immense auréole d'aigrettes roses. La femme descend; elle a l'aisance et la sécurité, et elle a aussi le ravissement. Nulle fierté empruntée, nulle distinction de commande, nulle froideur et nulle pose, mais un surprenant naturel, une simplicité inimitable, la grâce d'une parisienne aimant les hommages et une joie immense, une joie neuve et comme donnée, une joie du coeur et du visage, une joie persuasive qui gagne la salle entière, d'où l'ovation jaillit en hommage à l'étoile dont le sourire, sous l'émoi, s'attendrit. Ce n'est rien, et c'est une merveilleuse réussite. C'est un instant, mais cet instant résume le music-hall. C'est un moment de charme sensible, de panache et de gentillesse. C'est une entrée de Mistinguett."

23. Ibid., 62.

24. Martin Pénet, *Mistinguett: La Reine du music-hall* (Paris: Rocher, 1995), 11, quoting Mistinguett.

25. Ibid., 214.

26. Mistinguett, *Toute ma vie*, 1: 93: "Comment on devient la môme Flora, c'est difficile à dire. On se regarde dans la glace, mais on regarde surtout dans sa mémoire. Il ne s'agit pas d'avoir été la môme Flora, mais de l'avoir vue passer dans la rue, de l'avoir entendue parler, de l'avoir reconnue, de l'avoir suivie. Ce n'est pas un don. C'est de la mémoire, de l'expérience, de l'imagination. Et du travail. Il faut avoir vu, avoir senti, avoir rêvé. Avoir pensé. Etre chiffonnière à la scène, ça représente beaucoup d'éducation. Pas l'éducation en conserve. Celle de la rue."

27. Pénet, *Mistinguett*, 206, quoting Nozière: "Soudain, un demi-jour et la rôdeuse rencontre l'ami au visage blafard. Ils sont entrés dans le bal parce qu'ils étaient las d'errer sur le boulevard. Peut-être s'y est-il réfugié parce qu'il vient de faire un mauvais coup. Sa main est tachée de sang. Il cherche à s'étourdir. Et, soudain, il a saisi la femme. Impérieux, brutal, il la tient. Elle tremble, mais elle est dominée par la puissance du regard qui brille en cette face livide comme l'absinthe. Ah! Comme il la regarde! Quelle expression de cruauté tord sa bouche! Elle voudrait se dégager. Elle y parvient; elle semble y parvenir . . . D'un mouvement de bras, il la remène à lui; il l'étreint. Va-t-il l'adorer ou la tuer? Ses doigts de criminel frôlent le cou féminin, secouent la toison de la chevelure. La fille ne résiste plus, soumise, acceptant l'amour et la mort. Il s'est penché sur ses lèvres: un baiser furieux qui semble une morsure . . . Et, d'une brusque poussée, elle est rejetée loin de lui, comme l'écorce d'un fruit, comme le flacon d'un vin qui donne l'ivresse. Et, plus pâle encore, plus redoutable, il poursuit sa route— vers quels attentats?"

28. Pénet, *Mistinguett*, 203.

29. The apache, in fact, inspired an entire genre of writing about crime in turn-of-the-century France. For an analysis of the crime story in mass circulation daily newspapers, popular novels, and early cinema, see Dominique Kalifa, *L'Encre et le sang: Récits de crimes et société à la Belle Epoque* (Paris: Fayard, 1995). Robin Walz provides a compelling analysis of the *Fantomas* novels in *Pulp Surrealism: Insolent Popular Culture in Early Twentieth-Century Paris* (Berkeley: University of California Press, 2000).

30. Bernard Marchand, *Paris: Histoire d'une ville, XIXe–XXe siècle* (Paris: Seuil, 1993) 211.

31. Ibid., 211.

32. Fréjaville, *Au music-hall*, 76: With regard to the apache dance, "[La danse] exprime en quelques gestes simples et graves la violence du désir, le charme des premières étreintes, le vertige des sens, la soumission passionnée de l'amante, l'orgueil tendre et cruel de la possession."

33. For more information on Mistinguett's films, see the useful filmography in Pénet, *Mistinguett*, 736–46.

34. Richard Abel, *The Ciné Goes to Town: French Cinema, 1896–1914* (Berkeley: University of California Press, 1994), 40–41.

35. Publicity material on *Mistinguett Détective*, Collection Rondel, 4 Rk 6485, Bibliothèque de l'Arsenal.

36. The film was directed by Albert Capellani and written by a well-known playwright, Pierre Decourcelle. I have relied upon Richard Abel's description of *L'Épouvante* in *Ciné Goes to Town*, 214.

37. I thank Richard Abel for sharing his knowledge of this film with me. Abel notes that the film is interesting for "the way in which a French film negotiates its connections to the USA during the war, a negotiation that literally splits Mistinguett into two characters."

38. The composer, arranger, and songwriter Maurice Yvain (1891–1965), who worked in nearly every area of French show business, including music hall, cabaret, operetta, and cinema, composed the musical scores for *Prix de beauté* (1930), *Paris-Béguin* (1931), and *Coeur de Lilas* (1931), films analyzed in this book, as well as for *La Belle Équipe* (Duvivier, 1936) and *Le Plaisir* (Ophuls, 1952). See Alain Lacombe and François Porcile, *Les Musiques du cinéma français* (Paris: Bordas, 1995), 61.

39. For this summary of Carco's play, I have relied upon Pénet, *Mistinguett*, 542–43.

40. "My Man" would have a long career in America as well. Fanny Brice performed it on Broadway and in the film *My Man* (1929); Alice Faye sang it in *Rose of Washington Square* (1938), and Barbara Streisand sang it in *Funny Girl* (1968). "My Man" was also performed by Billie Holliday, Ella Fitzgerald, and Helen Merrill (Pénet, *Mistinguett*, 562).

41. "C'est vrai" (1933), lyrics, Albert Willemetz; music, Casimir Oberfeld.

42. Léon-Paul Fargue, *Music-Hall* (Paris: Bibliophiles du Palais, 1948), 73.

43. Lucienne Cantaloube-Ferrieu, *Chanson et poésie des années 30 aux années 60: Trenet, Brassens, Ferré ou les "enfants naturels" du surréalisme* (Paris: A. G. Nizet, 1981), 48: "Quand Mistinguett, attendrie sans doute, mais surtout blagueuse, clame 'Je suis née dans l'faubourg Saint-Denis' ou 'En douce,' la vérité et la satire social affleurent sous le sourire qui raille. Lorsqu'elle chante 'J'en ai marre' ou 'Mon homme,' sa voix, le ton, la démarche font naître un sourire qui écarte le mélodrame facile et c'est alors peut-être que, plus durement et le mieux, Mistinguett représent comme le pensait Mac Orlan, 'l'expression stylisée pour le music-hall d'un subconscient infiniment tragique.'"

44. "Ça c'est Paris" (1926), lyrics, Lucien Boyer, Jacques-Charles; music, José Padilla.

45. Brunschwig, Calvet, and Klein, *Cent ans de chanson française*, 268, quoting Jean Cocteau.

46. Léon-Martin, *Music-Hall et ses figures*, 64: "Elle aime à manier les étoffes, les rubans, les paillettes, les chiffons et les soieries. Elle y apporte le goût d'une arpète et l'oeil d'une parisienne. J'écris parisienne à dessein. On sait le rayonnement de la parisienne dans le monde. Mistinguett—malgré ses origines—personifie la parisienne avec un étonnant bonheur, une exactitude saisissante, bonheur et vérité qui sont à l'origine même de son universelle renommée."

47. Pierre Mac Orlan, "Mademoiselle Mistinguett," in *Lanterne sourde*, 72: "Si, dans ses chansons—fort bien faites d'ailleurs—Mlle Mistinguett évoque, le

plus souvent, une silhouette de pauvresse sous la bise, c'est avec les mains vio-
lettes d'avoir tenue les premiers brins de muguet et la voix douloureuse pour
avoir crié *l'Intran* qu'elle nous offre le coeur toujours inédit d'une fillette de
Belleville à qui rien n'interdit un avenir doré."

48. Fargue, *Music-Hall*, 73: "Elle est parisienne par la repartie prompte et
souvent dure, par le coup d'oeil, le sourire, la vitesse des réaction, le sens du
ridicule, du raté, du soufflé; elle est parisienne par le balancement des épaules, la
ruse du regard, la facilité du geste, le scepticisme, l'incrédulité, la raillerie toujours aiguisée. Elle est parisienne par ses mains aux hanches, ses paupières méfi-
antes de jeune chatte, ses chevilles et ses jarrets uniques au monde, son talent de
faire quelque chose d'énorme avec rien du tout. Enfin sa foi. C'est une parisienne du Paris le moins surfait, le plus vrai, le moins imitable et le plus sensible.
Par elle, loin de mon appartement et de mes bouquins, me revenaient toujours
les murmures odorants de la rue Lepic, de la Bastille, de la Cité, des Batignolles,
de Saint-Ouën. Je revoyais, à la faveur d'un disque ou d'une photo, les porce-
lainiers de la rue de Paradis, les camions des Halles, le canal de l'Ourcq, ses hor-
logues et ses briques, les mecs assis aux terrasses, le vin blanc des boulevards, les
bouquetières, les kiosques, les taxis, les tabacs, le marbre des bistros, l'ardoise et
le téléphone, les stations de métro, le P.M.U., les trains de banlieue. Par elle, dans
l'Indre, dans les Alpes-Maritimes, à Marseille, à Murano, à Bâle, à Amsterdam,
partout le nom de Mistinguett, évoqué, chanté ou prononcé, me rendait Paris
manquant, Paris maternel et tragique, Paris si nécessaire et si rassurant."

49. Bost, *Le Cirque et le music-hall*, 142: "Je reconnais volontiers qu'elle a
eu une influence considérable sur l'évolution du music-hall, à Paris, depuis de
longues années; qu'elle est d'autre part la seule vedette féminine française capable de tenir l'affiche d'une revue à grand spectacle; qu'elle est seule capable (on
nous l'a tant dit!) de descendre un escalier suivie de sept mètres de plumes et
coiffée de quinze livres d'aigrettes, qu'elle est une danseuse acrobatique de
bonne force; qu'elle a le sens du music-hall, de la décoration et de la mise en
scène; qu'elle est en quelque sorte l'auteur responsable des revues où elle n'est
nommèe que comme interprète; que sa vie est toute de labeur, de recherches et
d'amour du métier; que, surtout, le public l'adore et ne se lasse pas de l'ap-
plaudir; que les chansons qu'elle a lancées, de 'J'en ai marre' à 'Mon homme' ou
à 'Valencia' ont fait le tour du monde treize fois dans les deux sens. . . . La question est de savoir s'il peut suffire d'avoir de l'abatage pour faire une grande
vedette de music-hall, et si le répertoire faubourien, les histoires de la pauvre
môme battue, amoureuse et héroïque, peuvent être supportables. . . . Ah! ces
sketches écrits pour que Mistinguett, sous un projecteur, lance la chanson destinée à couvrir, par la vente en album, disques et rouleaux perforés, la moitié des
frais de la revue! Vraiment, vraiment, pourquoi de tels spectacles ont-ils encore
du succès?"

50. Ibid., 138.

51. Dudley Andrew, "Family Diversions: French Popular Cinema and the
Music Hall," in *Popular European Cinema*, ed. Richard Dyer and Ginette Vincendeau (New York: Routledge, 1992), 18.

52. Anne-Marie Sohn, "Entre deux guerres: Les Rôles féminins en France et en Angleterre," in *Histoire des femmes,* ed. Georges Duby and Michelle Perrot, vol. 5: *Le XXe Siècle,* ed. Françoise Thébaud (Paris: Plon, 1992), 97; James McMillan, *Housewife or Harlot: The Place of Women in French Society, 1870–1940* (New York: St. Martin's Press, 1981), 132.

53. McMillan, *Housewife or Harlot,* 117. In 1906, some 779,000 women were employed in commercial jobs; by 1921, that figure had risen to 1,008,000. In 1906, there were 293,000 women working in the liberal professions and public services; by 1921, there were 491,000.

54. Ibid., 117.

55. Ibid., 118.

56. Eugen Weber, *The Hollow Years: France in the 1930s* (New York: Norton, 1994), 59.

57. Anne Higonnet, "Femmes, images et représentations," in *Histoire des femmes,* ed. Georges Duby and Michelle Perrot, vol. 5: *Le XXe Siècle,* ed. Françoise Thébaud (Paris: Plon, 1992), 329.

58. Weber, *Hollow Years,* 76–78.

59. Sohn, "Entre deux guerres," 93.

60. Ibid., 109.

61. Weber, *Hollow Years,* 76.

62. Ibid., 301.

63. For a full account of this battle, see Laurence Klejman and Florence Rochefort, *L'Egalité en marche: Le Féminisme sous la Troisième République* (Paris: Presses de la Fondation nationale des sciences politiques, 1989).

64. Between 1880 and 1910, 72 percent of abortion cases ended in acquittal. In the period 1925–34, fewer than 20 percent did. Weber, *Hollow Years,* 77.

65. McMillan, *Housewife or Harlot,* 182–92.

66. Ibid., 157.

67. Weber, *Hollow Years,* 83

68. *Cinématographie française,* March 19, 1937.

69. Mistinguett's performance style hardly varies between the lullaby and the nightclub performance, and this is one of the many weaknesses of *Rigoloboche.* It appears that, after nearly fifty years of performing in the music hall, Mistinguett found it difficult to modulate her performance style in a way that was appropriate for the cinema by the mid 1930s.

70. "Oui! Je suis d'Paris" (1936), lyrics, Pierre Bayle and Léopold de Lima; music, Casimir Oberfeld.

71. The scene echoes a passage in Mistinguett's autobiography, in which she recounts how she turned down an offer of marriage from the aristocratic father of her child in favor of her music hall career.

72. Georges Sadoul, "Apropos Several Recent Films" (1936), in *French Film Theory and Criticism: A History/Anthology, 1907–1939,* vol. 2: *1929–1939,* ed. Richard Abel (Princeton, N.J.: Princeton University Press, 1988), 219.

73. Andrew, "Family Diversions."

74. Ibid., 24.

75. Ibid., 18. Andrew is right to point out this casting irony, for the music hall of the 1930s bore very little resemblance to the café-concert of the 1860s, the environment that produced the popular dancer Rigolboche.

76. George Stuart, "Un soir d'autrefois à Bobino, aujourd'hui ..." *Le Soir*, January 25, 1928: "Un tableau de la super-revue d'un grand music-hall nous offre, en ce moment, l'évocation du vieux Caf'-Conc'. C'est charmant, délicat et un peu nostalgique. Comme on savait rire et sourire, alors, comme la gaieté y résonnait honnête, fraîche et franche! Que de choses la guerre et le jazz-band ont tuées sur la piste et sur les plateaux! Cependant, on peut respirer encore cette atmosphère, évanouie partout ailleurs, entre les murs repeints de ce vieux Bobino. . . . J'imagine que l'ombre de Richepin, celles de Goudeau, de Métra et de François Coppée le viennent hanter comme jadis. Elles y retrouvent sans surprise le comique traditionnel qui est, cette semaine, M. Miss, tirant de sa voix, de ses jambes, de ses mains. . . . Enfin Yvette Guilbert nous donne le régal de son répertoire d'autrefois. Elle a quitté ses longues mitaines et sa robe au fourreau étroit. C'est en flottant costume d'apparait que la reine de la chanson française paraît aujourd'hui sur la scène. Comique ou tendre, narquoise ou pitoyable, elle dit, chante, vit. . . . et, de l'orchestre où les gens chic sont venus de lointains quartiers, au poulailler où les habitués, debout, grignotent les beignets et les frites, c'est le silence absolu, parfait. Ce silence qui est, pour l'artiste, l'hommage le plus précieux et le plus délicat et qui se résout tout à coup dans le tonnerre des applaudissements, quand le Fiacre ... cahin-caha ... a fini sa joyeuse course."

77. Sallée and Chauveau, *Music-Hall et café-concert*, 160–61.

78. Ibid., 161, quoting José de Bérys.

79. Ibid., 124.

80. Ibid.

CHAPTER 3. VOICES FROM THE PAST

1. Pierre Mac Orlan, "La Seine et les ponts de Paris," in *Lanterne sourde*, 11–16.

2. One particularly interesting example is *Envoûtement de Paris* (1938), an essay about Paris by Francis Carco (pseudonym of François Carcopino-Tusoli) with photographs of the city by René Jacques, which mixes nonfiction and fiction, in that the photographs' captions are excerpted from Carco's novels. For example, an image of a street in a poor neighborhood is captioned "Le quartier sentait la misère" (The neighborhood smelled of misery), which is identified as a quotation from Carco's novel *Paname* ("Paname" is slang for Paris). See also Léon-Paul Fargue's *Le Piéton de Paris* (1932; reprint, Paris: Gallimard, 1995), and Eugène Dabit's collected essays on Paris from the 1930s in *Ville lumière* (Paris: Dilettante, 1990).

3. Mac Orlan, "La Seine et les ponts de Paris," 13: "C'est ordinairement dans l'ombre d'un pont, au bord de la berge où les flots clapotent que l'on retrouve quelques pièces détachées de femmes coupées en morceaux. Ces dernières années furent particulièrement prodigues de ce genre d'assassinat qui donne une

coloration perverse aux ombres de la Seine et surtout aux locaux dont les murs furent témoins de ce genre d'opération. Cette image appliquée à l'une de ces mille maisons, entremêlées de guinguettes que l'on trouve au bord de la Seine, dans les faubourgs de la ville, donne une singulière qualité littéraire à des logements, au demeurant terrorisées par les punaises. On rencontre dans ces parages des figures latines, que les poils bruns, mal rasés sur des peux verdies par le sommeil à la belle étoile, rendent merveilleusement responsables de tout ce que les promeneurs solitaires, qui appartiennent à un autre genre, peuvent imaginer. Mais que dire des filles, des jeunes filles dédiées à cette détresse sans remède?"

4. Ibid.: "Les filles chantées par Fréhel naissent sous des ponts. C'est sous un pont, peut-être un pont plus nuptial, à cause de la richesse de son ornementation, que leur chair secrète s'émut pour la première fois. . . . [C]elles-ci, nées sur la pierre humide, participent des paysages urbains de la Seine et connaissent, peut-être, la farouche volupté d'être les déesses de l'égout, celles de la fumée noire des remorqueurs et du sombre silence qui accueille l'adieu à la vie des suicidés inconsistants."

5. For further examples of the importance of décor in the writings of Mac Orlan and other interwar writers, see Cantaloube-Ferrieu, *Chanson et poésie*, 32–34. For more information on the literary influences of poetic realist films, see Dudley Andrew, *Mists of Regret: Culture and Sensibility in Classic French Film* (Princeton, N.J.: Princeton University Press, 1995), 148–92.

6. Andrée Turcy (1891–1974), a contemporary of Damia and Fréhel, performed the realist song in the cabaret and the music hall beginning in 1910.

7. Andrew, *Mists of Regret*, 157.

8. Mac Orlan wrote the preface to Atget's 1930 *Photographie de Paris* and the text for Brassaï's volume of photographs, *The Secret Paris of the Thirties*. Andrew, *Mists of Regret*, 158.

9. Brunschwig, Calvet, and Klein, *Cent ans de chanson française*, 245.

10. Cantaloube-Ferrieu, *Chanson et poésie*, 148–49. For a sampling of Mac Orlan's songs, see Pierre Mac Orlan, *Chansons pour accordéon* (Paris: Gallimard, 1953). Mac Orlan's songs of the *pègre*, the légionnaires, the sailors—the *petit peuple*—were, according to Cantaloube-Ferrieu, resolutely backward-looking and quite at odds with the light-hearted songs of Charles Trenet, who made his debut in 1932. "En 1936 ses chansons semblent donc déjà entièrement tournées vers le passé, vers un monde en train de mourir sinon déjà mort [In 1936 his songs thus seemed already completely oriented toward the past, toward a world in the process of dying, if not already dead]." Cantaloube-Ferrieu places Mac Orlan, instead, in the romantic universe of Villon and Rimbaud. "Le mérite de Mac Orlan paraît se situer essentiellement dans l'achèvement d'un style plus que dans le renouvellement d'un genre, Mac Orlan donnant une existence littéraire aux chansons dites réalistes qui firent les délices des années 1920 [The merits of Mac Orlan seem to be essentially located in the accomplishment of a style more than in the renewel of a genre, with Mac Orlan giving a literary existence to songs known by the name *réaliste* that were the delight of the 1920s]."

11. Montero [b. 1909] made her debut in Madrid in the late 1930s and then

performed Spanish songs for the Parisian public. She also sang the songs of Jacques Prévert, Léo Ferré, and Aristide Bruant. Brunschwig, Calvet, and Klein, *Cent ans de chanson française*, 276.

12. Ibid., 191.

13. Rifkin, *Street Noises*, 73.

14. Brunschwig, Calvet, and Klein, *Cent ans de chanson française*, 82. "Le Doux Caboulot" (1931), lyrics, Francis Carco; music, Jacques Larmanjat.

15. *Paris-Béguin* and *Paris la nuit* are discussed in chapter 4.

16. *Cinématographie française*, March 31, 1939.

17. Andrew, *Mists of Regret*, 101–5.

18. Francis Carco [François Carcopino-Tusoli], *Prisons de femmes* (Paris: Éditions de France, 1931).

19. The close friendship between Juliette and Régine is the only vestige of the lesbian prison relationships explored by Carco in his nonfiction work *Prisons de femmes*.

20. "Je n'ai pas le temps d'aimer" (1938), lyrics, R. Jolivet and J. Lenoir; music, Jean Lenoir.

21. Fréhel, "La Complainte de ma vie," *Point de vue—Images du monde*, no. 31 (January 6, 1949): 16. Fréhel's life story was right at home in the sensationalistic *Point de vue*. Alongside the first installment of her memoirs are an excerpt from one of Georges Simenon's novels, photographs of bloody car accidents and stars' weddings, crime stories, and articles on yoga, acupuncture, and tattoos. "La complainte de ma vie, la complainte de ma vie. . . . Et comment n'appellerais-je pas ma vie une complainte, moi, qui depuis l'âge de cinq ans, n'ai cessé de pousser la romance, moi qui, à cinq ans, paraît-il, sans rien savoir de l'existence, faisait passer dans mes chansons toute la misère du coeur humain, toute la frénésie de l'amour et toute sa tristesse? Coups durs, coups de cafard, joies, triomphes et déchéances, ma vie roule tout cela pêle-mêle. Un seule moment me retrouve chaque soir pareille à moi-même, c'est celui où, devant la rampe, tout fait silence en moi; où, à l'être tumultueux que je suis, se substitue l'image que le public s'est faite de moi: Fréhel, la complainte de Paris. J'ai eu de bons instants et d'autres atroces, j'ai été pauvre, j'ai été riche, j'ai fait des folies et même des bêtises, j'ai aimé avec passion et détésté avec force, j'ai roulé ma bosse ici et là et j'ai vu beaucoup de choses. En somme, ça ne fait pas une trop mauvaise complainte."

22. In addition to the series published in *Point de vue—Images du monde*, see Maurice Verne's account of Fréhel's life in *Les Amuseurs de Paris* (Paris: Éditions de France, 1932).

23. Her performance of this song gave her the nickname "Pervanche" (Periwinkle) for the first part of her career. "Fréhel," which she later adopted as her permanent stage name, comes from the Bretonne location Cap Fréhel.

24. The success Montéhus's songs and performances with working-class audiences relied heavily upon stereotypical images, opposing the working man in a cloth cap to the *monsieur' à chapeau*. His working-class audiences became disillusioned, when, after World War I, he began performing for bourgeois audi-

ences wearing a worker's cap and a red belt. Brunschwig, Calvet and Klein, *Cent ans de chanson française*, 274–75.

25. "Je chantais le répertoire de Montéhus, des complaintes de misère et de douleur. En chantant, je revoyais tous les coups durs de mon enfance, l'escalier noir, la tentative du vieux monsieur dans le champ vague, les taloches, le manque de tendresse autour de moi, l'abandon, et j'ai mis ce jour-là, comme je l'ai toujours fait depuis, toute mon âme dans ces complaintes." Fréhel, " La Complainte de ma vie," *Point de vue—Images du monde*, no. 32 (January 13, 1949): 18.

26. Colette, *La Vagabonde* (1910), trans. Charlotte Remfry Kidd (New York: Bantam Books, 1994), 14–15.

27. "[E]n pleine beauté, en pleine vogue, en plein bonheur, je brulais la vie. Pouvais-je me douter que les jours sombres étaient si proches, les jours de colère, les jours de désespoir?" Fréhel, "La Complainte de ma vie," *Point de vue—Images du monde*, no. 33 (January 20, 1949): 21.

28. Verne, *Amuseurs de Paris*, 175.

29. "Foulard rouge à l'abandon, jupe plissée, poing sur les hanches et aux lèvres, une 'goualante,' c'est moi, Fréhel, telle qu'on pouvait me voir sur les scènes du music-hall parisien, à l'époque où le père Poincaré promenait sa barbichette sur les finances de la France. Ah! certes, j'avais bien changé. La 'Pervenche' de la douceur de vivre, mince comme une cigarière de Carmen, avait fait place à une grosse mémère, mafflue et truculente, avec des bras de République. Mais ce qui restait, c'était ma verdeur et ma franchise, ces deux armes essentielles pour qui veut s'essayer aux glorioles illuminées du caf' conc' où le public est le plus difficile du monde." Fréhel, "La Complainte de ma vie," *Point de vue—Images du monde*, no. 39 (March 3, 1949): 12.

30. Brunschwig, Calvet, and Klein, *Cent ans de chanson française*, 171.

31. See Vincendeau's superb analysis of Gabin's star image in Gauteur and Vincendeau, *Jean Gabin*, 93–203.

32. Andrew, *Mists of Regret*, 160.

33. Alain Lacombe and Nicole Lacombe, *Fréhel* (Paris: Pierre Belfond, 1990), 216, quoting Pierre La Mazière.

34. For more on this extraordinary film, see Andrew, *Mists of Regret*, 166–68.

35. "Et v'la pourquoi" (1936), lyrics, Sacha Guitry; music, A. Borchard. "Voilà pourquoi/Chaque dimanche/Je n'remets plus ma robe blanche/Pour me prom'ner dans la forêt/Avec celui que j'adorais."

36. Ginette Vincendeau, *Pépé le Moko* (London: British Film Institute, 1998), 22.

37. Mireille Ballin again plays the kept woman of a wealthy Parisian to Jean Gabin's working-class good guy—this time a soldier and then a printer—in *Gueule d'amour* (Grémillon, 1937).

38. Vincendeau, *Pépé le Moko*, 22.

39. "Où est-il donc?" lyrics, A. Decaye and Lucien Carol; music, Vincent Scotto.

40. Vincendeau, *Pépé le Moko,* 24.

41. Verne, *Amuseurs de Paris,* 182: "L'agressive passion de ce visage presque viril, aux joues larges, la silhouette charnue d'un massif nerveux, le rire qui engueule, et cette voix brisée entraînent vers des paysages de la zone, dans ces bicoques que dominent les fours jamais éteints, les cheminées fumantes des Saint-Denis ou des Aubervilliers du boue, de travail, et les taules des poisses et de leurs amies, mesdames les pierreuses. C'est Fréhel, la chanteuse réaliste, une fille mal couvée d'Aristide Bruant et de l'Yvette Guilbert des débuts. Mais elle, elle en est du peuple."

42. "Elle exprimait pour nous une certain sentimentalité populaire, une certaine gouaille, avec le physique approprié. . . . Elle était Montmartre et davantage encore." Louis Chevalier, *Montmartre du plaisir et du crime* (1980; reprint, Paris: Payot & Rivages, 1995), 352–53.

43. Ibid., 354.

44. Vincent Scotto, one of the most prolific composers of popular songs, operettas, and film scores from the 1930s through the 1950s, wrote the music to both "Où est-il donc?" and the song Jean Gabin sings in celebration of his love affair with Gaby, "Pour être heureux dans la vie."

45. The French artist Francisque Poulbot (1879–1946) was known for his drawings of poor children from Montmartre.

46. Rodolphe Salis (1852–97) was the creator of the Montmartre cabaret Le Chat noir.

47. According to Norma Evenson, *Paris: A Century of Change, 1878–1978* (New Haven, Conn.: Yale University Press, 1979), working-class dwellings in Paris were notoriously substandard at this time. Haussmann's urban renovation in the mid nineteenth century provided a large volume of new, comfortable housing for the middle class, particularly in the west of Paris, but the poor continued to live in deplorable conditions. Workers tended to live in minuscule rooms, typically measuring 1.5 by 2 meters, that lacked running water, heat, or adequate light and ventilation. Tuberculosis thrived in densely built neighborhoods and, although plans to demolish these *îlots insalubres* (unsanitary pockets) were repeatedly considered from the turn of the century onward, the project was delayed due to the onset of the war. The postwar era saw a renewed effort to improve housing conditions when another municipal study conducted in 1919 identified seventeen *îlots insalubres.* The slums were concentrated in eastern Paris in the nineteenth, twentieth, and eleventh arrondissements, particularly in La Villette and Belleville. One *îlot insalubre* was located in Clignancourt, just outside the *barrières* of the city north of the seventeenth and eighteenth arrondissements; others were clustered in the center of Paris. Once again, however, the demolition of the *îlots insalubres* was delayed repeatedly, due to financial problems and legal complexities in procedures of expropriation. Demolition did not begin in earnest until the 1930s, and when it did, the poor tended to be displaced, pushed farther and farther out from the center of Paris (ibid., 211–13). The area Fréhel sings of—from Abbesses to the place du Tertre—was not one of the *îlots insalubres* designated for the demolition of apartment build-

ings. No doubt this area was being cleared and developed with typical modern shortsightedness (the village of Montmartre, which still boasts a vineyard, detached houses, and enclosed yards, is now protected by historical classification, as is most of the city today). But, clearly, her song evoked the chaotic and problem-plagued removal of working-class dwellings during this era for her listeners. The communes evoked in the realist songs, decrepit though they may have been, enjoyed more life and activity on the street. The smaller houses and apartment buildings were never higher than three or four stories, which allowed everyone to hear the street singers and to lean out of their windows to gossip, eavesdrop, and generally know the business of everyone in the faubourg.

48. For a more extensive summary of the new currents in French popular song in the 1930s, see Klein, *Chanson à l'affiche,* 75–87.

49. Lacombe and Lacombe, *Fréhel,* 147.

50. "Dans la rue" (Éditions Salabert, 1931), lyrics, Serge Veber; music, Maurice Yvain.

51. The realist song performed in *Dans les rues,* an important precursor to poetic realism, is "L'Amour commence" (Love Begins), by Jean Nohain. Charlotte Davuia, a second-tier realist singer in the 1930s, sings this pessimistic ballad to the film's young lovers, played by Madeleine Ozeray and Jean-Pierre Aumont.

52. "C'est la rue sans nom" (Éditions Fortin, 1938), lyrics M. A. Malleville; music, Lionel Casaux and Pierre Guillermin. "La Rue de notre amour" (Paul Beuscher Éditions, 1940), lyrics, Maurice Vandair; music, Maurice Alexander.

53. "C'est la rue qui m'a dressée, la rue qui ma faite telle que je suis, avec mes qualités et mes défauts, la rue qui m'a appris à chanter. En passant devant les bistrots, les premiers phonographes à manchons m'envoyaient de leurs voix nasillardes, amplifiées par d'énormes pavillons, les refrains à la mode. Je m'arrêtais net, je restais parfois sous une pluie glaciale ou mes petites jupes soulevées par la bourrasque, en extase pendant des heures. La chanson s'enregistrait en moi, air et paroles: je n'oubliais plus jamais une chanson entendue." Fréhel, "La Complainte de ma vie," *Point de vue—Images du monde* 31 (January 6, 1949): 16.

54. "[L]a Chapelle . . . ce cirque grouillant et sonore où le fer se mêle à l'homme, le train au taxi, le bétail au soldat. Un pays plutôt qu'un arrondissement, formé par des canaux, des usines, les Buttes-Chaumont, le port de la Villette." Fargue, *Piéton de Paris,* 20.

55. "[Q]uartier pur, à la fois riche et serré, ennemi de Dieu et du snobisme." Ibid., 21.

56. "Le soir . . . la Chapelle est bien ce pays d'un merveilleux lugubre et prenant, ce paradis des paumés, des mômes de la cloche et des costauds qui ont l'honneur au bout de la langue et la loyauté au bout des doigts. . . . C'est aussi la Chapelle nocturne que je connais le mieux et que je préfère. Elle a plus de chien, plus d'âme et plus de résonance." Ibid., 24.

57. Chevalier, *Montmartre du plaisir et du crime,* 268–90.

58. Ibid., 270.

59. "Et de même que les images de Zola et de Bruant sont devenues la réalité de Carco et Mac Orlan, les images de Carco et de Mac Orlan deviendront la réalité de Prévert et de Carné dont les images, à leur tour, seront le pain quotidien des jeunes qui viendront après." Ibid.

60. *Cinématographie française*, February 20, 1932.

61. For a full discussion of the protracted process of the destruction and redevelopment of the military fortifications and the Zone, see Evenson, *Paris*.

62. Ibid., 206.

63. Ibid.

64. Rifkin, *Street Noises*, 28.

65. The connection between the realist singers and the geographical margins of Paris continues to be elaborated. An exhibition on the architectural history of the Parisian *faubourgs*, entitled "Paris des Faubourgs," held at the Pavillon de l'Arsenal in Paris October 1996–January 1997, featured, among its maps and photographs, a jukebox offering songs by Fréhel, Damia, Mistinguett, and other popular singers.

66. Klein, *Chanson à l'affiche*, 71.

67. Eugène Dabit, "Un Bal à Belleville," in *Ville Lumière* (1935; reprint, Paris: Dilettante, 1990), 39–44.

68. Brassaï, *Paris secret des années 30*, 73–83.

69. Léger, *Functions of Painting*, 74–77.

70. Gauteur and Vincendeau, *Jean Gabin*, 150.

71. André Sallée, *Les Acteurs français* (Paris: Bordas, 1988), 124.

72. I was unable to locate any further information about this song. Its sheet music can be found at the Département de l'Audiovisuel, 4°Vm15 18920, Bibliothèque nationale.

> N'te plains pas qu'on p'lote ta donzelle
> N'te plains pas quand on te la prendra,
> Ne te plains pas, ne te plains pas!
> Fallait pas la choisir si bell' qu'elle excit' notr' désir.
> Ell' aurait un' sal' gueul'
> On t'la lass' rait pour toi tout seul.
> N'te plains pas qu'la mariée soit trop belle,
> N'te plains pas qu'elle ait de beaux appas,
> Ne te plains pas, ne te plains pas!

73. There is another curious intertexutal link between the film, the realist song, and the performers' autobiographies. Shortly after making *Coeur de Lilas*, Marcelle Romée, the prostitute character dubbed "la Marlène Dietrich française," drowned herself in the Seine after struggling with depression, thus living out the narrative of a typical realist song. [R.M.] "La mort de Marcelle Romée," *Ciné-Miroir*, n.d., PHO 01 106, Bibliothèque de l'Arsenal.

74. Compared to Gabin, André Luguet, the male lead in the film, is rather insipid. *La Cinématographie française*, February 20, 1932, observed that the acting in *Coeur de Lilas* is "exceptional, except for Luguet, who is discreet, but

without real emotion." Luguet is better remembered for his Occupation-era films, including *Battement de coeur* (Henri Decoin, 1939), *Jeunes filles en détresse* (Pabst, 1940), and the sparkling comedy *L'Honorable Catherine* (L'Herbier, 1942). Luguet had acted at the Comédie-Française in the mid 1920s, then spent three years in Hollywood. He returned to the Parisian boulevard theater and to the cinema in the early 1930s, bringing to his film roles an aura of sophistication. André Sallée, *Acteurs français,* 163, compares him to Melvyn Douglas and William Powell, saying: "Dark, malicious, delicately mustached, Luguet is the prototype of the boulevard actor, with an audacity tempered by English tact."

75. Alain Corbin, *Women for Hire: Prostitution and Sexuality in France after 1850,* trans. Alan Sheridan (Cambridge, Mass.: Harvard University Press, 1990), 337.

76. "Sans lendemain" (1939), lyrics, Maurice Vaucaire; music, Georges Van Parys.

77. Burch and Sellier, *Drôle de guerre des sexes,* 48.

78. Ibid., 47.

79. Vincendeau, "Melodramatic Realism," 63.

80. See ibid. for a discussion of the rise in the late 1930s of women's magazines such as *Marie-Claire* and *Confidences,* which offered more modern (yet still deeply contradictory) discourses aimed at women on the family, work, and personal grooming. Michèle Morgan, Vincendeau points out, was one of the first French film stars to appear on the cover of *Marie-Claire* (in 1938). Charles Spaak tailored the character of Suzy to fit Morgan's image. Morgan had already appeared in *Gribouille* (M. Allégret, 1937).

81. Useful analyses of *Le Crime de M. Lange* include Alexander Sesonske, *Jean Renoir: The French Films, 1924–1939* (Cambridge, Mass.: Harvard University Press, 1980); Christopher Faulkner, *The Social Cinema of Jean Renoir* (Princeton, N.J.: Princeton University Press) 1986; Keith Reader, "Renoir's Popular Front Films, Texts in Context," in *La Vie est à nous,* ed. Keith Reader and Ginette Vincenau (London: British Film Institute, 1986), 37–61; Christopher Faulkner, "Paris, Arizona; or, The Redemption of Difference: Jean Renoir's *Le Crime de Monsieur Lange* (1935)," in *French Film: Texts and Contexts,* 2d ed., ed. Susan Hayward and Ginette Vincendeau (New York: Routledge, 1992) 15–30; and Andrew, "Family Diversions."

82. Sesonske, *Jean Renoir: The French Films, 1924–1939,* 191.

83. Yet another film in which the realist singer is invoked as a symbol of community is *La Goualeuse* (Street Singer) (Fernand Rivers, 1938), which was written specifically for Lys Gauty (Alice Gauthier, 1908), who was known primarily for her interpretations of realist songs and the Brecht and Weill repertoire in the Parisian cabaret of the 1930s. She had a successful recording career and is remembered particularly for "Le Chaland qui passe," the song imposed on *L'Atalante* by its producers, and "Quatorze juillet," the song used in René Clair's film of the same name. In her only film appearance, she plays a street singer living on a barge in *La Goualeuse,* a kind of populist melodrama/*policier,*

which polarizes *le peuple* and the police. A banker is murdered near a bar where her barge is docked; La Goualeuse's down-and-out boyfriend is suspected. When called before the judge, La Goualeuse gives an impassioned, bitter speech about the social shame of poverty. Like Florelle in *Le Crime de Monsieur Lange*, La Goualeuse makes an apologia for a crime committed by a marginalized person, thus linking the realist singer with social justice.

84. Andrew, "Family Diversions," 21.

85. Sesonske, *Jean Renoir: The French Films, 1924–1939*, 208.

86. Vincendeau, "French Cinema in the 1930s."

87. Jacques Siclier, *La Femme dans le cinéma français* (Paris: Cerf, 1957), 69: "Le sourire, les yeux, le physique de Florelle, sa façon de marcher, de parler, de se vêtir sont la marque parfaite de cette époque à laquelle l'actrice ne devait pas, ne *pouvait* pas échapper. . . . [Elle est] la synthèse d'un type femme—'femme 1935.'"

88. Biographical information on Florelle from Florelle, "Mes mémoires," *Marianne*, November 2, 16, and 23, 1932; Jean Huguet, "Et si l'on vous contait Florelle," in *Florelle*, exhibition catalogue, April 11–June 6, 1987, Musée de l'Abbaye Sainte-Croix, Sables d'Olonne, *Cahiers de l'Abbaye Sainte-Croix* 56 (1987): 53–61; Raymond Chirat, "Florelle, aux yeux du souvenir," in ibid.: 63–66; and Brunschwig, Calvet, and Klein, *Cent ans de chanson française*, 163.

89. "Florelle seule, à cette époque, pouvait rendre acceptable le romantisme de la prostituée hugolienne. Faite pour interpréter les héroïnes populaires, Florelle crevait l'écran par son naturel et faisait croire à tous les personnages." Siclier, *Femme dans le cinéma français*, 66.

90. Dominique Païni, "Pour Florelle," in *Florelle*, exhibition catalogue, April 11–June 6, 1987, Musée de l'Abbaye Sainte-Croix, Sables d'Olonne, *Cahiers de l'Abbaye Sainte-Croix* 56 (1987): 8.

91. "Florelle personnifie fortement . . . l'essential de ce qui constitue les fictions des années 30 et qui se résume dans le mélodrame. Tout les signes que l'on pourrait aisément organiser selon une fiction insensée, sont réunis ici: le bonheur de vivre trop débordant, l'insouciance amoureuse menacée, la rencontre fatale du destin sous les traits inquiétants d'un homme sombre, la maladie, le malheur, la déchéance, l'exil et le travestissement qui l'accompagne, la tendresse retrouvé." Ibid., 7.

92. Brassaï, *Paris secret des années 30*.

93. [Remaining verses of "A la belle étoile"]

Boulevard Richard Lenoir	Boulevard Richard Lenoir [the black]
J'ai rencontré Richard Le blanc.	I met up with Richard Le blanc
Il était pâle comme l'ivoire	[the white].
Et perdait tout son sang.	He was as pale as ivory
"Tire-toi d'ici, tire-toi d'ici"	And was losing all his blood.
Voilà ce qu'il m'a dit	"Get out of here, get out of here,"
"Les flics viennent de passer	That's what he said to me:
	"The cops just came by

Histoire de s'réchauffer	In order to warm themselves up,
Ils m'ont 'assaisonné.' "	They 'spiced me up' a bit."
Boulevard des Italiens	Boulevard des Italiens
J'ai recontré un Espagnol	I met up with a Spaniard
Devant chez Dupont.	In front of Chez Dupont.
Tout est bon	Everything is good
Après la fermeture.	After closing time.
Il fouillait les ordures	He rummaged through the trash
Pour trouver un croûton.	To find a crust.
"Encore un sale youpin,"	"Another dirty yid,"
Dit un monsieur très bien,	Said a very fine man,
"Qui vient manger notre pain."	"Who has come to eat our bread."
Boulevard de Vaugirard	Boulevard de Vaugirard
J'ai aperçu un nouveau-né	I spotted a newborn
Au pied d'un réverbère	At the foot of a lamp-post
Dans une boîte à chaussures.	In a shoe-box.
Le nouveau-né dormait	The newborn slept
Dormait, ah!	Slept, ah!
Quelle merveille	What a wonder
De son dernier sommeil	His last slumbers
Un vrai petit veinard	A real lucky one
Boulevard de Vaugirard.	Boulevard de Vaugirard.

94. Incidentally, there is another aspect of *Crime*'s sexual economy that is fairly rare in 1930s French film: its creation of two couples whose partners are close in age. (Estelle and Charles appear to be around twenty years old; Valentine and Lange appear to be in their mid-thirties.) As Vincendeau shows in "Daddy's Girls," this decade's cinema is dominated by couples consisting of mature men and young woman. Here, Lange thinks he loves the younger Estelle initially but backs off when he learns that she loves Charles, a boy her age. Valentine confirms the "rightness" of this by observing that the young should be with the young.

95. A *Cahiers du cinéma* critic describes it best: "[A]u fond, dans ce film qui a l'air de s'occuper d'autre chose, c'est très précisément à la vengeance d'une femme qu'on assiste, la vengeance de Valentine [In the end, with this film that seems to be about something else, it's specifically a woman's vengeance that we watch, Valentine's vengeance]." Claire Simon, *"Le Crime de Monsieur Lange,"* *Cahiers du cinéma*, July–August 1994, special issue on Jean Renoir. Valentine gets revenge on the exploitative men in her past by achieving financial stability (she could loan Batala money when he tries to scrape together money for his getaway, but refuses to do so) and by forging a relationship with Lange, a guileless, gentle man of integrity.

96. Sesonske, *Jean Renoir: The French Films, 1924–1939*, 208.

97. Interest in the mythology of the laundress is still so strong that a magnificently illustrated, very costly history of laundry was published in 1994.

Françoise de Bonneville, *Rêves de blanc: La Grande Histoire du linge du maison* (Paris: Flammarion, 1994).

98. Laurence Berrouet and Gilles Laurendon, *Métiers oubliés de Paris: Dictionnaire littéraire et anecdotique* (Paris: Parigramme, 1994), 22.

99. Raymond Durgnat, *Jean Renoir* (Berkeley: University of California Press, 1974), 122.

100. Jean Renoir, *Renoir on Renoir,* trans. Carol Volk (Cambridge: Cambridge University Press, 1989), 221.

101. Charles Bernheimer, *Figures of Ill Repute: Representing Prostitution in Nineteenth-Century France* (Cambridge, Mass.: Harvard University Press, 1989) 163.

102. Jean Renoir and Jacques Prévert, "*Le Crime de Monsieur Lange:* Tentative de Synopsis," Jean Renoir Collection, UCLA, Coll. 104, *Le Crime de Monsieur Lange,* script, box 2, folder 9.

103. Ibid., 3.

104. André Bazin, *Jean Renoir* (New York: Simon & Schuster, 1973).

105. Ibid., 166.

106. Ibid., 170.

CHAPTER 4. THE REVUE STAR AND THE REALIST SINGER

1. Jean-Jacques Meusy, *Paris-Palaces, ou, Le Temps des cinemas (1894–1918)* (Paris: CNRS, 1995), 118.

2. Abel, *Ciné Goes to Town,* 16. Film programs in the café-concert and music hall usually lasted around twelve minutes (Meusy, *Paris-Palaces,* 118).

3. Sallée and Chauveau, *Music-Hall et café-concert,* 34.

4. See ibid., 34–35, on other French films with music hall settings.

5. Morlay was so closely associated with the theater, in fact, that most of her 100-odd films are seen as documenting French theatrical performance in the early twentieth century, according to Sallée, *Acteurs français,* 176.

6. The neon sign for Le Palace advertises the "Revue Argentine, Gloria Guzman." I have been unable to discover whether such a revue ever existed.

7. Georges Champeaux, "Faubourg-Montmartre," *Gringoire,* October 2, 1933.

8. Ibid.

9. Georges Charensol, "Faubourg Montmartre," *Faubourg Montmartre* dossier, Collection Rondel, Bibliothèque de l'Arsenal. Original source unknown.

10. Ibid.: "Nul quartier de Paris n'a plus complètement changé de visage en vingt années, et dans un aussi brillant décor ce drame de la misère et de la prostitution se trouve singulièrement dépaysé."

11. Sallée and Chauveau, *Music-Hall et café-concert,* 174.

12. Ibid. Varna and Dufrenne also owned the illustrious Casino de Paris beginning in 1929, which was famous for the revues headed by Mistinguett, Josephine Baker, and Maurice Chevalier.

13. Fittingly, in light of *Faubourg Montmartre's* valorization of the inti-

mate realist song over the glitzy revue number later in the film, the Palace changed its formula the year after *Faubourg Montmartre* film was made. Varna, now alone after the 1933 murder of his business partner, attempted to recreate the turn-of-the-century café-concert. He changed the music hall's name to the Alcazar, in honor of the former monument to Parisian song where Thérésa had performed in the 1860s. In 1933 and 1934, Varna presented a series of variety programs and hired stars like Mayol, Georgius, Charles Trenet, Lys Gauty, Marianne Oswald, Yvette Guilbert, Damia, and Fréhel—comic and realist singers, as opposed to *meneuses de revues*. But the retreat to an old formula did not take; the Alcazar closed its doors in 1939. It reopened at the end of year under the name of Le Palace, only to fail once more. The Palace's last revue was performed in 1940; in 1946, it became a cinema.

14. "Faubourg Montmartre" (1931), lyrics, Raymond Bernard; music, André Roubaud.

15. "C'est lui" (1934), lyrics, Roger Bernstein; music, Georges Van Parys. This song was one of Baker's signature songs. Baker's voice was not that of the traditional realist singer; her soprano singing voice is closer to that of Florelle, or of the operetta singer Yvonne Printemps.

16. "Fifine," or "La Java des Marsiallo" (1934), lyrics, Géo Koger, Henri Varna, and E. Audiffred; music, Vincent Scotto.

17. Gabin's performance functions here much like Albert Préjean's singing performances in *Sous les toits de Paris* and in *Un Soir de rafle*. A sustained analysis of male singing performances in 1930s French cinema is, however, beyond the scope of this study. The star images and cinema performances of Préjean, Jean Sablon, Tino Rossi, Charles Trenet, and Maurice Chevalier clearly merit closer analysis.

18. "Haïti" (1934), lyrics, Géo Koger and E. Audiffred; music: Vincent Scotto.

19. The singing woman imprisoned in a cage recalls the repeated image of a birdcage, symbolizing a woman's confinement in marriage, in *Prix de beauté*, a film (discussed in chapter 6) that has much in common with *Zouzou*. The birdcage motif also recalls the cagelike mask worn by the only other black actress to star in a 1930s French film, Laurence Clavius, whose performance in Jean Grémillon's 1931 film about an elegant black woman's encounter with a working-class white man on a cruise ship, *Daïnah la Métisse*, is a fascinating contrast to Baker's roles. This extraordinary film, written by Charles Spaak and starring Charles Vanel and Clavius, was brutally cut to a sixty-minute version by its producers, Gaumont-Franco-Film-Aubert, prompting Grémillon to disavow the work. See Geneviève Sellier's discussion of *Daïnah la Métisse* in *Jean Grémillon: Le Cinéma est à vous* (Paris: Meridiens Klincksieck, 1989), 91–100.

20. Francis Carco crosses paths once again with the realist singer—he wrote the film's scenario, as well as the lyrics to its two songs. Serge Veber, who also wrote the lyrics for *Coeur de Lilas*, co-wrote the songs for *Paris-Béguin*. The music was composed by the ubiquitous operettist Maurice Yvain, who also wrote Mistinguett's "Mon homme." Francis Carco, as I mentioned, had already

written a scenario for a film about the encounter between a rich woman and the *bas-fonds* of Paris: *Paris la nuit* (Diamant-Berger, 1930). In *Paris la nuit*, Marguerite Moreno—a "madam" figure somewhat similar to those played by Françoise Rosay in *Jenny* and *Le Grand Jeu*—plays an underworld extortionist who takes a young rich woman and her American boyfriend on a tour of a seedy dance hall. The film contains a performance of a realist song "Je t'aime d'amour," written by the film's director, Henri Diamant-Berger, and an important composer of popular songs, Jean Lenoir. All the themes of the realist song are here: a woman's frank expression of sexual desire, the initiation of a prostitute, and depression. Floryse, a realist singer who sang in the music hall during the 1920s and early 1930s, performs the song.

21. Corbin, *Women for Hire*, 136. Léon-Paul Fargue's love letter to La Chapelle (*Piéton de Paris*, 24), discussed in chapter 4 in the analysis of *Coeur de Lilas*, also speaks of the prostitutes on the rue de la Charbonnière: "Rue de la Charbonnière, les prostituées en boutique, comme à Amsterdam, donnent à l'endroit un spectacle de jeu de cartes crasseuses. Des airs d'accordéon, minces comme des fumées de cigarettes, s'échappent des portes, et le Bal du Tourbillon commence à saigner de sa bouche dure." ("Rue de la Charbonnière, prostitutes in their boutiques, like in Amsterdam, lend the place the spectacle of a filthy card game. Accordion melodies, thin as the smoke of a cigarette, escape from doors, and the Bal du Tourbillon starts to bleed from its hard mouth.")

22. *Paris-Béguin* dossier, Collection Rondel, 40 Rk 7.152, Bibliothèque de l'Arsenal: "[C]onscience professionnelle et souci de la vérité poussés à la limite extrême . . . qui font honneur à la production française."

23. Gabin's character is coded more as Gaby's *amant de coeur* [lover] than her pimp. Although the *amant de coeur* of a prostitute was quite often, in fact, her pimp, Gabin's main occupation seems to be that of a thief. As in *Pépé le Moko*, Gabin's gangster avoids the unsavory characterization of pimp. See Corbin, *Women for Hire*, 155–61, for a discussion of the different modes of procurement and the representation of the *souteneur*.

24. "C'est pour toi que j'ai le béguin" (1931), lyrics, Francis Carco; music, Maurice Yvain.

25. "Le Bonheur n'est plus un rêve" (1935), lyrics, Louis Poterat; music, Billy Colson.

26. Mary Ann Doane, *The Desire to Desire: The Woman's Film of the 1940s* (Bloomington: Indiana University Press, 1987).

27. Andrew, *Mists of Regret*, 121.

28. It could be said that the real life queens of the revue, Baker and Mistinguett, desired both of these things, as well. In any case, they achieved them, to a large extent. And while the melodramatic narratives are fiction, there is enough evidence from what is known of their lives to suggest that their successes and power did not come without some personal cost. As I have pointed out, both Mistinguett and Baker mobilized rags-to-riches and rise-to-stardom scenarios in their autobiographies, in addition to their glamorous "queen" identities. Moreover, Baker participated in the realist singer tradition of going from

"riches" back down to "rags" when, impoverished owing to her own misman-agement, she was forced to sell her château in the Dordogne. In a gesture as well publicized as those of the fund-raisers of Buffet and Fréhel at the fin-de-siècle and the late 1940s, respectively, Baker camped out in the kitchen of the château on the day she was to leave the property, forcing the new owners to have her carried out in her bathrobe. Princess Grace of Monaco, moved by Baker's plight, offered her and her twelve adopted children a free residence in Monte Carlo. Phyllis Rose, *Jazz Cleopatra: Josephine Baker in Her Time* (New York: Double-day, 1989), 248–50.

CHAPTER 5. VIOLENT SPECTATORSHIP

1. Marina Warner rightly points out that this is a space of the modern city. "Its early juke-boxes, glass booths, brass dials, dangling earphones and polished irregular surfaces give Kaufman [the film's cinematographer] his final opportu-nity to depict the graphic strength of the city of modern life." Warner, *L'Ata-lante* (London: British Film Institute, 1993), 63.

2. Fargue, *Piéton de Paris*, 17–18.

3. Ibid., 18: "Les tripiers . . . les figurants des Bouffes du Nord, les employés de la navigation fluviale, les marchands de vins du quai de l'Oise et les garagistes de la place de Joinville sont pour le confort, et ne dédaignent pas d'écouter *Faust* ou la *Neuvième* quand leur haut-parleur huileux et courtaud vomit de la bonne musique."

4. Weber, *Hollow Years*, 64.

5. Anouk Adelmann, *Chansons à vendre* (Paris: Cujas, 1967), 19: "la 'sono' avec ses chambers d'échos, ses micros et tout son attirail a, en quelque sorte, 'inventé' une nouvelle audition, comme la photo et le cinema ont donné une nouvelle vision."

6. Ibid., 20: "le public . . . est impuissant avec ses seules cordes vocals à con-currer l'écho magnétique."

7. Simone Missia was Fréhel's contemporary. In the early 1930s, she was one of the performers associated with the "good old days" of the *café-concert*. Like Fréhel, she appeared at Casino-Montparnasse on the rue de la Gaîté in the 1931–32 season, when an attempt was made to attract an audience nostalgia for the *café-concert*. Mac Orlan writes in *Lanterne sourde*, 67–69, of Missia and the "sensualité criminelle" she evokes.

8. For a fuller discussion of the process by which the center of Parisian bohemia shifted from Montmartre to Montparnasse, see Nicholas Hewitt, "Shifting Cultural Centres in Twentieth-Century Paris," in *Parisian Fields*, ed. Michael Sheringham (London: Reaktion Books, 1996), 30–46.

9. Maurice Verne, *Aux usines du plaisir* (Paris: Portiques, 1929) 190.

10. It is possible that one of the reasons Damia's star image relied less heav-ily than that of Fréhel or Piaf on biographical information about tumultuous love affairs with high-profile men, her sexual initiation, and the like, is that she was lesbian. In the context of a passage describing the close friendship between

Damia and René Clair in his book on the filmmaker, Pierre Billard refutes the rumor that Damia and Clair had an amorous relationship, arguing instead that Damia was lesbian and that she made no secret of her sexual orientation. Billard, *Le Mystère René Clair* (Paris: Plon, 1998) 55.

11. Pierre Philippe, interviewed in the documentary *Damia: Concert en velours noir* (Juliet Berto, 1989).

12. [Gustave Fréjaville?], December 22, 1919, Collection Rondel, Ro 15,934 (1), Bibliothèque de l'Arsenal: "Elle est l'Eve dont le péché enfanta nos peines, elle est la grisette sentimentale qui souffre du mal d'amour, elle est la fille de barrière que son mâle terrifie, elle est la criminelle hantée par le remords, elle est la rouleuse, elle est une Nana qui aurait du génie. Elle est tout cela parce qu'elle se croit tout cela, parce qu'elle croit à tout cela."

13. Georges Saint-Bonnet, "Damia à l'Européen," *Le Soir*, April 2, 1928: "Damia exprime, avec cette sorte de morbidesse tragique si souvent exploitée depuis Carco, toute la poésie des existences troubles, louches, douteuses, souvent malsaines, mais toujours si profondément humaine qui grouillent dans les faubourgs."

14. Chevalier, *Montmartre du plaisir et du crime*, 352.

15. Ibid.

16. Fréjaville, *Au music-hall*, 108: "Damia commence à chanter. La diction est fortement marquée; l'articulation presque brutale. La voix est grave, un peu sourde; je ne cacherai pas qu'elle nasille parfois et surprend l'oreille par des défaillances soudaines suivies de brusques sursauts qui ne doivent rien aux méthodes d'école. Mais bientôt elle s'échauffe, s'enfle, s'étale en larges nappes, s'exalte en appels déchirants, roule des sanglots comme un fleuve roule des graviers. Elle sait aussi se faire enfantine et langoureuse, s'adoucir en murmures, se fondre en soupirs. Voix sans doute difficile à classer, où les notes riches et profondes du violoncelle s'allient à des plaintes de hautbois et à des appels de cor. Quand Damia vit ses chansons, les défauts même de cette voix ajoutent au pathétique de sa déclamation et de son geste: on n'imaginerait pas une plus parfaite harmonie."

17. Darius Milhaud, *Études* (Paris: Claude Aveline, 1927), 86.

18. Henri Béraud, "Le Secret de Damia," *Comoedia* 8 May 1933: "[S]a voix fameuse, faite d'un sanglot et d'une révolte même—cette voix qui n'est en rien de cantatrice, ni même une voix de diseuse, cette vraie voix de chair, faite en tout et pour tout d'un souffle de femme, une voix qui livre le ton même d'un être et qui plainte ou cri, ne sait que se tendre jusqu'aux limites de notre angoisse, pour se briser sans faute au moment où notre résistance va s'épuiser."

19. Bost, *Le Cirque et le music-hall*, 139.

20. I have relied upon the following for the basic outline of Damia's biography: Pierre Barlatier, "Aux temps de *Marius* et de 'la chanson de Paris,'" *Le Soir*, November 15, 1963; Brunschwig, Calvet, and Klein, *Cent ans de chanson française*, 115–17; René Bizet, "Et voici l'histoire de Damia," *L'Intransigeant*, February 22, 1938; and Damia, "Je suis une fille de Paris," *Vedettes*, December 7, 1940, Collection Rondel, Ro 15934 (1), Bibliothèque de l'Arsenal.

21. The Pépinière was located in the eighth arrondissement at 9, rue de la Pépinière, and was frequented largely by the domestics and soldiers of the neighborhood. There is some confusion as to the exact year in which Damia made her singing debut. Sallée and Chauveau, *Music-Hall et café-concert*, report the date as 1909; Brunschwig, Calvet, and and Klein report 1911.

22. Fréjaville, *Au music-hall*, 100.

23. [G. S.], "Damia." *Comoedia*, April 19, 1928.

24. André Levinson, *Paris Journal*, November 21, 1924.

25. Chevalier, *Montmartre du plaisir et du crime*, 356.

26. Ibid.

27. Fréjaville, *Au music-hall*, 109: "Damia ne décrit pas, elle vit. Son commentaire est tout psychologique et intérieur. Elle traduit en gestes stylisées, en attitudes synthétiques, les mouvements de son âme."

28. Gina Manès was an important film actress in the 1920s, appearing in *Coeur fidèle* (Jean Epstein, 1923), *Âme d'artiste* (Germaine Dulac, 1924), *L'Homme sans visage* (Louis Feuillade, 1919), and *Thérèse Raquin* (Jacques Feyder, 1928).

29. Anonymous critic quoted in Raymond Chirat, *"La Tête d'un homme,"* *Premier Plan* 50 (December 1968): 45: "Si l'interprète de cette mélodie n'était pas Damia, peut-être, en effet, pourrait-on dire qu'elle n'ajoute rien à la valeur du film, mais il suffit de cette voix douloureuse pour que ces simples couplets deviennent au contraire un puissant élément dramatique."

30. "Tu ne sais pas aimer" (1931), lyrics, Maurice Aubrey; music, Guy Zoka. The song enjoyed considerable success. Damia recorded it for Columbia and nine other singers, including the realist singers Odette Barencey and Berthe Sylva, recorded the song for other record companies during the same period. Basile and Gavouyère, *Chanson française*, 91.

Un soir ton corps s'est donné	One night you gave your body
Oui, mais ton coeur tu l'as gardé.	Yes, but you kept your heart.
C'est pourquoi, malgré toutes sourires	This is why, despite your smiles,
Mon regret ne cesse te dire:	My regret never ceases to tell you:
Tu ne sais pas aimer,	You don't know how to love
tu ne sais pas.	you don't know.
En vain, je tends les bras,	In vain, I open my arms
Je cherche une âme,	I look for a soul,
Au fond de tes grands yeux	Deep in your big eyes
Une âme!	A soul!
et ne vois rien qu'un peu de bleu.	and see nothing but a little blue.

31. The theme of exile is emphasized in the dialogue earlier in the film when the manager of the cabaret in Singapore, a former singer at the Opéra de Toulouse who has lived in Singapore for thirty years (Marguerite Moreno), warns Jeff that returning to France might be difficult. "People save to go back to France and, at the last minute, wind up staying." He replies, "One is always exiled somewhere." For other treatments of the female voice and the Frenchman

in exile, see *Amok* (Fédor Ozep, 1934), *La Maison du Maltais* (Pierre Chenal, 1938), and *Le Grand Jeu* (Jacques Feyder).

32. Pierre de Lacretelle, *Gringoire*, February 20, 1931: "L'idée, c'est d'avoir supposé qu'un disque de gramophone peut, dans certains cas, prendre une existence propre, que la voix mécanique agit sur un homme au point d'exercer sur lui l'influence d'une présence réelle artificiellement construite par son imagination. Autrefois, dans les romans, on voyait des fous fastueux se promener sur la terre à la recherche du modèle d'une statue ou d'un portrait. Aujourd'hui, c'est une plaque de cire noire qui suffit à développer l'illusion."

33. Émile Vuillermoz, "Autour de *Sola*," *Temps*, May 16, 1931.

34. François Vinneuil, *Action française*, February 24, 1931: "De la photographie, des acteurs, de la mise en scène, il est impossible de dire quoi que ce soit. La nullité n'est plus même un défaut. Il reste Damia. Des dilettantes du music-hall dont nous ne voulons pas contester le goût, ont créé autour d'elle une petite littérature assez ingénieuse: l'humanité, la tragédie à propos de chansons insignifiantes. Il se peut. Personnellement, nous n'aimons pas beaucoup cela. Nous constatons que Damia possède assez de tours dans son sac pour ne pas faire au studio plus mauvaise figure que telle autre vedette, mais elle ne sait pas transposer son numéro de scène. Allez donc voir plutôt les réactions spontanées de Marlène Dietrich devant les caméras. Voilà qui est vivant et cinématographique."

35. Philippe Soupault, "Sola avec Damia," *L'Europe nouvelle*, March 28, 1931: "Damia n'a rien d'une comédienne. . . . Mais, habilement, on la fait beaucoup chanter et on retrouve la puissance étrange de la vraie Damia."

36. Roger Icart, *La Revolution du parlant vue par la presse française* (Perpignan: Institut Jean Vigo, 1988), 237.

37. Cécil Jorgefélice, *Courrier cinématographique*, May 17, 1930, quoted in Roger Icart, *La Révolution du parlant, vue par la presse française* (Perpignan: Institut Jean Vigo, 1988), 238: "La partition musicale, judicieusement composée, soutient fort bien les images. Les paroles sont brèves, réduites à l'essentiel, en généralement assez expressives pour ne pas donner l'impression de 'remplissage'. En tout cas, bien peu apparaissent comme superflues ou insuffisantes."

38. For a history of the bob haircut and an astute assessment of Brooks's image, see Peter Wollen, "Brooks and the Bob," *Sight and Sound*, February 1994, 22–25.

39. "Je n'ai qu'un amour, c'est toi" (1930), music, W. Zeller; lyrics, Jean Boyer and Sylviano.

40. René Jeanne, *Tu seras star! Introduction à la vie cinématographique* (Paris: Nouvelle Société d'Édition, 1929), 15.

41. *Prix de beauté* and *Zouzou* both confront and contain the threat of the "spectating" woman, thus almost literally representing the repression of the feminine. For a comparison of these two films in terms of how they foreclose the possibility of female spectatorship and subjectivity, see Kelley Conway, "La Femme-Spectacle du cinéma français des années 30: *Prix de beauté, Zouzou, Le Bonheur*" (D.E.A. mémoire, Sorbonne Paris-III, 1992). For an analysis of this

mechanism in the American woman's film, see Mary Ann Doane's analyses of *Caught* and *Rebecca* in *Desire to Desire,* 155–75.

42. Archives René Clair, RC 31 (001–006), Bibliothèque de l'Arsenal.

CONCLUSION

1. Sallée and Chauveau, *Music-hall et café-concert,* 40, calls Piaf "la plus grande, la plus populaire, la plus admirée des chanteuses françaises."

2. Even a brief look at the thousands of web sites devoted to Edith Piaf conveys a sense of her continued relevance to fans today. For a tiny sampling of Piaf biographies and autobiographies, see Simone Bertaut, *Piaf,* trans. Ghislaine Boulanger (London: W. H. Allen, 1971); David Bret, *Piaf: A Passionate Life* (London: Robson, 1998); Pierre Duclos and Georges Martin, *Piaf* (Paris: Seuil, 1993); Monique Lange, *Piaf,* trans. Richard S. Woodward (New York: Seaver Books, 1981); and Edith Piaf, *My Life,* with Jean Noli, trans. and ed. Margaret Crosland (London: Peter Owen, 2000).

3. My outline of Piaf's biography comes from Brunschwig, Calvet, and Klein, *Cent ans de chanson française,* 307–9, but similar accounts can be found in the numerous biographies noted above.

4. Cantaloube-Ferrieu, *Chanson et poésie,* 294.

5. Cited in Brunschwig, Calvet, and Klein, *Cent ans de chanson française,* 308.

6. Maurice Laporte, "Edith Piaf, Salle Pleyel," *Libération,* August 3, 1944: "La rue, la peine de la fille qui un soir s'est attachée à un passant, l'amour humble et battu d'une ouvrière pour un mauvais garçon, dix chanteuses pour qui on avait inventé le qualificatif de 'realiste' les ont chantés avant elle. Mais malgré leur robe noire et leur foulard rouge c'était 'du dehors' qu'elles racontaient leurs chansons. C'était en mots littéraires qu'elles exprimaient leurs amours sans phrases. . . . [Mais Piaf est éclairée] . . . de l'intérieur par cette ardeur authentique, on s'aperçoit que les mots banaux ont été choisis avec quelle infaillibilité, avec quel sens du symbole!"

7. Cited in Berteaut, *Piaf,* 241.

8. Cantaloube-Ferrieu, *Chanson et poésie,* 295.

9. Bertaut, *Piaf,* 112.

10. Jean Cocteau, *Le Foyer des artistes* (Paris: Plon, 1946), 190.

11. Claude Nougaro, "Elle était l'amour de chanter," *Lettres françaises* 999 (October 1963): 17–23. Cited in Cantaloube-Ferrieu, *Chanson et poésie,* 295.

12. Cantaloube-Ferrieu, *Chanson et poésie,* 298.

13. For a complete Piaf filmography, see Duclos and Martin, *Piaf,* 368–73.

14. "Quand même, fais-moi valser" (1936), lyrics, Léon Poterat; music, Jean Wiener.

15. Alan Williams, *Republic of Images: A History of French Filmmaking* (Cambridge, Mass.: Harvard University Press, 1992), 263.

16. Ibid., 264.

17. Gauteur and Vincendeau, *Jean Gabin.*

18. Nearly every review of Piaf's singing performance mentions her relative immobility on stage followed by a sudden movement that takes on an explosive intensity. See the Rondel Collection dossier on Edith Piaf at the Bibliothèque de l'Arsenal in Paris.

19. Vincendeau, *"Mise-en-scène."*

20. Gauteur and Vincendeau, *Jean Gabin,* 173–96.

21. Vincendeau, "French Cinema in the 1930s," 277.

Select Bibliography

Abel, Richard. *The Ciné Goes to Town: French Cinema, 1896–1914*. Berkeley: University of California Press, 1994.

———. *French Cinema: The First Wave*. Princeton, N.J.: Princeton University Press, 1984.

Adelmann, Anouk. *Chansons à vendre*. Paris: Cujas, 1967.

Andrew, Dudley. "*Casque d'or, Casquettes,* a Cask of Aging Wine: Jacques Becker's *Casque d'or* (1952)." In *French Film: Texts and Contexts,* edited by Susan Hayward and Ginette Vincendeau, 112–26. 2d ed. New York: Routledge, 2000.

———. "Family Diversions: French Popular Cinema and the Music Hall." In *Popular European Cinema,* edited by Richard Dyer and Ginette Vincendeau, 15–30. New York: Routledge, 1992.

———. *Mists of Regret: Culture and Sensibility in Classic French Film*. Princeton, N.J.: Princeton University Press, 1995.

Baker, Jean-Claude, and Chris Chase. *Josephine: The Hungry Heart*. New York: Random House, 1993.

Baker, Josephine. *Les Mémoires de Joséphine Baker*. Edited by Marcel Sauvage. Paris: Kra, 1927.

Basile, Giusy, and Chantal Gavouyère. *La Chanson française dans le cinéma des années trente: Discographie*. Paris: Bibliothèque nationale, 1996.

Bazin, André. *Jean Renoir*. New York: Simon & Schuster, 1973.

Benjamin, Walter. *The Arcades Project*. Translated by Howard Eiland and Kevin McLaughlin. Cambridge, Mass.: Harvard University Press, Belknap Press, 1999. Originally published as *Die Passagen-Werk,* edited by Rolf Tiedemann (Frankfurt a/M: Suhrkamp, 1983).

Bergstrom, Janet, and Mary Ann Doane. "The Female Spectator: Contexts and Directions." *Camera Obscura* 20–21 (1989): 5–27.

Bernheimer, Charles. *Figures of Ill Repute: Representing Prostitution in Nineteenth-Century France*. Cambridge, Mass.: Harvard University Press, 1989.

Bernstein, Henry. *"Le Bonheur." L'Avant Scène Théâtre* 819–20 (December 1–15, 1987).

Berrouet, Laurence, and Gilles Laurendon. *Métiers oubliés de Paris: Dictionnaire littéraire et anecdotique.* Paris: Parigramme, 1994.

Bertaut, Simone. *Piaf.* Translated by Ghislaine Boulanger. London: W. H. Allen, 1971.

Billard, Pierre. *Le Mystère René Clair.* Paris: Plon, 1998.

Bizet, René. *L'Epoque du Music-Hall.* Paris: Pamphlets du Capitole, 1927.

Bost, Pierre. *Le Cirque et le music-hall.* Paris: René Hilsum, 1931.

Brassaï. *Paris de nuit.* Paris: Arts et Métiers graphiques, 1933.

———. *Le Paris secret des années 30.* Paris: Gallimard, 1976. Translated by Richard Miller as *The Secret Paris of the Thirties* (New York: Pantheon Books, 1976).

Bret, David. *Piaf: A Passionate Life.* London: Robson, 1998.

Bruant, Aristide. *Dans les rues: Chansons et monologues.* 2 vols. Paris: Aristide Bruant, 1889.

Brunschwig, Chantal, Louis-Jean Calvet, and Jean-Claude Klein. *Cent ans de chanson française.* Paris: Seuil, 1981.

Buck-Morss, Susan. *The Dialectics of Seeing: Walter Benjamin and the Arcades Project.* Cambridge, Mass.: MIT Press, 1989.

———. "The Flaneur, the Sandwichman and the Whore." *New German Critique* 39 (1986): 99–140.

Buffet, Eugénie. *Ma vie, mes amours, mes aventures.* Paris: Eugène Figuière, 1930.

Buhler, James, Caryl Flinn, and David Neumeyer, eds. *Music and Cinema.* Hanover, N.H.: Wesleyan University Press/University Press of New England, 2000.

Burch, Noël, and Geneviève Sellier. *La Drôle de guerre des sexes du cinéma français, 1930–1956.* Paris: Nathan, 1996.

Calvet, Louis-Jean. *Chanson et société.* Paris: Payot, 1981.

Cantaloube-Ferrieu, Lucienne. *Chanson et poésie des années 30 aux années 60: Trenet, Brassens, Ferré ou les "enfants naturels" du surréalisme.* Paris: A. G. Nizet, 1981.

Caradec, François, and Alain Weill. *Le Café-Concert.* Paris: Atelier Hachette/Massin, 1980.

Carco, Francis [François Carcopino-Tusoli]. *Jésus-la-Caille.* 1914. Reprint. Paris: Albin Michel, 1985.

———. *Prisons de femmes.* Paris: Éditions de France, 1931.

Carco, Francis, and René Jacques. *Envoûtement de Paris.* Paris: Grasset, 1938.

Chevalier, Louis. *Montmartre du plaisir et du crime.* 1980. Reprint. Paris: Payot & Rivages, 1995.

Chirat, Raymond. *Catalogue des films français de long métrage: Films sonores de fiction, 1929–1939.* 2d ed. Brussels: Cinémathèque royale de Belgique, 1981.

———. *Le Cinéma français des années 30.* Paris: Hatier, 1983.

———. "Florelle, aux yeux du souvenir." In *Florelle*, exhibition catalogue, April

11–June 6, 1987, Musée de l'Abbaye Sainte-Croix, Sables d'Olonne. *Cahiers de l'Abbaye Sainte-Croix* 56 (1987): 63–66.

———. "*La Tête d'un homme.*" *Premier Plan* 50 (December 1968): 45.

Clark, T. J. "The Bar at the Folies-Bergère." In *Popular Culture in France: The Wolf and the Lamb,* Edited by Jacques Beauroy, Marc Bertrand, and Edward T. Gargan, 233–52. Saratoga, Calif.: Anma Libri, 1977.

———. *The Painting of Modern Life: Paris in the Art of Manet and His Followers.* 1984. Rev. ed. Princeton, N.J.: Princeton University Press, 1999.

Cocteau, Jean. *Le Foyer des artistes.* Paris: Plon, 1946.

Colette. *La Vagabonde.* 1910. Translated by Charlotte Remfry Kidd. New York: Bantam Books, 1994.

Condemi, Concetta. *Les Cafés-Concerts: Histoire d'un divertissement (1849–1914).* Paris: Quai Voltaire Histoire, 1992.

Conway, Kelley. "La Femme-Spectacle du cinéma français des années 30: *Prix de beauté, Zouzou, Le Bonheur.*" D.E.A. mémoire, Sorbonne Paris-III, 1992.

Corbin, Alain. *Women for Hire: Prostitution and Sexuality in France after 1850.* Translated by Alan Sheridan. Cambridge, Mass.: Harvard University Press, 1990.

Crisp, Colin. *The Classic French Cinema, 1930–1960.* Bloomington: Indiana University Press, 1997.

Dabit, Eugène. *L'Hôtel du Nord.* 1921. Reprint. Paris: Denoël, 1977.

———. *Ville Lumière.* Paris: Dilettante, 1990.

Dall'Asta, Monica. *Un Cinéma musclé: Le Surhomme dans le cinéma muet italien (1913–1926).* Paris: Éditions Yellow Now, 1992.

Doane, Mary Ann. *The Desire to Desire: The Woman's Film of the 1940s.* Bloomington: Indiana University Press, 1987.

Duclos, Pierre, and Georges Martin. *Piaf.* Paris: Seuil, 1993.

Durgnat, Raymond. *Jean Renoir.* Berkeley: University of California Press, 1974.

Dyer, Richard. *Stars.* London: British Film Institute, 1990.

Evenson, Norma. *Paris: A Century of Change, 1878–1978.* New Haven, Conn.: Yale University Press, 1979.

Ezra, Elizabeth. *The Colonial Unconscious: Race and Culture in Interwar France.* Ithaca, N.Y.: Cornell University Press, 2000.

Fargue, Léon-Paul. *Music-Hall.* Paris: Bibliophiles du Palais, 1948.

———. *Le Piéton de Paris.* 1932. Reprint. Paris: Gallimard, 1995.

Faulkner, Christopher. "Paris, Arizona; or, The Redemption of Difference: Jean Renoir's *Le Crime de Monsieur Lange* (1935)." In *French Film: Texts and Contexts,* 2d ed., edited by Susan Hayward and Ginette Vincendeau, 15–30. New York: Routledge, 2000..

———. *The Social Cinema of Jean Renoir.* Princeton, N.J.: Princeton University Press, 1986.

Ferguson, Priscilla Parkhurst. "The *Flâneur* on and off the Streets of Paris." In *The Flâneur,* edited by Keith Tester, 22–42. New York: Routledge, 1994.

Flinn, Caryl. *Strains of Utopia: Gender, Nostalgia, and Hollywood Film Music.* Princeton, N.J.: Princeton University Press, 1992.

Flitterman-Lewis, Sandy. *To Desire Differently: Feminism and the French Cinema.* Urbana: University of Illinois Press, 1990.

Fréhel. "La Complainte de ma vie." *Point de vue—Images du monde* 31–41 (1949).

Fréjaville, Gustave. *Au music-hall.* Paris: Monde nouveau, 1922.

Friedberg, Anne. *Window Shopping: Cinema and the Postmodern.* Berkeley: University of California Press, 1993.

Gauteur, Claude, and Ginette Vincendeau. *Jean Gabin: Anatomie d'un mythe.* Paris: Nathan Université, 1993.

Giret, Noëlle. "Le Cinéma selon Madame Yvette Guilbert." In *Yvette Guilbert: Diseuse fin de siècle,* 41–47. Paris: Bibliothèque nationale, 1994.

Giteau, Cécile. "Yvette Guilbert et la Bibliothèque nationale." In *Yvette Guilbert: Diseuse fin de siècle,* 67–69. Paris: Bibliothèque nationale, 1994.

Gledhill, Christine, ed. *Stardom: Industry of Desire.* New York: Routledge, 1991.

Gorbman, Claudia. *Unheard Melodies: Narrative Film Music.* Bloomington: Indiana University Press, 1987.

Gordon, Rae Beth. *Why the French Love Jerry Lewis: From Cabaret to Early Cinema.* Stanford, Calif.: Stanford University Press, 2001.

Guilbert, Yvette, and Harold Simpson. *Yvette Guilbert: Struggles and Victories.* London: Mills & Boon, 1910.

Guillaume-Grimaud, Geneviève. *Le Cinéma du Front populaire.* Paris: Lherminier, 1986.

Hansen, Miriam. *Babel and Babylon: Spectatorship in American Silent Cinema.* Cambridge, Mass.: Harvard University Press, 1991.

Hayward, Susan, and Ginette Vincendeau, eds. *French Film: Texts and Contexts.* 2d ed. New York: Routledge, 2000.

Hewitt, Nicholas. "Shifting Cultural Centres in Twentieth-Century Paris." In *Parisian Fields,* edited by Michael Sheringham, 30–46. London: Reaktion Books, 1996.

Higonnet, Anne. "Femmes, images et représentations." In *Histoire des femmes,* edited by Georges Duby and Michelle Perrot, vol. 5: *Le XXe Siècle,* edited by Françoise Thébaud, 315–73. Paris: Plon, 1992..

Hughes, Alex, and James S. Williams, eds. *Gender and French Cinema.* New York: Berg, 2001.

Hughes, Alex, "The City and the Female Autograph." In *Parisian Fields,* edited by Michael Sheringham, 115–32. London: Reaktion Books, 1996.

Huguet, Jean. "Et si l'on vous contait Florelle." In *Florelle,* exhibition catalogue, April 11–June 6, 1987, Musée de l'Abbaye Sainte-Croix, Sables d'Olonne. *Cahiers de l'Abbaye Sainte-Croix* 56 (1987): 53–61.

Huysmans, J. K. *Parisian Sketches.* 1886. Translated by Richard Griffiths. London: Fortune Press, 1962.

Huyssen, Andreas. *After the Great Divide: Modernism, Mass Culture, Postmodernism.* Bloomington: Indiana University Press, 1986.

Icart, Roger. *La Révolution du parlant, vue par la presse française.* Perpignan: Institut Jean Vigo, 1988.

Jacobs, Lea. *Wages of Sin: Censorship and the Fallen Woman Film, 1928–1942.* Madison: University of Wisconsin Press, 1991.

Jeancolas, Jean-Pierre. *15 ans d'années trente: Le Cinéma des Français, 1929–1944.* Paris: Stock, 1983.

Jeanne, René. *Tu seras star! Introduction à la vie cinématographique.* Paris: Nouvelle Société d'Édition, 1929.

Kalifa, Dominique. *L'Encre et le sang: Récits de crimes et société à la Belle Époque.* Paris: Fayard, 1995.

Kalinak, Kathryn. *Settling the Score: Music and the Classical Hollywood Film.* Madison: University of Wisconsin Press, 1992.

Kassabian, Anahid. *Hearing Film: Tracking Identifications in Contemporary Hollywood Film Music.* New York: Routledge, 2001.

Kear, Jon. "*Vénus noire:* Josephine Baker and the Parisian Music-hall." In *Parisian Fields,* edited by Michael Sheringham, 46–70. London: Reaktion Books, 1996.

Kertész, André. *Paris vu par André Kertész.* Text by Pierre Mac Orlan. Paris: Plon, 1934.

Klein, Jean-Claude. "Borrowing, Syncretism, Hybridisation: The Parisian Revue of the 1920s." *Popular Music* 5 (1985): 175–87.

———. *La Chanson à l'affiche: Histoire de la chanson française du café-concert à nos jours.* Paris: Du May, 1991.

———. *Florilège de la chanson française.* Paris: Bordas, 1989.

Klejman, Laurence, and Florence Rochefort. *L'Egalité en marche: Le Féminisme sous la Troisième République.* Paris: Fondation nationale des sciences politiques, 1989.

Knight, Arthur, and Pamela Robertson Wojcik, eds. *Soundtrack Available: Essays on Film and Popular Music.* Durham, N.C.: Duke University Press, 2001.

Lacombe, Alain, and Nicole Lacombe. *Fréhel.* Paris: Pierre Belfond, 1990.

Lagny, Michèle, Marie-Claire Ropars, and Pierre Sorlin. *Générique des années 30.* Paris: Presses universitaires de Vincennes, 1986.

Lange, Monique. *Piaf.* Translated by Richard S. Woodward. New York: Seaver Books, 1981.

Léger, Fernand. *Functions of Painting.* Translated by Alexandra Anderson. New York: Viking, 1973.

Legrand-Chabrier. "Le Music-Hall." In *Les Spectacles à travers les âges,* 247–88. Paris: Cygne, 1931..

Léon-Martin, Louis. *Le Music-Hall et ses figures.* Paris: Éditions de France, 1928.

Mac Orlan, Pierre. *Chansons pour accordéon.* Paris: Gallimard, 1953.

———. *Images Secrètes de Paris.* Paris: René Kieffer, 1930.

———. "Mademoiselle Mistinguett." In *La Lanterne sourde.* 1953. Reprint, Paris: Gallimard, 1982.

———. *Quai des brumes.* Paris: Gallimard, 1927.

———. "La Seine et les ponts de Paris." 1925. In *La Lanterne sourde.* 1953. Reprint. Paris: Gallimard, 1982.

Marchand, Bernard. *Paris: Histoire d'une ville, XIXe–XXe siècle.* Paris: Seuil, 1993.

Mayne, Judith. *Cinema and Spectatorship.* New York: Routledge, 1993.

———. *Directed by Dorothy Arzner.* Bloomington: Indiana University Press, 1994.

McClary, Susan. *Feminine Endings: Music, Gender, and Sexuality.* Minneapolis: University of Minnesota Press, 1991.

McMillan, James. *Housewife or Harlot: The Place of Women in French Society, 1870–1940.* New York: St. Martin's Press, 1981.

Meusy, Jean-Jacques. *Paris-Palaces, ou, Le Temps des cinemas (1894–1918).* Paris: CNRS, 1995.

Milhaud, Darius. *Études.* Paris: Claude Aveline, 1927.

Mistinguett. *Toute ma vie.* 2 vols. Paris: René Julliard, 1954.

Mizejewski, Linda. *Ziegfeld Girl: Image and Icon in Culture and Cinema.* Durham, N.C.: Duke University Press, 1999.

Morin, Edgar. *Les Stars.* Paris: Seuil, 1972.

Mulvey, Laura. "Visual Pleasure and Narrative Cinema." In *Visual and Other Pleasures,* 14–26. Bloomington: Indiana University Press, 1989.

Nesbit, Molly. *Atget's Seven Albums.* New Haven, Conn.: Yale University Press, 1992.

Païni, Dominique. "Pour Florelle." In *Florelle,* exhibition catalogue, April 11–June 6, 1987, Musée de l'Abbaye Sainte-Croix, Sables d'Olonne. *Cahiers de l'Abbaye Sainte-Croix* 56 (1987): 8.

Parsons, Deborah L. *Streetwalking the Metropolis: Women, the City and Modernity.* Oxford: Oxford University Press, 2000.

Pénet, Martin. *Mistinguett: La Reine du Music-Hall.* Paris: Rocher, 1995.

Petro, Patrice. "Feminism and Film History." *Camera Obscura* 22 (1990): 9–28.

Piaf, Edith, with Jean Noli. *My Life.* Translated and edited by Margaret Crosland. London: Peter Owen, 2000.

Rancière, Jacques. "Good Times, or, Pleasure at the Barriers." In *Voices of the People: The Social Life of "La Sociale" at the End of the Second Empire* translated by John Moore, edited by Adrian Rifkin and Roger Thomas, 45–94. New York: Routledge & Kegan Paul, 1988.

Reader, Keith. " 'Mon cul est intersexuel?': Arletty's Performance of Gender." In *Gender and French Cinema,* edited by Alex Hughes and James S. Williams, 63–76. New York: Berg, 2001.

———. "Renoir's Popular Front Films, Texts in Context." In *La Vie est à nous,* edited by Keith Reader and Ginette Vincendeau, 37–61. London: British Film Institute, 1986..

Rearick, Charles. *The French in Love and War: Popular Culture in the Era of the World Wars.* New Haven, Conn.: Yale University Press, 1997.

———. *Pleasures of the Belle Epoque: Entertainment and Festivity in Turn-of-the-Century France.* New Haven, Conn.: Yale University Press, 1985.

Renoir, Jean. *Renoir on Renoir.* Translated by Carol Volk. Cambridge: Cambridge University Press, 1989.

Rieger, Dietmar. " 'J'cass'rai la gueule aux proprios': Aristide Bruant et la chanson 'naturaliste' fin-de-siècle." In *La Chanson française et son histoire*, edited by Dietmar Rieger, 203–24. Tübingen: Gunther Narr, 1988.

Rifkin, Adrian. *Street Noises: Parisian Pleasure, 1900–40.* Manchester: Manchester University Press, 1993.

Roberts, Mary Louise. *Civilization without Sexes: Reconstructing Gender in Postwar France, 1917–1927.* Chicago: University of Chicago Press, 1994.

———. *Disruptive Acts: The New Woman in Fin-de-Siècle France.* Chicago: University of Chicago Press, 2002.

Rose, Phyllis. *Jazz Cleopatra: Josephine Baker in Her Time.* New York: Doubleday, 1989.

Sadoul, Georges. "Apropos Several Recent Films." In *French Film Theory and Criticism: A History/Anthology, 1907–1939*, vol. 2: *1929–1939*, edited by Richard Abel. Princeton, N.J.: Princeton University Press, 1988. Originally published in *Commune* 39 (November 1936): 372–79.

Sallée, André, and Philippe Chauveau. *Music-hall et café-concert.* Paris: Bordas, 1985.

Sallée, André. *Les Acteurs français.* Paris: Bordas, 1988.

Schwartz, Vanessa. *Spectacular Realities: Early Mass Culture in Fin-de-Siècle Paris.* Berkeley: University of California Press, 1998.

Sellier, Geneviève. *Jean Grémillon: Le Cinéma est à vous.* Paris: Meridiens Klincksieck, 1989.

Sesonske, Alexander. *Jean Renoir: The French Films, 1924–1939.* Cambridge, Mass.: Harvard University Press, 1980.

Siclier, Jacques. *La Femmes dans le cinéma français.* Paris: Cerf, 1957.

Slavin, David. *Colonial Cinema and Imperial France, 1919–1939.* Baltimore: Johns Hopkins University Press, 2001.

Sohn, Anne-Marie. "Entre deux guerres: Les Rôles féminins en France et en Angleterre." In *Histoire des femmes*, edited by Georges Duby and Michelle Perrot, vol. 5: *Le XXe iècle*, edited by Françoise Thébaud, 91–113. Paris: Plon, 1992.

Squier, Susan Merrill, ed. *Women Writers and the City.* Knoxville: University of Tennessee Press, 1984.

Strebel, Elizabeth Grottle. *French Social Cinema of the Nineteen-Thirties: A Cinematic Expression of Popular Front Consciousness.* New York: Arno, 1980.

Sweeney, Regina M. *Singing Our Way to Victory: French Cultural Politics and Music during the Great War.* Middletown, Conn.: Wesleyan University Press, 2001.

Tester, Keith, ed. *The Flâneur.* New York: Routledge, 1994.

Thérésa. *Mémoires de Thérésa.* 2d ed. Paris: E. Dentu, 1865.

Toulet, Emmanuelle, ed. *Le Cinéma au rendez-vous des arts: France, années 20 et 30.* Paris: Bibliothèque nationale, 1995.

Turk, Edward Baron. *Child of Paradise: Marcel Carné and the Golden Age of French Cinema.* Cambridge, Mass.: Harvard University Press, 1989.

Verne, Maurice. *Les Amuseurs de Paris.* Paris: Éditions de France, 1932.
——— *Aux usines du plaisir.* Paris: Portiques, 1929.
Veuillot, Louis. *Les Odeurs de Paris.* 1867. Paris: J. M. Dent et fils, 1920.
Vincendeau, Ginette. "Community, Nostalgia and the Spectacle of Masculinity."
    Screen 26, no. 6 (1985): 18–38.
———. "Daddy's Girls (Oedipal Narratives in 1930s French Films)." *Iris* 8
    (1988): 70–81.
———. "French Cinema in the 1930s: Social Text and Context of a Popular
    Entertainment Medium." Diss., University of East Anglia, 1985.
———. "Melodramatic Realism: On Some French Women's Films in the
    1930s." *Screen* 30, no. 3 (1989): 51–65.
———. "The *Mise-en-scène* of Suffering: French *Chanteuses réalistes.*" *New
    Formations* 3 (1987): 107–28.
———. *Pépé le Moko.* London: British Film Institute, 1998.
Viviani, Christian. "Société de spectacle, société en spectacle." *Cahiers de la
    Cinémathèque* 23–24, dossier 2, "Le Cinéma du Sam'di Soir" (1977): 14–18.
Walz, Robin. *Pulp Surrealism: Insolent Popular Culture in Early Twentieth-
    Century Paris.* Berkeley: University of California Press, 2000.
Warehime, Marja. *Brassaï: Images of Culture and the Surrealist Observer.*
    Baton Rouge: Louisiana University Press, 1996.
Warnaud, André. *Visages de Paris.* Paris: Firmin-Didot, 1930.
Warner, Marina. *L'Atalante.* London: British Film Institute, 1993.
Weber, Eugen. *The Hollow Years: France in the 1930s.* Norton: New York, 1994.
Williams, Alan. *Republic of Images: A History of French Filmmaking.* Cam-
    bridge, Mass.: Harvard University Press, 1992.
Wilson, Elizabeth. *The Sphinx in the City: Urban Life, the Control of Disorder,
    and Women.* Berkeley: University of California Press, 1991.
Wolff, Janet. "The Artist and the *Flâneur:* Rodin, Rilke and Gwen John in Paris."
    In *The Flâneur,* edited by Keith Tester, 111–37. New York: Routledge, 1994.
———. *Feminine Sentences: Essays on Women and Culture.* Berkeley: Univer-
    sity of California Press, 1990.

Index

Text:	10/13 Aldus
Display:	Aldus
Indexer:	Patricia Deminna
Compositor:	BookMatters, Berkeley
Printer and binder:	Edwards Brothers